THE

CONQUEST OF CALIFORNIA

AND

NEW MEXICO,

BY THE FORCES OF THE UNITED STATES,

IN THE YEARS 1846 & 1847.

BY

JAMES MADISON CUTTS.

HORN & WALLACE, PUBLISHERS
P.O. BOX 4204
ALBUQUERQUE, NEW MEXICO

© Copyright 1965
HORN & WALLACE, Publishers
Albuquerque, New Mexico

LIBRARY OF CONGRESS
CARD CATALOG NO.
65-26214

Printed by ARTMASTER, INC.,
OLATHE, KANSAS
Bound by INTERSTATE BINDERY
KANSAS CITY, MISSOURI

1965

A

Foreword

At mid 19th century, the United States was at a turning point in its history. In two centuries, the nation had expanded slowly (but solidly) from the Atlantic seaboard to the Missouri River. There the western boundary of the nation paused, facing many Indian tribes which had been removed to reservations across that dividing line. Farther to the South and West were the Spanish colonies of Texas, New Mexico and California.

These factors proved only a temporary barrier to the occasional hunter, explorer (private or official), or trader who probed freely the character and resources of this vast area, or to the settlers who soon followed in their footsteps. By 1820, Missouri had been occupied by pioneers who liked its fertile soil. Others moved into Texas, now under the

Mexican flag, while a small army of fur traders, filled with adventure and courage, led by associates of William H. Ashley, explored the Rocky Mountains and the unknown lands beyond.

The 1840's found the nation at the peak of its power and its faith in its ultimate "Manifest" destiny. This meant nothing less than taking over the vast stretch of country between Missouri and the Pacific Ocean. Exuding assurance and self-confidence, the United States recognized no obstacle to the achievement of that goal. The year 1846 became the "Year of Decision," because its neighbor, Mexico, as heir of Spain, claimed much of the same territory by right of discovery, if not actually by right of occupancy, and had no intention of surrendering that right. And Texas, having declared its independence from Mexico, was determined to remain a part of the union of States—the United States of America.

The clash that ensued between Mexico and the United States marked a collision of irresistible ideas and forces. President James K. Polk, spokesman for the free nation, championed the right of the pioneers to make beneficial use of the lands and resources of the West. General Antonio Lopez de Santa Anna of Mexico, a master in the art of political leadership, saw in the situation an opportunity for self-advancement, as well as a patriotic duty to protect the borders and possessions of his country. Unhappily for him, the military might of his armies was no match for that of his opponent. In the war that followed, the forces of the United States, ineptly organized and equipped, but led by men of superb training, experience and determination, soon overcame the forces of their enemies.

The story of this conflict, as it related to New Mexico, Arizona, and the Pacific Coast, and how the campaigns were conceived and executed, is told by Cutts in good style and spirit. He did not propose to give a discussion of the political issue involved, but wrote an informative volume on the Western areas over which the fighting took place, its geography, and the men who fought and won that struggle.

Cutts wrote a highly important book that ranks even today as an enviable contribution to American history. After giving the reader a preliminary account of Mexico and its various states, with emphasis on those along its northern fringes, he devotes the major portion of his study to the unfolding of the American conquest.

Leading the American army into the Southwest was a professional soldier, Col. Stephen W. Kearny, recently appointed to head the "Army of the West," as it was called. Efficient rather than colorful or spectacular, Kearny performed his duties with consummate skill, guiding his forces through the Southwest in the heat of summer, and taking New Mexico without the firing of a shot or the shedding of a drop of blood. At Las Vegas, first major town to be occupied, he accepted the allegiance of the citizens on August 15, 1846, promised them protection under the laws of the United States, and secured their friendship and support. Particularly important to many was the guarantee of religious liberty, which Kearny freely promised. As Catholics, they feared that they might be denied the religion of their choice.

Three days later Kearny and his army were in Santa Fe, having marched unmolested through Apache Canyon, where Governor Manuel Armijo of New Mexico had stationed his forces but which he had withdrawn before Kearny's arrival, afraid to match arms with the invader. With the road to Santa Fe open, Kearny and his men soon bivouacked around the plaza of New Mexico's capital, as the Mexican forces fled southward. In Santa Fe, Kearny, following instructions, acted with the same generosity toward the inhabitants, guaranteeing them freedom and liberty under the laws of the United States. For their guidance he issued a legal code for the government of the territory and appointed civil officials to enforce them. These laws were drafted by Col. A. W. Doniphan with the assistance of

Willard P. Hall, a member of his regiment. As governor he named the famous Charles Bent, and as secretary of the territory, Donaciano Vigil. He himself, in recognition of his services, was promoted to the title of brigadier general.

Kearny's orders provided that, in case of successful conquest, he was to go on to California, leaving a part of his troops in Santa Fe. Others were to be sent to Chihuahua to support General Wool, since it appeared that there was no danger of an uprising in New Mexico.

On the march of Kearny's dragoons down the Rio Grande, Kit Carson met him near Socorro with the news that California had already been conquered. Changing his plans, in view of the altered military situation, Kearny detached 200 men to remain in New Mexico, while he went on with about 100, confident of an uneventful march to the Pacific. One rainy morning, however, at a place called San Pasqual, some 35 miles east of San Diego, he was surprised by a party of Californians, well mounted, who cleverly led their enemy into a trap by feigning retreat, but who then turned and attacked, killing seventeen Americans and wounding several, including Kearny. Forced to await reinforcements from San Diego, the Americans a few days later marched to the port city, where Commodore Robert F. Stockton already had the province under control. By order of the Secretary of War William L. Marcy, General Kearny was to become the civil and military commander of California, but Stockton refused to yield to him and retained the office himself. Kearny, deferring to the naval officer, joined forces with him and marched to Los Angeles, where they were met by Captain John C. Fremont coming down from the north with 400 men. Against these combined forces the Californians were powerless, and on January 13, 1847, signed the Treaty of Cahuenga, near Los Angeles, effectively ending any resistance in California and making the province a part of the United States.

For Mexico, the situation was indeed desperate, after General Winfield Scott had seized the capital city late in

1847. Into the Southwest, not far behind Kearny's troops, came the Mormon Battalion of some 500 men, and in March, 1847, the first contingents of Colonel John D. Stevenson's regiment of New York Volunteers reached San Francisco by sea. With the end of the war, all troops were mustered out of the service, those in California ready to settle in the newly conquered region. With the gold discovery early in 1848, they were among the first to profit from the miraculous opportunities that opened on every hand. The presence of so many able-bodied and ambitious young men gave a tremendous boost to the economy, as well as to the strength of the Anglo-American portion of the population. Many of them became leading citizens of the new territory, so soon to become the 31st state in the Union.

The above outline, given in such sketchy fashion, is expanded by Cutts with the color and substance that only a well-informed and intelligent observer could. Each chapter tells of what happened in this great national adventure with a charm and thoroughness of detail that makes the book useful and exciting. Interspersed in the narrative are original documents of great significance, some of which are not found elsewhere. All add an intimate and authoritative tone to the author's descriptions.

The name of James Madison Cutts brings up visions of the great leaders of the infant republic of the United States, when the fathers of the Federal system—Jefferson, Madison and Monroe—all great presidents and all still living, were universally recognized as men of exceptional stature. Of these, Madison had met a young widow, Dorothea Payne Todd (commonly called Dolly), and married her in 1794. Her first husband, John Todd, a Pennsylvania lawyer had died of yellow fever, leaving her with a boy about a year old. The union proved to be one of the most romantic and striking of the day. When Madison became Jefferson's successor in the White House in 1809, Dolly Madison, a beauty of regal bearing, presided as the nation's first lady with a dignity and charm that has become legendary in American history.

Dolly's favorite sister, Anna, to whom she was deeply devoted, married Richard Cutts (1771-1845) in April, 1804. He was a member of the House of Representatives from what is now Maine, then still a part of Massachusetts. A Harvard graduate and lawyer (1790), Cutts served a term in the legislature, and then was elected to Congress from 1801-1813. Having been defeated for re-election in 1812, he was appointed superintendent of military supplies and served for four years, then became Second Comptroller of the Treasury, an office he filled from 1817 to 1829.

The eldest son of Richard and Anna Cutts was James Madison Cutts, born July 29, 1805. When Anna's sister, Dolly, became the first lady of the land on Madison's elevation to the presidency, this family moved in the nation's foremost social and political circles. In 1834, the young Cutts married Ellen, a member of the prominent Neale family of Maryland. The wedding was held at Montpelier, with ex-president Madison, rather frail, greeting the guests. (Ellen's sister was Rose Adele Greenhow, celebrated as a Confederate spy during the Civil War. She was the widow of Robert Greenhow, who had died in 1854. He had been translator and librarian of the State Department, and author of a famous *History of Oregon and California*, first published in 1844.) Of James Madison Cutts' two children, Adele became the second wife of Senator Stephen A. Douglas of Illinois in 1856 when she was not quite 21 years of age; his son, named after his father, became a colonel in the U. S. Army, holder of the Medal of Honor and an active member of the Columbia Historical Society until his death in 1903.

Our James Madison Cutts began a public career at an early age. According to Navy lists of the period, he was commissioned a midshipman in June, 1812, as he was approaching his seventh birthday. Perhaps he was assigned to duty with his uncle, President Madison, in some capacity. He was carried on the Navy lists, without pay, until 1821.

In the meantime, he probably went to school in Washington, but details are lacking. On April 9, 1821, he was employed by the Treasury in the Second Comptroller's office (then held by his father) as one of its lowliest clerks at a rate of $800. Through the years, he rose in the ranks until in 1857 he had become one of the senior clerks, at double his original pay. He was then advanced by President Buchanan to his father's old job.

This appointment occasioned some controversy, as is evidenced by published correspondence between Senator Stephen A. Douglas and the president. The press charged that Douglas was guilty of nepotism in attempting to secure the position for his father-in-law, but the senator insisted to the president that the promotion, if made, should not be chargeable to Illinois, which he said had never enjoyed its share of federal patronage. Thus Cutts was given the office in seeming recognition of his long years of service in the Treasury Department. He continued to serve as Second Comptroller until his death in May, 1863, during Lincoln's first term as president.

On Cutt's death, the obituary notices spoke of him as "one of the most liberal and public spirited citizens of the Federal capital," a man of large experience, integrity and knowledge. So it would seem that James Madison Cutts, an intelligent and well-placed man, had ample opportunity and inspiration to write *The Conquest of California and New Mexico*. Closely associated with the leaders of the capital, moving in the highest circles through the favoritism of his Aunt Dolly, who from 1834 to her death in 1849 presided over Washington social life from the old Richard Cutts home on Lafayette Square, he must have given the family additional cause for pride with his book describing the latest great adventure in the expansion of the United States.

George P. Hammond

The Bancroft Library
University of California
August, 1965

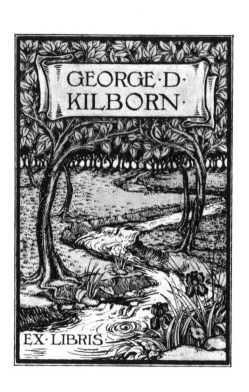

GEORGE·D·
KILBORN·

EX·LIBRIS·

BRIG.GEN.KEARNY.

THE CONQUEST OF

CALIFORNIA AND NEW MEXICO

J. C. Frémont,

BY J. MADISON CUTTS.

PHILADELPHIA

PUBLISHED BY CAREY AND HART.

THE

CONQUEST OF CALIFORNIA

AND

NEW MEXICO,

BY THE FORCES OF THE UNITED STATES,

IN THE YEARS 1846 & 1847.

BY

JAMES MADISON CUTTS.

WITH ENGRAVINGS, PLANS OF BATTLE, ETC.

PHILADELPHIA:
PUBLISHED BY CAREY & HART.
1847.

STEREOTYPED BY L. JOHNSON AND CO.
PHILADELPHIA.
PRINTED BY T. K. AND P. G. COLLINS.

INTRODUCTION.

THE AUTHOR'S PURPOSE.

WHETHER by emigration or by war—by conquest or by purchase—*New Mexico*, and the *Californias*, one or all, are to become territories of the *United States* of *North America*, is no part of this work to discuss. Their geographical position and the course of events may tend to this result. It is, however, left to others to canvass the possibilities or probabilities, along with the policy of such consummation.

A general outline of the geography of these countries, together with *a concise and continuous narrative* of recent military and naval operations connected with the *Conquest of California and New Mexico*, embodying marches and exploits "*among the most wonderful of the age*,"* is apparently demanded by their romantic and "*almost fabulous*" interest, as well as by the universal attention bestowed upon the *Mexican war*, and its consequences.

The purpose is here to sketch the geographical and histo-

---

* Senator Benton.

rical outlines with entire impartiality, and with such fidelity as the records now admit of; so that the Public may have before them an unpretending, yet useful *compendium*. At least, such is the Author's only design, and this he hopes to accomplish satisfactorily, the more that he makes no literary pretensions, and that it must be obvious to all, that the materials of history are not sufficiently developed for the more studied and philosophical research, which may hereafter occupy the minds of some of those historians of whose fame America is so justly proud.

CONTENTS.

CHAPTER I.

CHAPTER VI.

CHAPTER VII.

CHAPTER VIII.

CHAPTER IX.

CHAPTER X.

THE CONQUEST

OF

CALIFORNIA AND NEW MEXICO.

CHAPTER I.

Historical Summary of Mexico—National Boundary—Departments and Popula-
tion—Yucatan and Texas—Mountains and Table-land of Mexico—Salubrity—
Rivers—Lakes—Volcanoes—Harbours—Mixed Races—Slavery—Commerce
—Manufactures—Mines—Military Force—Revenue—Debt.

MEXICO, once the powerful and populous empire of Montezuma,
chief of the native Aztec race; afterwards, by the conquest of
Cortez, in 1521, one of the brightest gems in the Spanish crown,
asserted, in 1810, her independence, and at the end of a prolonged
and bloody struggle, in which some 500,000 perished, adopted, in
1824, a constitution of government formed nearly on the model
of the United States, with two essential exceptions. One which
established the Catholic Roman Apostolic Religion, and declared
that the nation will protect it by wise and just laws, and prohibited the exercise of any other. The second, whereby their Congress was authorized, in times of national danger, to create a
dictator, for a limited time; or, in other words, " to grant extraordinary powers to the executive, for a limited time, upon a full
knowledge of the cause."

Amid civil dissensions, this constitution preserved a nominal
existence until 1835, when the general Congress suppressed the
state legislatures, and provided for the division of the country into
departments; the president to be chosen by an indirect vote, and
the two houses of Congress by direct popular vote; the executive
head of each department to be appointed by the supreme national
government.

Successive revolutions, headed by military chiefs who more or less exercised unlimited power, or claimed to restore the constitution of 1824, followed, until, the republican party once more in apparent ascendency, the re-establishment of the constitution of 1824 was, on the 22d August, 1846, decreed, and with it the dissolution of the departmental assemblies and the reorganization of the several departments into sovereign and independent states.

On the 20th of April, 1847, the Mexican Congress conferred on the executive—then General Santa Anna—"extraordinary powers" restricted by the following provisoes : that it shall not have power to make peace ;—to conclude a negotiation with foreign powers ;—to alienate the territory of the republic ;—to enter into colonization contracts ;—to impose penalties ;—or lastly, to confer other civil and military employments than those expressly sanctioned by the constitution of 1824.

On the 6th of June, 1847, a coalition of the states of Jalisco, San Louis Potosi, Zacatecas, Mexico, Queretara and Aguascalientes was formed at Largos, which, looking to the fall of the capital, was prepared to maintain their independence and the federal system through all the vicissitudes of war and to the resistance to peace.

Lord Palmerston had, May 31, 1847, assured the minister of the Mexican republic, Don Joaquin Mora, "In regard to the contemplated abandonment of the Mexican capital by the executive, to which Señor Mora refers in his letter, the undersigned (Palmerston) has the honour of assuring Señor Mora, that the English minister accredited to the Mexican government, will consider it his duty to follow the government, and maintain his relations with it, in whatever part of the Mexican territory said government may fix its residence." From whatever causes, whether from corruptions and abuses of power introduced into the administration ; from the mixture of races ; want of education and enlightenment among the masses, it has happened that Mexico, since her emancipation from Spain, has exhibited the spectacle of a republic convulsed by the disputes of political parties and of rival chiefs, ending at times in sanguinary struggles and civil warfare ; in fact, "peace seems not to be the element in which Mexican statesmen gain or maintain their personal ascendency."

The Mexican nation or republic is now bounded on the north by the Oregon Territory of the United States; on the south by Yucatan and Guatamala: on the east by the United States, and the Gulf of Mexico; and on the west and south-west by the Pacific ocean. This territory extends from latitude 15° to latitude 42° north, or about 1800 miles from north to south.

Geographical and political details of the original divisions, and of the subsequent territorial subdivisions, cannot find space in this work; sufficient to state that, on 10th November, 1843, a decree for the election of delegates to the new Congress to convene in the city of Mexico on 1st June, 1844, fixed the ratio of representation as one delegate for 70,000 souls, agreeably to the census prepared by the National Institute of Geography and Statistics, and named the departments as follows:—

Departments.	Population.
Mexico,	1,389,520
Jalisco,	679,111
Puebla,	661,902
Yucatan,	580,948
Guanaxuato,	513,606
Oajaca,	500,278
Michoacan,	497,906
San Louis Potosi,	321,840
Zacatecas,	273,575
Vera Cruz,	254,380
Durango,	162,618
Chihuahua,	147,600
Sinaloa,	147,000
Chiapas,	141,206
Sonora,	124,000
Queretara,	120,560
Neuvo Leon,	101,108
Tamaulipas,	100,068
Coahuila,	75,340

Aguascalientes, ...	69,693
Tabasco, ...	63,580
Neuvo Mexico, ...	57,026
Californias, ...	33,439
Texas, ...	27,800
Total,	7,044,140

Yucatan has since dissolved the connection. Texas had declared and conquered her independence at the time, and claims, as embraced within her boundaries, the parts lying east of the Rio Grande, of four of the departments enumerated above; namely, of New Mexico, Chihuahua, Coahuila, and Tamaulipas.

The vast ridge which runs through Mexico connects the Andes of the south and the Rocky Mountains of the north. In the centre of Mexico, this chain presents a broad table-land from 6000 to 8000 feet in height, diversified by detached mountains, rising into the regions of perpetual snow, while it falls off rapidly as it spreads towards the eastern and western sea-coasts. Hence, on an almost continuous level, wheel carriages may run from the capital to Santa Fé, in New Mexico, while laterally the communication is extremely difficult, and, in most cases, can be carried on only by mules.

The summit of this vast table-plain is devoid of vegetation from the absence of moisture; its first slopes afford a vegetation of uncommon strength and beauty, while the narrow plain along the sea-coast produces the richest tropical productions, with a luxuriance scarcely to be paralleled.

On the other hand, health and salubrity of air retrograde with as decided steps as fertility advances towards the coasts.

Of the rivers of Mexico, not numerous or of great magnitude, the Rio Grande del Norte is the principal, running a south-easterly course, about 1600 miles to the Gulf of Mexico. The Sacramento and San Joachim are large rivers of Upper California. The Colorado of the West is also a large river, and falls into the Gulf of California, after receiving the Gila. From the structure of the country, the rivers of tropical Mexico mostly become mere torrents. The Panuco, the San Fernando, and the Santander, are considerable streams on the eastern coast ; and the Zacatula, Rio Grande, (or Tololotlan,) and Hiaqui on the western. The lakes of Mexico are very numerous, and appear to be the remains of others of vast extent. There are five active volcanic mountains, Tuxtla, Orizava, Popocatepetl, Jarullo, and Colima, connected by a chain of intermediate ones, evidently of similar origin.

The principal port on the Gulf of Mexico is the insecure harbour of Vera Cruz ; Tampico is much frequented, north-east of which are several natural harbours less used, while south are Alvarado and Huascualco. On the Pacific, are the bays of San Francisco, Monterey, Tehuantepec, Acapulco, and San Blas. The want of good harbours must prevent Mexico proper from ever becoming a great maritime power. In the Gulf of California there are tolerable harbours, but few considerable settlements.

The population of Mexico is variously rated, almost universally larger than the estimate given by the Mexican National Institute of Geography.

Its mixed character is singularly different from that of other countries. The following statement concisely enumerates the classes.

1. Europeans, or persons of pure Spanish blood, not natives of Mexico, powerless in a political point of view, but wealthy, though of small number.

2. Crillos or Creoles ; persons of unadulterated white blood. During the revolution, these and the first class were known as Gauchupinos, and, generally opposing the revolution, were called Realists or Royalists.

3. Meztizos, or half-bloods, the descendants of the white and aboriginal races ; this class comprises a great portion of the population of Mexico.

4. The native unmixed Indians, now rapidly being amalgamated with the others, yet still powerful in a numerical point of view.

B

5. Mulattoes, as with us, the descendants of whites and
Africans.

6. Africans, and persons of unmixed African blood.

7. Zambos, the descendants of Indian and African parents.

Besides, there are numerous descendants of emigrants from the
Canary Islands, with a great admixture of Moorish, not African
blood. Gitanos or Gipseys, and, it is said, on the Pacific coast,
near Acapulco, a large proportion of the population have a mixture of Malay and Chinese blood.

Slavery was abolished on the 13th of July, 1824, and from that
date, every imported slave was declared to be a free man from the
moment he landed upon the Mexican coast. They have, however,
a system of quasi servitude, called peonage.

The commerce of Mexico does not correspond with its capa-
bilities of production. On the " temperate lands," the finest plants
of the most genial temperate climates are produced in higher per-
fection than in most other parts of the world ; while the different
elevations of its great tabular mass of territory afford scope for
such vast variety of productions as to render Mexico celebrated as
an agricultural country.

Manufactures spread slowly among them, yet they are now
being established; principally in Puebla.

The mines, however, have given the idea of unbounded wealth
and romantic splendour to the name of Mexico, whence, indeed,
since the first discovery, more silver has been produced than from
all the rest of the world. The amount coined at the mint of
Mexico, since the conquest, amounts to 443,000,000 dollars. The
number of mines already known is between three and four thousand. Their largest yield in any one year was, in 1796,
25,644,566 dollars, and for some years previous to 1810, the
average annual yield was 24,000,000. During the revolution,
the amount was greatly reduced, water having been, in many
instances, allowed to rush in, the machinery destroyed, and the
workmen dispersed. In 1825, numerous British capitalists undertook to restore and extend the produce of the mines. German
companies were also formed, as also were two American ; the

expenses in the outset were enormous, and the results discouraging; their subsequent special operations are not known, further than that Europeans have now an interest in the mines of Mexico, of some twenty millions of dollars. This would appear to be a glittering prospect, but, classed with other industrial pursuits, the yield, compared to the capital and labour, may not be found to be greater than an equal amount invested in agriculture, commerce or manufactures.

The unsettled state of the country gives little value to its statistical statements. Nothing certain can be told of its military force, nor of its annual revenue, which has been stated as about 16,000,000 dollars. The national debt is equally unascertainable—computed, however, by those most competent to determine, at about 100,000,000 dollars, subject to the addition which the present war entails. On the 13th of September, 1847, the consolidation and acknowledgment of the Mexican debt to English bond-holders was formally announced in London, by authority of the Mexican legation at that court, as having been consummated in Mexico, to the amount of £10,241,650;—represented at the Mexican par, as about forty-six millions of dollars. What other foreign obligations may exist cannot be ascertained with any accuracy.

CHAPTER II.

Geographical Outline of California and New Mexico.

THE conquest of California and New Mexico embodied a class
of men whose intelligence, enterprise, and capacity, might well
be confided in to develop the character of the country, or to discover its utmost resources. Their marches and counter-marches,
in a great measure, afforded occasion, if not facilities. But it was
not alone that our forces embraced the profession of arms, the
citizen soldier, and the anticipated emigrant, but that the government had also provided men of science, from whose reports more
might be accurately known of California and New Mexico. Time
has not sufficiently elapsed to hear fully from these conjoined
sources of intelligent and extensive exploration much that must
hereafter serve to the attainment of a certain fixed knowledge of
the geography, soil, climate, &c. of these countries.

At present the accounts received vary materially. It is necessary, however, for the purposes of this narrative, that some general outline of the geography of the scenes of many a gallant contest here sketched, should be given, and in this the author deems
old authorities, as Humboldt, and more modern, " The United
States Exploring Expedition," Greenhow, &c., as, on the whole,
altogether preferable to the newspaper paragraphs which so seldom agree one with another. Whatever exception may be made
in the compilation of the geographical outline of California and
New Mexico will be accompanied with names.

"Upper California extends, upon the Pacific, from the 32d
parallel of latitude, about seven hundred miles north-westward to
Oregon, from which it is divided, nearly in the course of the 42d
parallel—that is in the latitude of Boston—by a chain of highlands
called the Snowy Mountains ; the Sierra Nevada of the Spaniards.
Its boundaries on the west are not, as yet, politically determined

by the Mexican government ; nor do geographers agree with regard to natural limits in that direction. By some, it is considered
as embracing only the territory between the Pacific and the summit of the mountains which border the western side of the continent : others extend its limits to the Colorado ; while others include
in it, and others again exclude from it, the entire regions drained
by that river. The only portion occupied by Mexicans, or of
which any distinct accounts have been obtained, is that between
the great chain of mountains and the ocean ; the country east of
that ridge to the Colorado appears to be an uninhabitable desert.

 " Northward from the Peninsula, or Lower California, the great
westermost chain of mountains continues nearly parallel with the
Pacific coast, to the 34th degree of latitude, under which rises
Mount San Bernardin, one of the highest peaks in California,
about forty miles from the ocean. Further north the coast turns
more to the west, and the space between it and the summit line
of the mountains becomes wider, so as to exceed eighty miles in
some places ; the intermediate region being traversed by lines of
hills, or smaller mountains, connected with the main range. The
principal of these inferior ridges extends from Mount San Bernardin north-westward to its termination on the south side of the
entrance of the great Bay of San Francisco, near the 38th degree
of latitude, where it is called the San Bruno Mountains. Between
this range and the coast run the Santa Barbara Mountains, terminating on the north at the Cape of Pines, on the south-west side
of the Bay of Monterey, near the latitude 36½ degrees. North of
the San Bruno Mountains is the Bolbones ridge, bordering the
Bay of San Francisco on the east ; and still farther in the same
direction are other and much higher lines of highlands, stretch-
ing from the great chain, and terminating in capes on the Pacific.

 " The southern part of Upper California, between the Pacific and
the great westermost chain of mountains, is very hot and dry, except during a short time in winter. Further north the wet season
increases in length, and about the Bay of San Francisco the rains
are almost constant from November to April, the earth being moist-

cned during the remainder of the year by heavy dews and fogs. Snow and ice are sometimes seen in the winter on the shores of this bay, but never further south, except on the mountain-tops. The whole of California is, however, subject to long droughts."* Heavy rains are of rare occurrence, and two years without any is not unusual; notwithstanding which, vegetation does not suffer to the extent that might be inferred, because, in the first place, many small streams descend from the mountain ranges, supplying the means of both natural and artificial irrigation; and, next, that the country near the coast is favoured with a diurnal land and sea breeze; and, from the comparatively low temperature of the sea, the latter is always in summer accompanied with fogs, in the latter part of the night, and which are dissipated by the morning's sun, but serve to moisten the pastures and nourish a somewhat peculiar vegetation abounding in beautiful flowers.

"Among the valleys of Upper California are many streams, some of which discharge large quantities of water in the rainy season; but no river is known to flow through the maritime ridge of mountains from the interior to the Pacific, except perhaps the Sacramento, falling into the Bay of San Francisco, though several are thus represented on the maps. The valleys thus watered afford abundant pasturage for cattle, with which they are covered; California, however, contains but two tracts of country capable of supporting large numbers of inhabitants, which are that west of Mount San Bernardin, about the 34th degree of latitude, and that surrounding the Bay of San Francisco, and the lower part of the Sacramento; and even in these, irrigation would be indispensable to insure success in agriculture."

In reply to inquiries of the author of these sketches, as to the area of Upper California, William Darby, the well-known American geographer, writes: "The provincial terms of New Mexico, and of Upper and Lower California, have been, and are yet, rather designations of indefinite tracts than of real defined political sections. The Pacific ocean limits on the west, and by treaty, N. lat. 42° on the north; but inland and southward, it is in vain

---

* Greenhow.

to seek any definite boundary. In order, however, to give as distinct a view as the nature of the case will admit, let us adopt the mouth of the Colorado and Gila, or the head of the Gulf of California, as a point on the southern boundary of Upper California. The point assumed coincides very nearly with N. lat. 32°, and, if adopted, would give to that country a breadth of ten degrees of latitude, or in round numbers 800 statute miles from south to north. As already stated, the Pacific Ocean bounds this country on the west, and lat. 42° on the north. To separate it on the east from New Mexico, we must assume the mountain chain of the Sierra Madre, or Anahuac, which, in this region, inclines but little from north and south : whilst the Pacific coast extends in general course north-west and south-east. These opposite outlines contract the southern side to about 500 miles, and open the northern side to rather above 800 miles ; giving a mean breadth of 650 miles. The area, for all general purposes, may be safely taken at 500,000 square miles. The general slope or declination of this great region is westward, towards the Pacific and Gulf of California."

Mr. Darby adds : " The climate of the western slope of North America has a warmth ten degrees at least higher than the eastern, upon similar latitude. The cause of this difference is the course of prevailing winds in the temperate zones of the earth, from the western points. Thus the winds on the western side of the continent are from the ocean, and on the eastern from the land. I have in the present case given *ten degrees* of difference, in order to be within bounds ; but am confident that above N. lat. 32°, and within two or three hundred miles from the ocean, the climatic difference in winter, on equal elevations of surface, is far nearer *twenty* than *ten.*" The author's investigations would lead him to the conviction that the climatic difference is considerably above ten degrees, and that Mr. Darby may be correct as to the higher point. It is, however, a subject yet undetermined, and one which the author is aware now engages the philosophical investigation of one of the ablest and most deservedly honored sages of America, Albert Gallatin, from whose conclusions the public will need no appeal.

The visit of Captain Wilkes, of the United States Exploring Expedition, was made in 1841. He refers to very great difficulty in obtaining accurate information in relation to Upper California; the country, at the time of his visit, and for several years previous, having been in a state of revolution. He found it suffering under a drought of eleven months' continuance, and hence his first view was unfavourable as to its beauty or fertility, nor did subsequent experience materially alter this impression, except as to the regions to which allusion has been already made.

"The soil is as variable as the face of the country. On the coast range of hills there is little to invite the agriculturist, except in some vales of no great extent. These hills are, however, admirably adapted for raising herds and flocks, and are at present the feeding-grounds of numerous deer, elk, &c., to which the short, sweet grass and wild oats that are spread over them afford a plentiful supply of food." Captain Wilkes concludes: "The valley of the Sacramento, and that of San Juan are the most fruitful parts of California. particularly the latter, which is capable of producing wheat, Indian corn, rye, oats, &c., with all the fruits of the temperate, and many of the tropical climates. It likewise offers pasture grounds for cattle. This region comprises a level plain, from fifteen to twenty miles in width, extending from the bay of San Francisco, beyond the mission of that name, north and south. This may be termed the garden of California; but although several small streams and lakes serve to water it, yet in dry seasons or droughts, not only the crops but the herbage also suffers extremely, and the cattle are deprived of food." The most extensive portion of Upper California—the inland plain between the "California" and the Colorado range of mountains—is an arid waste, destitute of the requisites for supplying the wants of man. "This plain is a waste of sand, with a few detached mountains (some of which rise to the region of perpetual snow) whose positions are unknown; from these flow small streams that are soon lost in the sand. A few Indians are scattered over the plain, the most miserable objects in creation."

The climate varies as much or more than its natural features and soil. On the coast range, it has as high a mean temperature in winter as in summer. In fact, the latter is the coldest part of the year owing to the prevalence of cold, damp and uncomfortable north-west winds, rendering fire often necessary for comfort in mid-summer. Thirty miles, however, from the coast, the climate undergoes a great change, and according to Captain Wilkes, "in no part of the world is there to be found a finer or a more equable one than in the valley of San Juan," and none can be more salubrious.

The Sacramento is the largest river in California. The San Joachim is next in importance. "There are many small streams that flow through the different valleys, and afford partial opportunities for irrigating the land; but there are none of them navigable except the Sacramento."

Upper California has one of the finest harbours in the world, in which the combined fleets of all the naval powers of Europe might ride in safety. "This, however, is the only real good harbour which the country possesses; for the others so called may be frequented only during the fine season, being nothing more than roadsteads, affording little safety and but few supplies to vessels."

"Among these bays are that of Monterey, the capital of Upper California, and that of Santa Barbara and San Pedro. The two last are partly protected from the swell of the Pacific ocean by the islands that cover them."*

The yield of wheat, small grain and vegetables, is said to be great, and very remarkable, but, as agriculture cannot succeed in Upper California, but by irrigation, it has hitherto happened that it has been principally occupied as a pastoral country—as costing least labour to rear cattle, for which it is only necessary to provide keepers, and have them marked. The numerous animals which are there slaughtered for little more than their hides and tallow, do not putrefy and become offensive as they would in other climates, but, as wood is not everywhere as abundant as their

---

* Captain Wilkes.

bones, the last are sometimes used to supply the place of the former, in the construction of garden fences, &c.

The principal towns are enumerated by M. de Mofras, together with their population. His account of the soil, exports, &c., is interesting, and accurate, doubtless, of the time to which it refers. Since then, however, the population has been increased by emigration. M. de Mofras gives a very minute account of the state of affairs in California, in 1842. His work was published under the immediate direction of the French minister, Marshal Soult, by order of the king of France.

The area of Upper California he gives at 500,000 square miles, and the population exclusive of Indians scattered over this extent he classifies as follows :

Californians descended from Spain, ...	4000
Americans from United States, ...	360
English, Scotch, and Irish, ...	300
European Spaniards, ...	80
French and Canadians, ...	80
Germans, Italians, Portuguese and Sandwich islanders,	90
Mexicans, ...	90
Total, . .	5000

Among the English and Americans, he states, are many runaway seamen, but most of them are immigrants from the west. The location of this population is given as follows :

San Diego, ...	1300
Santa Barbara, ...	800
Monterey, ...	1000
San Francisco, ...	800
Scattered, ...	1100
Total, . .	5000

The three most important establishments in the country, are the factories of the Hudson Bay company, and the most important of all, New Helvetia, founded by Captain Sutter, a retired officer of the Swiss Guards of Charles X., disbanded at the revolution of the three days of 1830. This enterprising gentleman emigrated from

Missouri to California, in 1838, 1839, and has formed the nucleus of the future empire on the Pacific. Captain Fremont, on his visit to Captain Sutter, 1844, states that on his first settlement he had some trouble with the Indians, but by the occasional exercise of well-timed authority, converted them into a peaceable and industrious people. On application to the chief of a village, he obtained as many boys and girls as he can employ; and there was at that time a number in training for a woollen factory. He bought out the stock of a Russian establishment, the owners of which wished to leave the country, consisting of a large number of cattle, artillery, &c., and makes payment for them annually in grain. His fort mounts twelve cannon, and can hold 1000 men, but is garrisoned with forty Indians, in uniform. The imports and exports of California, M. de Mofras gives as follows:

	Imports.	Exports.
Mexican flag,	50,000	65,000
United States flag,	70,000	150,000
English flag,	20,000	45,000
Miscellaneous flag,	10,000	20,000
Total,	150,000	280,000

The articles exported are, hides $210,000; tallow $55,000; peltries, wood, &c. $15,000; total $280,000. The business done under the Mexican flag is not in Mexican vessels, but in those belonging to citizens of other countries, doing business in Mexico. In 1841, of eleven vessels that reached California under the Mexican flag, only one, a boat of eighty-six tons, in the service of the government, was Mexican. In relation to the soil of California, he remarks as follows:

"The soil is often in the valleys, two metres deep: the superior strata are formed in part of organic detritus, and are, of course, extremely fertile. The soil is never naked, grass covers it through the whole year. The gramineous plants attain the height of eight or ten feet. But the trees of California, if not the largest, are at any rate the tallest, on the globe.

"The seasons follow the same course as in (southern) Europe, and the year is divided into two well-marked parts, the season of

rains, which begins in October and ends in March, and the dry
season, which embraces the remaining six months of spring and
summer.   *   *   *

"Once only since the colonization of the country, has snow
been known to fall in the plains.

"To resume, Upper California is, on the whole, admirably fitted
for colonization. This province presents the greatest facilities for
raising cattle, for cultivating corn, plants, and for the grape; it
might contain twenty millions of inhabitants; and its ports are a
point of necessary communication for vessels going from China
and Asia to the western coasts of North America.

"It is beyond doubt, that so soon as an intelligent and laborious
population is established there, this country will occupy an elevated rank in the commercial scale; it would form the *entrepôt*
where the coasts of the great ocean would send their products,
and would furnish the greatest part of their subsistence in grains
to the north-west, to Mexico, to Central America, to Ecuador, to
Peru, to the north coast of Asia, and to many groups of Polynesia
—such as the Sandwich isles, the Marquesas, and Tahiti."

The number of emigrants that have arrived, as far as heard
from, may be estimated as about three thousand. Others are on
their way, to a much greater amount.

Of the present condition of the country, in addition to what
will be necessarily said in other chapters, as connected with military events, the following extract from the "California Star,"
edited by the chief of the Mormon emigrants, will, perhaps, suffice
for the purposes of our mere outlines:

"YERBA BUENA AND SAN FRANCISCO BAY.—The only journal
upon which the people at a distance can rely, with any degree of
certainty for facts and correct description, is the plain but well-
written work of Col. J. C. Fremont, which we recommend to every
one who feels an interest in learning any thing in relation to the
former history or late condition of the country.

"In consequence of the difficulty which Colonel Fremont laboured
under in getting access to the different parts of the country, he
was unable to give that accurate information relative to this

part, which he could and would have done under other circumstances. To supply the deficiency in all these works, (some of
which have obtained an extensive circulation,) so far as it relates
to this part of California, we have obtained from the most authentic sources the description of the town and bay, which follows :

" Yerba Buena, the name of our town, which means, GOOD HERB,
is situated on the south-west side of the principal arm of San
Francisco Bay, about five miles from the ocean, on a narrow neck
of land, varying from four to ten miles in width—the narrowest
place being sixteen miles south-west of the town. It is in latitude
37° 45′ north. This narrow slip of land is about sixty miles in
length, extending from the point formed by the bay and the ocean
to the valley of San Jose. The site of the town is handsome and
commanding, being an inclined plane of about a mile in extent
from the water's edge to the hills in the rear. Two points of
land—one on each side, extending into the bay—form a crescent,
or a small bay in the shape of a crescent, in front, which bears
the name of the town. These points afford a fine view of the
surrounding country—the snow-capped mountains in the distance—the green valleys beneath them—the beautiful, smooth,
and unruffled bay in front and on either side, at once burst upon
the eye. There is in front of the town a small island, rising high
above the surface of the bay, about two miles long and one wide,
which is covered, the greater part of the year, with the most exu-
berant herbage of untrodden freshness. This little island is about
three miles from the shore. Between it and the town is the principal anchorage. Here the vessels of all nations rest in safety
and peace, and their flags are displayed by the aromatic breeze.
Two hundred yards from the shore, there is twenty-four feet
water, and a short distance beyond that as many fathoms. The
beach, immediately in front of the now business part of the town,
is shelving, but it will, no doubt, in a short time be filled up, and
become the most valuable part of the place.

" The climate here is, in the winter, which is the rainy season,
damp and chilly. During the balance of the year, it is dry, but
chilly in consequence of the continual strong winds from north

c

and north-west. There is but little variation in the atmosphere throughout the year; the thermometer ranging from fifty-five to seventy degrees, Fahrenheit.

"Yerba Buena is one of the most healthy places on the whole coast of the Pacific. Sickness of any kind is rarely known among us. The salubrity of the climate—beauty of the site of the town—its contiguity to the mouth of the bay—the finest harbour on the whole coast, in front—the rich and beautiful country around it, all conspire to render it one of the best commercial points in the world.

"The town is new, having been laid off in 1839, by Captain John Viogt, and, notwithstanding all the troubles in the country, has gradually increased in size and importance. It now contains a population of about 500 permanent citizens. Two years ago there were but about 200.

"Three miles south is the mission Dolores, on Mission Creek, surrounded by a small valley of rich and beautiful land. The water from this creek can easily be brought by means of aqueducts to any point to supply vessels. For the supply of the citizens, the best of well-water is obtained in every part of the town, by boring the distance of forty feet.

"In going south from Yerba Buena, the traveller passes over this narrow neck of land; a most delightful region, interspersed with hills, valleys, and mountains—the valleys rich and beautiful—the hills covered with tall pines, red wood, and cedar, that have withstood the tempests and whirlwinds of a century, and the mountains rising in majestic grandeur to the clouds. In passing out, the valley of San Jose opens to the view in all the loveliness of the climate of Italy, and beauty of the tropics. This valley is about sixty miles in length, and ten in width. The Puebla (which means an incorporated town) is the principal place of business for the valley, and is about five miles from Santa Clara, the landing on the bay, or, as it is termed here, 'the embarcadero.' Passing on from here, north-east, the traveller, in a few hours' ride, reaches the straits which separate the Suisun Bay, formed by the confluence of the Sacramento and San Joaquin rivers, from that of San Pablo. Here it seems that the accumulated waters of a thousand years had suddenly rent the opposing mountain asunder, and flowed with tremendous force to the great bosom of the deep.

"On the north side of the bay, from the straits to Sausilita, is one of the finest districts of country in all Upper California.

"Next to Yerba Buena, Sausilita is the best point on the whole bay for a commercial town. It is seven miles, a little east of north, from this place, on the opposite side of the bay, and has long been a watering point for vessels.

"An attempt has recently been made to lay off and build up a town at the straits, to supersede the two last-mentioned places. It will, no doubt, however, be an entire failure.

"San Francisco bay being the safest and most commodious harbour on the entire coast of the Pacific, some point on it must be the great mart of the Western World. We believe Yerba Buena is the point, commanding, as it does now, all the trade of the surrounding country, and there being already a large amount of capital concentrated here.

"The town of Yerba Buena is called, in some of the old maps of the country, San Francisco. It is not known by that name here, however.

"The town takes its name from an herb to be found all around it, which is said to make good tea, and possessing excellent medicinal qualities; it is called good herb, or Yerba Buena."

The Honourable Willard P. Hall, member of the House of Representatives of the United States, who, it will be seen in a subsequent chapter, brought opportunity and intelligence to the proper determination of the geographical character of the country, thus expressed himself:—"As to California, I am not prepared to speak with much certainty. All I can say is, the climate is delightful, the situation is excellent, but the soil is not to compare with ours (of Missouri.) It rains but little, and crops can only be raised by irrigating the land. California is a good stock country, the grass is now green, and resembles ours in May. I am told every thing is parched up in summer. The valleys are small, and the mountains many and extensive."

On the other hand, publications giving an enthusiastic commendation of California have appeared in the newspapers of the day, but generally without the name of the author, whereby their experience might be tested.

New Mexico, lying eastward of Upper California, and separated from it by the mountain chain of the Sierra Madre, has, as already observed, never been accurately defined. It may, for all useful purposes, be restricted to the narrow valley of the Upper Rio Grande. The name of "New Mexico" was applied by the early Spanish conquerors to their possessions along the north-west coast. Under later Mexican viceroys, "New Mexico" referred to the intendancy on the Rio Grande. In 1803, Humboldt supposed this intendancy to contain 44,000 square miles, and 40,000 inhabitants. Lieut. Abert, who accompanied Gen. Kearny to Santa Fé, estimates the population, from official records that fell under his inspection at Santa Fé, at about 100,000. Humboldt and all others who have described this country, represent it as generally sterile, and, for its latitude, excessively cold—the coldness compared with its latitude proving its great elevation above the oceanic level. "It would be presumption to assign an area, even approximately, to a country not one outline of which we can fix with any exactness."* It is true that Humboldt lays down the boundary, but changes have so altered the acceptation of the geographical term "New Mexico," as to produce the conclusion at which Mr. Darby arrives. Of other particulars of this country, enough will, perhaps, be said in the course of the military narrative, to render our sketches intelligible to the general reader. Those who seek a more detailed knowledge of California and New Mexico, will doubtless refer to the very interesting and able works here quoted, as well as to others.

---

* Wm. Darby.

CHAPTER III.

Principal Military and Naval events of the Mexican War, antecedent to, and cotemporaneous with the operations of the forces in California and New Mexico.

A SERIES of military achievements more uninterruptedly successful than history has record of, already covers the reputation of *Scott and Taylor, and of their Generals*, together with that of their coadjutors, with such renown as will for ever form a part of the inheritance of American patriotism. It is not within the scope of this work to enlarge upon their fame, however grateful the undertaking, but rather to enumerate in this chapter, somewhat chronologically, their principal battles, &c.; so that when events, which so greatly distinguished the skill and energy of commanders and their conrades in another quarter of the war, come to be here spoken of, they may readily be compared in point of time with like heroic deeds of their fellow soldiers further south.

General Taylor took position, at Corpus Christi, on the 15th August, 1845; from thence moved westward, on the 11th March, 1846; and, on the 28th of same month, reached the east bank of the Rio Grande, opposite to Matamoras. These movements were made in pursuance of orders from the War Department, issued 28th May, 1845, and 13th January, 1846.

Mexican battery opened on Fort Brown, May 3d, 1846.

Matamoras occupied by the American forces under Major-general Taylor, May 18, 1846.

Tampico, in the Gulf of Mexico, taken possession of by Commodore Perry, November 14, 1846.

Saltillo occupied, by Major-general Taylor, Nov. 16, 1846.

Occupation of Victoria, by Brigadier-general Quitman, Dec. 29, 1846.

Alvarado occupied by Commodore Perry and Brigadier-general Quitman, April 2, 1847.

c 2

Tuspan taken by the naval forces, April 18, 1847.

Tabasco captured by Commodore Perry, June 16, 1847.

Brigadier-general Wool, in command of the centre division of U. S. Army, arrived, with an aggregate force of 1954 men, from San Antonio de Bexar, at the left bank of the Rio Grande, near Presidio, on the 8th October ; entered Santa Rosa, in Chihuahua, on the 24th of same month ; occupied Monclova, in Coahuila, on 3d November ; arrived at Parras, December 5, and thence, on same month of 1846, reached Saltillo, to participate afterwards, gloriously, in the battle of Buena Vista.

Major-general Scott departed from the capital of the United States, on 24th November, 1846, to assume command in chief of the army. Sailed from New Orleans on 23d December, 1846—visited, with his staff, Brazos Santiago, Tampico, and the Island of Lobos, and landed with the army from the fleet, on the 9th March, 1847.

As condensation is appropriate in matters which only collaterally appertain to our narrative, the most prominent battles of the south are collected, from official despatches, in the following tabular form :

AMERICAN.					MEXICAN.			
Battles.	Date.	Force engaged.	Killed.	Wounded.	Force estimated.	Killed.	Wounded.	Prisoners.
Palo Alto	May 8, 1846	2,288	9	44	6,000	100	400	
Res. de la Palma	May 9, 1846	1,700	39	82	6,000	100	400	135
Monterey	Sep. 23 & 24, 1846	6,645	120	368	10,000	500	800	
Buena Vista	Feb. 22 & 23, 1847	4,759	267	456	20,000	500	1,500	294
Vera Cruz	March 9 to 27, "	13,470	11	55	8,000	400	600	5,000
Cerro Gordo	April 17 & 18, "	8,500	63	407	12,000	500	700	2,837
Contreros	August 19, "	2,000 }	137	877	8,000	750	1,000	1,500
Churubusco	August 20, "	8,497 }			30,000	500	1,000	1,100
Molino del Rey	September 8, "	3,100	116	655	14,000	3000 kill'd, w'ded & pris.		
Chapultepec	Sept. 12 & 13, "	7,180 }	130	703	25,000 }	1000	2,000	3,000
City of Mexico	September 14, "	6,000 }			30,000 }			

Major-general Taylor's despatch, of 17th May, 1846, gives the enemy's loss in killed, wounded, and missing, in the two affairs of the 8th and 9th of May, as 1000 men, "moderately estimated." The

Mexican account sets down their loss, in the two actions, as 262 killed, 355 wounded, and 135 prisoners.

The despatch of March 6, 1847, from Major-general Taylor, fixes the Mexican force, at Buena Vista, at 20,000, "as stated in Santa Anna's summons, and as confirmed by all the information since obtained;" and states that their killed and wounded "may be fairly estimated at 1500, and will probably reach 2000."

The Mexican loss at Monterey was never ascertained; it was estimated at some one or two thousand killed and wounded.

The Mexicans estimated their loss, during the bombardment of Vera Cruz, at nearly one thousand killed and wounded.

Major-general Scott's despatch, of April 23d, 1847, gives our "whole force present, in action and in reserve," as 8500, and estimates the enemy's at 12,000 or more. "About 3000 prisoners, 4 or 5000 stand of arms, and 43 pieces of artillery were taken." And computes the enemy's loss, at Cerro Gordo, to have been from 1000 to 1200.

GENERAL SUMMARY

From Gen. Scott's Despatches of September 18, 1847.

AUGUST 19, 20.—Killed, 137, including 14 officers. Wounded, 877, including 62 officers. Missing, (probably killed,) 38 rank and file. Total, 1,052.

SEPTEMBER 8.—Killed, 116, including 9 officers. Wounded, 665, including 49 officers. Missing, 18 rank and file. Total, 789.

SEPTEMBER 12, 13, 14.—Killed, 130, including 10 officers. Wounded, 703, including 68 officers. Missing, 29 rank and file. Total, 862.

Grand total of losses, 2,703, including 383 officers.

On the other hand, this small force has beaten, on the same occasions, in view of their capital, the whole Mexican army, of (at the beginning) thirty odd thousand men, posted always in chosen positions, behind intrenchments, or more formidable defences of nature and art: killed or wounded of that number more than 7,000 officers and men; taken 3,730 prisoners, one-seventh officers, including 13 generals, of whom three had been Presidents of this Republic; captured more than 20 colours and standards, 75 pieces of ordnance, besides 57 wall-pieces, 20,000 small-arms, an immense quantity of shots, shells, powder, &c.

Of that enemy, once so formidable in numbers, appointments, artillery, &c., twenty odd thousand have disbanded themselves in despair, leaving, as is known, not more than three fragments—the largest about 2,500—now wandering in different directions, without magazines or a military chest, and living *at free quarters* upon their own people.

CHAPTER IV.

"Army of the West"—Purpose of the greatest importance—Gen. Kearny
—Orders and instructions for New Mexico and Upper California—Civil
governments—Forces organized at Fort Leavenworth—Capture of Santa Fé—
Proclamations, &c.—Legislative and Executive action thereon—Expedition
—Fort—Treaties with Indians, &c.—Orders to Col. Doniphan, &c.—Marches
for Upper California.

THE existence of the war with Mexico having been recognised
by the act of Congress of May 13, 1846, the Executive of the
United States prepared to prosecute it with the utmost vigour.
The ports of Mexico on the Gulf, and on the Pacific, were placed
under blockade, and her territory invaded at several important
points. The operations on the Gulf, and of our armies in the
south of Mexico, have been rapidly sketched in the last chapter;
and, if it be true, as it undoubtedly is, that their gallant achievements have afforded " *examples of courage and skill scarcely excelled in the history of military operations,*"* it is equally a
subject of patriotic exultation that our army and navy have earned
unfading laurels on the Pacific, and in the north.

The rapid and almost bloodless movements by which a territory,
vast and extensive as one-third of our entire Union, has been sub-
jugated, are not alone objects of the deepest interest from the mo-
mentous consideration, that the *Conquest of California and New
Mexico* may have finally dissolved the political ties which bound
these States to Mexico, and this consummation eventually become
the principal result of the Mexican war; but that an absorbing
interest is created by the romantic and perilous enterprises of the
small " Army of the West," led, for thousands of miles, through
unexplored regions—across trackless deserts and arid plains—or
over mountains and through defiles whither the foot of civilized
man had seldom, if ever penetrated—now victoriously contending

---

* W. L. Marcy, Secretary of War.

against vastly superior numbers of Mexicans, and anon chastising savage tribes of Indians for cruelties and robberies perpetrated on an enemy, from a bloody contest with whom they had issued, with scarce time enough to bind up their wounds, or wipe the dust of battle from their brows. In fact, it will be seen that an "*almost fabulous*" interest attended the expeditions of our military and naval forces in the west and north-west, apart from their great political importance, which has already engrossed so much legislative discussion, and still occupies the press and the minds of the people.

That the vigilance of our government was early directed to the vulnerable points of Mexico, was apparent from the position of our fleets and forces at the breaking out of the war. *The "Army of the West"* was one of those instruments chosen by the executive, at the earliest period of hostilities, to execute, in conjunction with the Pacific squadron, a purpose of "the greatest importance." And well and nobly did this little band of regulars and volunteers accomplish the object of their enrolment.

Simultaneously with the recognition of the war between the United States and Mexico, the President was authorized to accept the services of volunteers, not to exceed 50,000, to serve for the period of twelve months, or to the end of the war. Immediately twenty-six regiments were called for from the western and southwestern States. A regiment of mounted volunteers, thus called out from Missouri, were mustered into service, on the 6th of June, 1846, at Fort Leavenworth, where, under orders from the War Department, five companies of the First Regiment United States Dragoons, with one volunteer troop of horse, two companies of foot, and two of light artillery volunteers from St. Louis, were being concentrated to compose an expedition to Santa Fé.

To the command of this force, afterwards increased as its purposes were enlarged, *Col. Stephen W. Kearny,* of the First Regiment United States Dragoons, was designated.

Col. Kearny ranked very high as an energetic and accomplished officer, and his long service in the west, on the frontier and among the Indians, had admirably qualified him to direct this very difficult and distant enterprise to a successful termination.

3

The gallant achievements of Colonel, now Brigadier-general Kearny, require some biographical notice of one who has won for himself rank among the most distinguished of our American generals. It is hoped that the concise sketch here given will be found, at least accurate, though far short of the subject.

Stephen W. Kearny was born in New Jersey, where his parents then resided, although they belonged to one of the old colonial families of New York. At the age of sixteen years, young Kearny was placed at Columbia College, New York city, to complete his education. Here he much endeared himself to his classmates and companions ; always punctiliously respectful and courteous in his deportment, he never wounded the feeling of others, while the serenity and equableness of his temper, joined to his unpretending modesty, stern integrity, and cool and resolute determination of character, won the highest respect of all his acquaintances. In fact, he possessed in himself, and in his nature, so much of high and chivalrous feeling, that he may be almost said to have been born a soldier. It may not, therefore, be surprising that, when the late war with Great Britain was about to be declared, no persuasions of his friends or family could delay young Kearny from leaving his collegiate studies—though, as he was just about to graduate with honour to himself, it is presumed his diploma followed him in a few weeks—and seeking a commission, which was bestowed upon him, as first-lieutenant of Thirteenth Infantry, on the 12th March, 1812. He repaired promptly to his post on the Niagara frontier ; and, in the fall of 1812, participated in the battle of Queenstown Heights, where, with others, he was taken prisoner. Having been exchanged, we find him promoted to a captaincy in the First Infantry, on the 1st of April, 1813. He is known to have served through the war of 1812, with the reputation of a gallant, intelligent, and energetic officer, who gave every promise of rising to high distinction, should opportunity offer itself. On the 1st of May, 1829, he was appointed major of the Third Infantry, of which he had been brevet-major since April 1, 1823. On the organization of the First Dragoons, March 4, 1833, he was made the lieutenant-colonel ; and, on the 4th July, 1836, he became the colonel of that regiment. For the last fifteen or twenty years, he has been stationed in the far west—at St. Louis, and generally at Fort Leavenworth, on the Missouri—in the dragoon service. He has made frequent reconnoissances, in military expeditions, in that region. In 1845, he marched, with five companies of his regiment, at least 2200 miles, as a summer campaign, in 99 days, through the Indian country, a considerable portion of it a barren wilderness, carrying their provisions and stores with them, and their horses subsisting on the grass of the prairies. This tour swept westward until it fell on the Oregon trail; thence to the Nebraska, &c., to Fort Laramie; thence to the "South Pass," and to the waters of the Green river, on the Colorado of the West; and from thence returned, by a route leading them some hundreds of miles further south, to Fort Leavenworth, without the loss of a man. Thus Col. Kearny had acquired such knowledge of the physical features of the country, of the Indian habits, and of the resources of a western life, as amply qualified him to act the pioneer and commanding officer of the expedition which he so successfully conducted to Santa Fé, and afterwards extended to California. In personal appearance he has much the look and carriage of the soldier—of good stature, erect, and well formed, his sun-burnt and somewhat care-worn countenance presents still a face of oval proportions, intelligent, and dignified repose; while the short black hair, rapidly verging into gray, and keen eye, indicate the energy of the man and the soldier. Col. Kearny married the step-daughter of the celebrated Wm. Clark, of St. Louis, who penetrated, with Meriwether Lewis, to the Columbia river, in 1804-5-6; and is said to be rich, and independent of the profession of arms, which he has long followed, and for which he is said ever to have had an unconquerable predilection.

The projected movements of Col. Kearny on Santa Fé were looked to with the most intense interest in Missouri, where so many volunteers were anxious to get into the saddle, and take a part in the gallant enterprise. However great the enthusiasm, which even carried a delegation of seventy ladies up from St. Louis to Fort Leavenworth, to present a flag to the Clay county volun-

teers, it was not deemed necessary to accept the services of other
than eight companies of mounted men from Missouri, under Col.
Doniphan, and Capt. Hudson's company of dragoons, "Laclede
Rangers," of St. Louis, who served with the United States dragoons—a compliment to their discipline and efficiency; Major
Clark's flying artillery battalion, composed of Capt. Fischer's
and Capt. Weightman's companies, of St. Louis; and two companies of volunteer infantry, under Capts. Angney and Murphy,
from Missouri.

The preparations were pushed forward with the utmost vigour.
Ordnance, subsistence, near a thousand mules for draught, several
hundred horses for the ordnance, and for mounting the dragoons,
at least three hundred wagons, baggage trains, &c., and other stores
in proportion, were collected in June. The volunteers, during this
month, as they successively reached Fort Leavenworth, were
drilled and instructed, so that—containing within themselves many
an old campaigner and hardy trapper of the western wilds and
Rocky Mountains—it was then apparent, as it subsequently proved,
"*they could not be beat.*"

With an energy that "gave assurance of the end"—the faithful
and gallant performance of the duties assigned to them—four
talented young officers of the United States Topographical Engineers, Lieuts. William H. Emory, W. H. Warner, J. W.
Abert, and W. G. Peck, hurried on from the seat of government, and quickly completing, at St. Louis, their equipment for
the campaign, arranging their instruments, &c., reported to Col.
Kearny.

While thus preparing at the general rendezvous, rumours arrived from Santa Fé, of various species of hostile reception they
might expect—one, which was reasonably near the truth, that
Governor Armijo was at Moro, about ninety miles this side of
Santa Fé, with about four thousand men, ready to engage with
any force that the United States might send against them. Two
companies of dragoons were despatched to intercept a party of
Mexican traders, who were charged, erroneously as it appeared
afterwards, with conveying to Santa Fé a large quantity of arms

and ammunition, while other peaceful traders were assured that private property and rights would be respected.

It was while thus energetically occupied in mustering, ordering, and disciplining his forces, that Col. Kearny received, from the Secretary of War, the highly important instructions,* of June 3, 1846, informing him, that " it had been decided by the President to be of the greatest importance in the pending war with Mexico, to take the earliest possession of Upper California." That an expedition with that view was " hereby ordered," and that he was designated to command it. And that, to enable him to be in sufficient force to conduct it successfully, an additional force of a thousand mounted men had been called for, from the governor of the state of Missouri, to follow him in the direction of Santa Fé, and to be under his orders, or the officer he might leave in command at Santa Fé.

In this communication, Col. Kearny was told that it was deemed prudent the object of adding to the force under his command should not, at that time, become a matter of public notoriety.

It was supposed the additional force would be behind that ordered for the Santa Fé expedition, probably not more than three weeks. That, should he take possession of Santa Fé with the force already called out, and find himself in a condition to garrison it with a small part of his command, (as the additional force would soon be at that place,) he should with the remainder press forward to California, and make such arrangements as to being followed by the reinforcements before mentioned, as he might deem safe and prudent. The Secretary cautioned him to provide for retaining safe possession of Santa Fé, including the State of New Mexico; and should Col. Kearny deem it prudent to have still more troops for the objects designated in the communication, he should lose no time in forwarding to the department his opinion on that point, and on all others connected with the enterprise. In fact, he was authorized to make a direct requisition on the gover-

---

* As this is an interesting document, though here closely followed, it is given in the Appendix, No. 1.

D

nor of Missouri. He was informed that a large body of Mormon emigrants were *en route* to California, to settle there, and desired to use "all proper means to have a good understanding with them, to the end that the United States might have their co-operation in taking possession of, and holding, that territory." To aid in the expedition against California, he was authorized to induce to volunteer into the service a number not exceeding one-third of his entire force, to be paid as other volunteers, and to allow them, so far as it could properly be done, to designate their own officers. It was supposed that a considerable number of American citizens, well disposed towards the United States, were then settled on the Sacramento river, near Suter's establishment, called "Nueva Helvetia," and, should he find such to be the true state of things there, he was authorized to organize, and receive into the service, such portion of these citizens as he might think useful to aid him in holding possession of the country, allowing them to select their own officers so far as he should judge proper.

The choice of routes to enter California, was left to his judgment, and more ample means of accurate information, but a southern route (called the Caravan route, by which the wild horses are brought from that country into New Mexico) was intimated as practicable; and it was suggested as not improbable, that it could be passed over in the winter, or at least late in autumn.

The Secretary advised him, that, should the President be disappointed in his cherished hope of his being able to reach the interior of Upper California before winter, he should make the best arrangements he could for sustaining his forces during the winter, and make an early movement in the spring. That, though very desirable the expedition should reach California that season, (the President not doubting he would make every possible effort to accomplish it,) yet, if in his judgment it could not be undertaken with reasonable prospect of success, he should defer it, as before suggested, until spring.

Col. Kearny was informed it was expected the naval forces of the United States were there, or soon would be, in the Pacific, and in possession of all the towns on the sea-coast, and that they would co-operate with him in the conquest of California. That arms, ordnance, munitions of war and provisions, to be used in the country, would be sent by sea to the squadron in the Pacific for the land forces.

Should he conquer and take possession of New Mexico and California, or considerable places in either, Col. Kearny was ordered to establish civil governments therein—abolishing all existing arbitrary restrictions, so far as might be done with safety, and in this it would be wise and prudent to continue all such existing officers as were known to be friendly to the United States, and would take the oath of allegiance to them. He was advised the duties at the custom-houses ought, at once, to be reduced to such rate as would be barely sufficient to maintain the necessary officers. He was authorized to assure the people of those provinces, that it was the wish and design of the United States to provide for them a free government, with the least possible delay, similar to that which existed in the territories, and then they would be called on to exercise the rights of freemen in electing their own representatives to the territorial legislature.

That it was foreseen that what related to the civil government would be a difficult and unpleasant part of his duty, and much must necessarily be left to his own discretion, and his whole conduct must be so regulated as best to conciliate the inhabitants, and render them friendly to the United States.

The Secretary of War instructs him that it is desirable the trade between the citizens of the United States and the Mexican provinces should, as usual, be continued as far as practicable under the changed condition of things between the two countries; cautions him to increase his supply of goods to be distributed as presents to the Indians; informs him that he will be furnished with a proclamation, in the Spanish language, to be issued among the Mexican people by him on his entering into or approaching their country, and that he must use his utmost endeavours to have the pledges and promises therein contained carried out to the utmost extent; and, finally, the Secretary tells Col. Kearny, in conclusion of this communication, marked "confidential," that he was

directed by the President to say, that the rank of brevet brigadier-
general would be conferred on him as soon as he commenced his
movement towards California, and sent round to him by sea, or
over the country, or to the care of the commandant of our squadron in the Pacific, and that in that way cannon, arms, ammunition, and supplies for the land forces would be sent to him.

Two days after the date of the above instruction, the following
letter of the Secretary of War was forwarded to Col. Kearny.

WAR DEPARTMENT,
Washington, June 5th, 1846.

SIR :—I enclosed to you a few copies of a proclamation prepared for Gen. Taylor, to issue to the Mexicans.   I discover
that there are parts of it that will not answer our purpose for
Santa Fé or Upper California.   You will not, therefore, use these
copies.   It is intended to make the needful alterations in it, and,
thus altered, send on copies to you before you will have occasion
to distribute them.   I must, however, urge you not to use those
which have been forwarded.

Subsequently, Congress were informed that "no proclamation,
modified as proposed, was sent" to Col. Kearny—that "no proclamation for circulation was ever furnished to Gen. Kearny.
"A few copies of that prepared for, and sent to, Gen. Taylor,
were forwarded to Gen. Kearny, but he was requested not to use
them.   These copies were the only proclamations sent by the
War Department to him," and that the Department "are not
aware that he ever used any of them."

By the last days of June, the energy and activity of Col.
Kearny, of his officers, and of the Secretary of War, had per-
fected the arrangements at Fort Leavenworth.   All were impatient for action—every thing promised fairly—the troops were in
excellent health and spirits—the horses in better condition than
when they came there.   The trumpet sounded—then came the
joyous spring into the saddle of the dragoons and mounted men—
the roll of the infantry drums—the artillerists harnessing up their
draft horses and manœuvering with the "big guns"—and they

were off on their distant tramp, over a wild country, where, for hundreds of miles, a long train of baggage and provision wagons carried, through tribes of savage and thieving Indians, their only support—until " they met the enemy and they were theirs."

Col. Kearny's well-known experience had been fully exercised in putting the column in motion, so that the successive battalions, stock animals, trains, &c., might not interfere with the subsistence, foraging, and celerity of the march.

On the 27th, the Topographical Engineers started for the prairies, ahead of the main column. They had with them some eight or ten "*voyageurs*," several pack mules, a baggage wagon, and a spring car, with four mules harnessed to it, to carry the instruments.

The movement from Fort Leavenworth having been completed, the troops travelled uninterruptedly on a most interesting route—"the Santa Fé trace," too often described to be necessary here; until about the 1st of August, when the whole original force of about 1657 men concentrated at Bent's Fort, or rather, for the convenience of grazing, about nine miles below. They had then marched 564 miles from Fort Leavenworth, in excellent order and fine spirits, without an accident, and in improved health and discipline.

It is worthy of remark that the two infantry companies had outmarched, and reachèd, on foot, the fort in advance of the mounted companies; and, as showing the precision of experienced military combination, and the energy and discipline of the volunteers as well as regulars, it may be mentioned that many of the battalions arrived at the hour, and the whole force on the day fixed upon by the commander-in-chief.

The corrected longitude of Bent's Fort, as ascertained by Lieutenant Emory, and published by the Topographical Bureau, is 103° 25′ 45″ west; and latitude 38° 2′ 53″ north. It is distant from Santa Fé exactly 309 miles.

While the troops rested here, for four or five days, to recover from the fatigues of the march, three spies from New Mexico were brought in, and were so promenaded into—through—round and

D 2

about, and round about again the different encampments, as to be made to entertain a very lively and exaggerated conception of the number of the American forces, which they doubtless reported, in full, to Gov. Armijo, on being dismissed unharmed by Col. Kearny, with a message that he would see the governor in a few days.

At Bent's Fort, Col. Kearny held a talk with the Chyennes Indians, advising them to peaceful pursuits, &c. Here, also, was promulgated the following:

Proclamation to the citizens of New Mexico, by Colonel Kearny, commanding the United States forces.

The undersigned enters New Mexico with a large military force, for the purpose of seeking union with and ameliorating the condition of its inhabitants. This he does under instructions from his government, and with the assurance that he will be amply sustained in the accomplishment of this object. It is enjoined on the citizens of New Mexico to remain quietly at their homes, and to pursue their peaceful avocations. So long as they continue in such pursuits, they will not be interfered with by the American army, but will be respected and protected in their rights, both civil and religious.

All who take up arms or encourage resistance against the government of the United States will be regarded as enemies, and will be treated accordingly.   S. W. KEARNY,
Colonel First Dragoons.
Camp at Bent's Fort, on the Arkansas, *July* 31*st*, 1846.

At Bent's Fort, as at Fort Leavenworth, various rumours reached the camp of the movements of the enemy. By some it was said there would be little or no fighting; by others, that the Mexicans were straining every nerve to fortify Santa Fé and Taos, and were, elsewhere, marshalling their forces.

The ordnance was still on its way from Fort Leavenworth, whence, as soon as prepared, Lieut. Warner, of Topographical Engineers, had been left to bring it up with the column. This was an undertaking not so easily accomplished with the only means left—ox-teams—and, although this officer worked "like a beaver," and struggled ahead with characteristic energy and perseverance, yet he was unable to reach Col. Kearny with his charge, until after the occupation of Santa Fé, when his serviceable fatigue and labours were gratefully and very complimentarily acknowledged by the commander.

On the 3d of August, Col. Kearny, having determined not to wait for his ordnance train, or for the new levies, pushed rapidly on, that, by the celerity of his movements, he might frustrate any combination of the forces of the enemy.

On the march, several hundred horses and mules had to be left behind, unable longer to follow. On the 13th, their progress had overcome the sandy soil, bad quality of the grass, want of good water, and the inconvenience of almost insupportable heat and hot winds; for they had begun to ascend the great chain of mountains running north and south on the west side of the Rio Grande, and had reached the settlements.

The march now became intensely interesting. Messengers arrived from Armijo with a letter to Col. Kearny, in answer to one sent by Capt. Cooke, of Dragoons, some days previous. "It was a sensible, straight-forward letter, and if written by an American, or by an Englishman, would have meant this: You have notified me that you intend to take possession of the country I govern. The people of the country have risen in mass to my defence. If you get the country, it will be because you prove the strongest in battle. I suggest to you to stop at the Sapilla, and I will march to the Vegos. We will meet and negotiate on the plains between them."*

Messages reached the advancing columns from Americans at Santa Fé and other towns, stating they were very much alarmed for their own safety, the Mexicans having told them that, if they were defeated, they would return and take full vengeance on them. They stated variously the forces which had gone out to meet the Americans.

---

* Lieut. Emory's Journal, in " Union" of 22d Oct. 1846.

The Spy company, in advance, met four well-mounted and armed Mexicans, who summoned Capt. Bent and his small party to surrender, but quickly concluded it would be most advisable to surrender themselves, and accordingly they were added to other prisoners made of the scouts of the enemy. Some of these were disarmed, and sent forth to the villages with proclamations.

On the 14th, the order of march was the order of battle.—(Here the author finds a published description of the exciting events of this period, so graphical and authentic, that he fears to attempt its abridgment, as well on account of its great interest, as that he must avow his inability to do it justice, otherwise than by copying it entire.)*

" *Friday, August* 14.—Started at 7 o'clock ; at four miles met four Mexicans sent by Gov. Armijo to Gen. Kearny with a letter. They were dragoons, dressed in roundabout and pants of light blue cloth, similar to our own dragoons, with a red stripe down the outer seam of the pants. They all wore large Mexican hats ; there was a lieutenant, sergeant and two privates. They rode small horses. The lieutenant had a sabre ; the others were armed with carbines and lances. They made a very respectable appearance, but such soldiers cannot fight United States dragoons. Their heavy horses and superior equipment will conquer them. The four dragoons above spoken of, and those taken a day or two since, were set at large to-day. The colonel told them that he had come with a sufficient force to extend our laws over them. That he came as their friend. That he came to give protection alike to the poor man and the rich. That, although he had the power to do as he pleased, still his orders were to treat all who remained at home in the peaceful pursuit of their business, as friends. But, that if found in arms against him, the vengeance of his government and army would be poured out upon them. He told them that, not 'an onion or a pepper would be taken from them without a full equivalent in cash ;' that their persons, property and religion,

---

* It assumes the shape of a diary, and from the position of the author—near the general commanding—may be regarded, with all its statements, as of the most authentic character."—*St. Louis Republican*, Sept. 24, 1846, and *Washington* " *Union*," Oct. 2, 1846.

would be respected. That he would soon be in Santa Fé, and that he hoped to meet Gov. Armijo and shake hands with him as a friend; but if that were denied him, he had a force sufficient to put down all opposition, and that he would certainly do it. We are encamped at the Passes: at this place runs a small mountain stream, and near it, a village containing probably one hundred mud-built houses.

"There were 300 mounted men here yesterday. They have all gone to Santa Fé, no doubt to join the main army, which is said to be 12,000 strong—2,000 well armed, and four pieces of artillery, (one six-pounder taken from the Santa Fé prisoners.) The other 10,000 are said to be armed with bows and arrows, slings, and other weapons. The Mexican dragoons report that Capt. Cooke left Santa Fé with them, but as they got a change of horses, they out-rode him. (The captain had been sent from Bent's Fort, by Gen. Kearny, with letters to Gov. Armijo.) He will be with us to-morrow. From white men, who reside here, we learn that the governor exercises the most despotic sway over the common people, aided by the priests. They say to such men as we have met, 'Go on such a road, ascertain where Cooke and his men are, and return to me at such a time.' They furnish no man for the performance of the duty, and give no compensation. Yet no Mexican dare to refuse, or fail to perform the duty. What a change will be effected among these people when they are emancipated. If Gen. Kearny succeeds in this expedition without inflicting any pain, he will be the greatest man that has ever been in New Mexico. There are extensive fields of corn near us, cultivated by irrigation. After spring sets in, there is no rain here till in August, when they have refreshing showers, and the grass begins to grow again. The rain of this season commenced about ten days since, and grass is more abundant. But for this, it would be impossible to take our animals to Santa Fé, probably not beyond this place. Gen. Kearny's 'good luck' still attends him. We have passed, within the last two days, cattle and sheep enough to subsist the army all winter, and we have no fear of starving.

" *Saturday, August* 15.—Started at 7, A. M., and passed through the village. The colonel was overtaken at this place by Major Swords, from Fort Leavenworth, who brought him a commission as brigadier-general.

"After having passed through the village, the troops halted near it, while the general addressed the alcalde and people from the top of one of the houses. He told them 'that he came by order of the government of the United States to take possession of New Mexico, and to extend the laws of the United States over them. That he had an ample force with him, and that another army would soon join them. That, in future, they were absolved from all allegiance to the Mexican government and Governor Armijo, and must hold allegiance to the United States, and to *him* as their governor. That, for this allegiance, they would be protected by the United States government from the Indians, (who are dreadful scourges to them,) and from all their enemies. That he came to protect the poor man as well as the rich man. That, if they remained peaceably at home, they would be considered good citizens ; but, if found fighting against him, they would be considered traitors, and treated accordingly.'

"He continued the alcalde in his office, and told him to be governed by the laws of Mexico for the present.

"He stated to them that he had been well informed 'that some of the priests had endeavoured to make them believe that he was coming to destroy their religion, and to inflict grievous wrongs upon them.' This, he said, was false. He told them that their persons, property, and religion would not be interfered with. 'Now,' said he, 'under these circumstances, are you, Mr. Alcalde, and you, two captains of militia, willing to take the oath of allegiance to the United States?' Two of them readily consented, but one of the captains evaded the question. The general demanded a categorical answer. The captain said 'Yes,' but it was evident it was with a bad grace. They then raised their hands and made the sign of the cross with the thumb and finger, all present uncovering their heads, and the general in a solemn manner administered the following oath : 'You do swear to hold faithful allegiance to the United States, and to defend its government and laws against

all its enemies, in the name of the Father, Son, and Holy Ghost,'
or words to that effect. The general then said: 'I will shake
hands with them as good friends.' When he came to the captain,
who did not seem to enter fully into the matter, he took him by the
hand, and told the interpreter, 'Tell the man to look *me* in the eye.'
The general gave him one of his significant smiles, and with his
keen eyes fixed firmly on him, seemed to say, 'I know you are a
rascal;' (such he no doubt was,) but the others, I think, were
honest. He then told the people, (about two hundred,) 'I shake
hands with you all, through your alcalde, and hail you as good
citizens of the United States:' upon which they raised a general
shout. At this town are extensive fields of wheat and corn, cultivated by irrigation, from a beautiful creek. The water is taken
out on each side in canals, and spread over their fields. It was a
beautiful sight to see the clear mountain water rushing through
these canals, and producing luxuriant fields of corn and wheat,
where rain so seldom falls.

"Our camp was near these fields, and although sentinels were
placed very near together, with strict orders to keep every animal
out of them, yet some did get in, and some damage was done.
The general told the alcalde that he had used every precaution to
prevent 'any interference with their crops,' yet 'they had sustained some loss.' He told him to examine the fields and ascertain
what the damage was to each man, to send him a statement of it to
Santa Fé, and that full compensation should be paid them. They
seemed delighted with this exemplification of equal justice—a thing
not dreamed of in New Mexico, under the rule of Armijo.

"News reached the general last night, that we would have a fight
to-day in one of the mountain gorges, and our movement has been
in a strict military manner. When paasing through these narrow
defiles, (where an enemy would be most formidable,) the word
'draw sabre' was given, and we passed through at a fast trot.
But no enemy has been seen. The infantry passed over the mountain to take them in rear. We passed through several other villages, where the general assembled the inhabitants, and proceeded
as with the first. The two last appeared happy to be recognised

as citizens of the United States, and were seen to embrace each other in token of their joy at the change of government. At the last one, they brought forward their wives to receive the congratulations of the general, (whose manner on such occasions is most happy,) and it was evident that his words had gladdened their hearts, for they smiled upon him in a manner which woman alone knows how to do. We encamped at 4, P. M., in poor grass, having marched seventeen miles. Capt. Cooke met us to-day, from Santa Fé, and says Governor Armijo will meet us with an army. He had been kindly treated while in Santa Fé, and smoked many a 'segarito' from the fair lips of the ladies.

"The villages we have passed to-day are built of sun-burnt bricks. The houses have flat roofs, covered with earth, and are dry and comfortable from the absence of rain or moisture. Each one has a church, and a graveyard, with high walls of sun-burnt brick. There is more intelligence among them than I expected to find, and with a good government and protection from the Indians, they will become a happy people.

"The Eutaws have recently stolen their stock, and carried off several children. Well may they hail this revolution as a blessing. One of the alcaldes to-day said, that God ruled the destinies of men, and that as we had come with a strong army among them to change their form of government, it must be right, and he submitted cheerfully. Major Swords and Lieut. Gilmer brought us the mail to the 19th of July, and many a heart was made glad by tidings from wives, mothers, children, and dearly beloved ones. There are plenty of cattle, sheep, and goats in the country, and we shall fare well enough.

" *Sunday, August* 16.—Started at the usual hour, and at seven miles, came to the village of St. Miguel, built like the others, of sun-burnt brick, and with flat roofs. After much delay, the alcalde and padre were found, and presented to Gen. Kearny. They received him politely, but it was evident they did not relish an interview with him. This village contains a respectable church, and about two or three hundred houses. The general expressed a wish to ascend one of the houses, with the priest and alcalde, and to address the people of the town, informing them of the object of his mission. After many evasions, delays, and useless speeches, the padre made a speech, stating that " he was a Mexican, but should obey the laws that were placed over him for *the time*, but if the general should point all his cannon at his breast, he could not consent to go up there and address the people."

"The general very mildly told him, through the interpreter, Mr. Robideau, that he had not come to injure him, nor did he wish him to address the people. He only wished him to go up there, and hear him (the general) address them. The padre still fought shy, and commenced a long speech, which the general interrupted, and told him he had no time to listen to 'useless remarks,' and repeated, that he only wanted him to go up and listen to his speech. He consented. The general made pretty much the same remarks to the alcalde and people that he had made to the people of the other villages. He assured them that he had an ample force, and would have possession of the country against all opposition ; but gave them assurances of the friendship and protection of the United States. He stated to them that this had never been given them by the government of Mexico, but that the United States were able, and would certainly protect them, not only in their persons, property, and religion, but against the cruel invasion of the Indians. That they saw but a small part of the force that was at his disposal. Many more troops were near him on another road, (some of which he showed them a mile or two distant,) and that another army would, probably, be through their village in three weeks. After this, he said, 'Mr. Alcalde, are you willing to take the oath of allegiance to the United States ?' He replied, that 'he would prefer waiting till the general had taken possession of the capital.' The general told him, 'it was sufficient for him to know that he had possession of his village.' He then consented, and with the usual formalities, he said : ' You swear, that you will bear true allegiance to the government of the United States of America.' The alcalde said : 'Provided, I can be protected in my religion.' The general said : 'I swear you shall be.' He then continued, 'and that you will defend her

E   4

against all her enemies and opposers, in the name of the Father,
the Son, and Holy Ghost—Amen.'

"The general then said : 'I continue you as the alcalde of this
village ; and require you, the inhabitants of this village, to obey
him as such.   Your laws will be continued for the present, but as
soon as I have time to examine them, if any change can be made
that will be for your benefit, it shall be done.'   After shaking
hands with them, he left.   The padre then invited him to his
house, and gave them and his staff refreshments ; and after sun-
dry hugs, jokes, and professions of friendship, with an expression
from the general, that the 'better they became acquainted, the
better friends they would be,' and an invitation to the padre to
visit him at Santa Fé, (which he promised,) we left the village.
The padre was evidently the ruling spirit of the village, and the
alcalde was under great restraint by his presence.   The visit to
the priest, and the frank and friendly manner of the general had
the desired effect, and I believe they parted the best of friends,
and have no doubt that the inhabitants of St. Miguel will soon be
as good democrats as can be found in Missouri.

"The alcalde informed the general that 400 men left the village to
join the Mexican army, but that 200 had returned home.

"Soon after leaving this village, an express arrived from Santa Fé,
informing the general that a large force would oppose his march
fifteen miles from that place, in a deep ravine.   It was headed by
an individual known as Salazar.   That Gen. Armijo refused to
command them, and said he would defend the town.   The same
information was soon after brought by Puebla Indians, who said
there was a large force of their people among the Mexicans, armed
with bows and arrows ; that their people had been forced into the
service, and that their chiefs would not permit them to take their
guns.

"As it is not more than two days' march to Santa Fé, if we have
a fight, it will probably be to-morrow.   Marched seventeen miles.

"*Monday, August 17.*—Started at the usual time.   Our picket-
guard took a prisoner, the son of the noted Salazar, well remembered by the Texan prisoners for his cruelties to them.   He stated

that the Mexican army had left the cañon and gone home. The general told him he would keep him a prisoner, and if he found that he had told him falsely, he would hang him. We soon met others from Santa Fé, who congratulated the general on his arrival in the country, and their deliverance from the tyrannical rule of Armijo.

"They further said, that Armijo had taken one hundred dragoons and his cannon, and gone this morning towards Chihuahua. We passed, to-day, the ruins of the ancient town of Pecos. I visited it with some Mexicans, and an interpreter, who gave me a full account of it. It was said to have been built long before the conquest. It stands on an eminence. The dwellings were built of small stones and mud; some of the buildings are still so far perfect as to show three full stories. There were four rooms under ground, fifteen feet deep, and twenty-five feet across, in a circular form. In one of these rooms burned the 'holy fire,' which was kindled many centuries before the conquest; and when the Pecos Indians were converted to the Catholic faith, they still continued their own religious rites, and among them the 'sacred fire,' which never ceased to burn, till seven years since, when the village was broken up. The population is probably one thousand. The church is large, and although in ruins, was evidently a fine building. It was built after the conquest. The eastern roof of the main building is still good—it is filled with birds. As we came in front of it, the Mexicans took off their hats, and on entering the building did the same. The general learned, to-day, that Salazar had been in command at the cañon, and that he had passed round us and gone to St. Miguel, the town we passed yesterday. The general sent him word that he had his son a prisoner, and would treat him well, if the father remained peaceable, but if he took up arms, or excited the people to resistance, he would hang him.

"We encamped at 3, P. M., on the Pecos creek, in excellent grass, where was a beautiful farm, well watered—distance, to-day, fifteen and three-quarter miles.

"An abundance of vegetables have been brought into camp this evening, and we have fared better than since we left Missouri.

Bread, coffee, and bacon are excellent articles of food, when accompanied with other little 'fixings,' which ladies only can provide us with, but of themselves, after a few weeks, campaigners become a little tired.

"An American gentleman has just arrived in camp from Santa Fé; he left at 12, M., to-day, and says that after the governor's abdication, the alcaldes held a meeting, and *gravely* discussed the propriety of tearing down the churches to prevent their being converted into barracks, and that the American citizens interfered, and assured them that they had nothing to fear on that subject, and thereby saved the churches. A lady also sent for him this morning, and asked him if he did not think it advisable for her to leave the town, with her daughters, to save them from dishonour. He advised her by all means to remain at home, and assured her that she and her daughters were in no danger from the approach of the army.

"Most of the respectable people of the town have left, and many country people are going to town for protection.

" *Tuesday, August* 18.—Started as usual, and at six miles came to the cañon, where the Mexican army had been assembled. There had been 3000 troops there, but it seems that the nearer we approached them, the fewer they became, and when we passed through they had all gone. The position they chose was near the lower end, and it was one of great strength. The passage was not more than forty feet wide—in front, they had made an obstruction with timber, and beyond this, at 300 yards' distance, was an eminence in the road, on which their cannon had been placed; and it was thought by us that their position was equal to 5000 men. We reached the hill which overlooks Santa Fé, at 5, P. M. Major Clark's artillery was put into line, and the mounted troops and infantry were marched through the town to the palace, (as it is called,) on the public square, where the general and his staff dismounted, and were received by the acting governor, and other dignitaries, and conducted to a large room. The general stated, in a few words, the object of his visit, and gave assurances of safety and protection to all unoffending citizens. While this transpired,

the stars and stripes were hoisted on the staff which is attached
to the palace, by Major Swords, and as soon as it was seen to
wave above the buildings, it was hailed by a national salute from
the batteries of Capts. Fischer and Weightman, under the command
of Major Clark. While the general was proclaiming the conquest
of New Mexico, as a part of the United States, the first gun was
heard. 'There,' said he, 'my guns proclaim that the flag of the
United States floats over this capital.' The people appeared satisfied. The general slept in the palace, (we democrats must call it
the governor's house.) One company of dragoons was kept in the
city as a guard, and the business of the day was ended.

"Thus, in the short space of fifty days, has an army been
marched nearly 900 miles, over a desert country, and conquered
a province of 80,000 souls, without firing a gun—a success which
may be attributed mainly to the skill and ability with which Gen.
Kearny has managed this arduous and delicate business. In explaining his object in coming into the country, and the kindness
he felt for the inhabitants, he was mild and courteous; but then,
(would add,) 'I claim the whole of New Mexico for the United
States. I put my hand on it from this moment, (bringing his
hand firmly down on his thigh,) and demand obedience to its
laws.'

"*Wednesday, August* 19.—The general addressed the whole
people to-day, more at length than he had on other occasions, and
took particular care to give them the most positive assurances of
protection in their persons, property, and religion. Many families
had fled on his approach, and he told their friends to bring them
back, and to say to them that they would be more safe under his
administration than they had ever been. He stated, that in taking
possession of New Mexico, he claimed the whole of it for the
United States, without reference to the Rio Grande. He absolved
them from their allegiance to Mexico and Governor Armijo, and
proclaimed himself governor of New Mexico, and claimed them
as citizens of the United States.

"The acting governor and alcaldes then took the oath of allegiance to the United States, and the people, with a simultaneous

E 2

shout, exclaimed ' *Vive le General.*' The acting governor then addressed the people as follows :—

" 'John Baptist Vigil, alcalde, political and military governor, *pro tem.*, of the department of New Mexico, to the inhabitants of Santa Fé, the capital thereof, greeting : It having been out of my power, by all the exertions that I could put in practice, to calm the fears impressed on the inhabitants by the desertion of Gen. Don Manuel Armijo and his soldiers, and what was most frightful, he having made them conceive, on the approach of the military forces of the government of the United States of North America to the capital, that said forces were composed of cruel and sanguinary savages, and for which many families have left their homes to hide themselves in the desert—believing that no security, no protection of their lives or property was to be expected from the commander of said forces ; and in order to appease these fears, I thought, it convenient and necessary to order to be set up in the most public places, the proclamation of the chief of said forces, of which the following is its tenor.' He then read the proclamation which Gen. Kearny had sent among the Mexicans in advance.

" *Thursday, August 20, and Friday 21.*—The general sits in his room, and is constantly receiving visits from the officers of ex-Governor Armijo and others, who fled on his approach. To all who remain quiet and peaceable, he promises protection. Many of them come into his presence very much disquieted, but he has the happy faculty of calming all their fears, and he is winning laurels among them daily. Ex-Governor Armijo has certainly fled. The cannon he took from the place have been retaken by Capt. Fischer, and will be here soon. The gun taken from the Texan prisoners was left in a mountain, carriage destroyed ; the gun, a brass six-pounder, has been recovered.

" *Saturday, August 21.*—The general is still receiving visits and attending to matters and things which are referred to him. Capt. Waldo, of the volunteers, is translating the few written laws which can be found.

" *Sunday, August 23.*—The general and his staff, and some other officers went to church to-day. There are no seats in the

church, except one for the governor, and a bench on which his
subs sit. Gen. Kearny occupied the former, and we the latter.
The rich and the ragged kneel or sit on the floor, as best they can.
When the priests were ready, the service commenced with a piece
of music, not unlike what I have heard in the theatre, and pretty
well played. This continued with different pieces of music till
the ceremony was over. After which, they escorted the general
to his quarters with music.

"There is evidently a large proportion of very ignorant people
here, and many of them seem to think, judging from their deportment, that they have no rights, and are bound to obey their supe-
riors. When our laws and institutions are established here, the
resources of the country will be developed, and these people will
become prosperous and happy."*

It subsequently appeared, that Governor Armijo had actually
4000 men at his command, but very badly armed; and that on
the 16th, they left for the place appointed as the battle-ground.
When he got there, however, a council of his officers was called,
and they refused to fight. Very soon after this determination,
Gov. Armijo turned his head towards Chihuahua, followed by a
few dragoons.

In fact, the star-spangled banner now waved over the capital of
New Mexico. American sentinels guarded the town ; American
soldiers paraded on the public *plaza.* On the highlands south,
tent upon tent was to be seen, their inmates busily engaged clean-
ing their armour, drilling, and attending to their various military
duties; the cannon of Major Clark's battalion pointing signifi-
cantly with their muzzles towards the town—all denoting that the
war east of the Rio Grande was ended. The fall of the capital

---

* The "unofficial journal" of Lieut. Emory, chief of the Engineer staff of
Gen. Kearny's command, distinguished for his intelligence as an officer and a
man, and now Lieutenant-colonel of Col. G. W. Hughes's regiment, was published in the " Union" of 22d and 23d of October, and 5th of November, 1846. It
confirms and gives these incidents, &c., in greater detail. The limits of this
work preclude the insertion here, of what will be found exceedingly interesting
ọ those who desire fuller details than this work professes to give.

was in effect the fall of the country. Here a scarcity of forage was experienced, and portions of the troops were necessarily stationed with almost all the horses at villages around—some of them many miles distant—for the purpose of grazing the animals.

The highly efficient quartermaster, Major T. Swords, of United States Dragoons, wrote Gen. Jesup : "Should the additional regiment of Missouri Volunteers, under Col. Price, be stationed in this section of country during the coming winter, I see but little prospect of their animals getting through it, as there will be no surplus forage in the country, and the grazing for miles around is said to be entirely eaten up. The country round here is, indeed, too poor to sustain any living thing but the wretched inhabitants, their donkeys, goats, and sheep. Should a large military force be kept in the country, it must be attended with enormous expense— the country furnishing but few of the articles necessary for the support of an army."

Lieut. Emory, also, speaks of the country round about Santa Fé, as "poor and barren," but important in a military point of view, &c.

Of the gallant volunteers, officers and men, a most interesting and original, as gallant and noble—rough yet generous—kind yet brave—a set as ever mingled strangers with a strange people— strange manners—strange customs—they to the Mexicans, and the Mexicans to them—they and their adventures are too full of pleasant interest to venture upon here, else this work would be enlarged beyond its prescribed limits.

Colonel, now Brigadier-general Kearny, was laboriously occupied with his various responsible duties. He early ordered the erection of a fort, a site for which was selected within six hundred yards of the town, and from sixty to one hundred feet above it. The Engineer officers, Lieuts. Emory, Gilmer and Peck, laboured assiduously until, under their superintendence, arose a most imposing structure, called Fort Marcy. A tall flag-staff, erected by the quartermaster's department—spire upon spire towering towards the heavens, and bearing the American banner, excited the wonder of the natives so far that old men were said to have walked sixty miles to look upon it.

The chiefs and head men of the Puebla Indians came in to give in their adhesion. These are represented as a large and formidable band, yet among the most peaceful of New Mexico.

A band of Navahoes were told of their plundering habits, and, if the Mexicans were again disturbed, they would be hung.

Here was issued the following :—

Proclamation to the Inhabitants of New Mexico, by Brigadier-general S. W. Kearny, commanding the troops of the United States in the same.

As, by the act of the republic of Mexico, a state of war exists between that government and the United States ; and as the undersigned, at the head of his troops, on the 18th instant, took possession of Santa Fé, the capital of the department of New Mexico, he now announces his intention to hold the department, with its original boundaries, (on both sides of the Del Norte,) as a part of the United States, and under the name of the Territory of New Mexico.

The undersigned has come to New Mexico with a strong military force, and an equally strong one is following close in his rear. He has more troops than is necessary to put down any opposition that can possibly be brought against him, and therefore it would be but folly or madness for any dissatisfied or discontented persons to think of resisting him.

The undersigned has instructions from his government to respect the religious institutions of New Mexico—to protect the property of the church—to cause the worship of those belonging to it to be undisturbed, and their religious rights in the amplest manner preserved to them—also to protect the persons and property of all quiet and peaceable inhabitants within its boundaries against their enemies, the Eutaws, the Navajoes, and others ; and when he assures all that it will be his pleasure, as well as his duty, to comply with those instructions, he calls upon them to exert themselves in preserving order, in promoting concord, and in maintaining the authority and efficacy of the laws. And he requires of those who have left their homes and taken up arms against the troops of the United States to return *forthwith* to them, or else they will be considered as enemies and traitors, subjecting their persons to punishment and their property to seizure and confiscation for the benefit of the public treasury.

It is the wish and intention of the United States to provide for New Mexico a free government, with the least possible delay, similar to those in the United States ; and the people of New Mexico will then be called on to exercise the rights of freemen, in electing their own representatives to the territorial legislature. But until this can be done, the laws hitherto in existence will be continued until changed or modified by competent authority ; and those persons holding office will continue in the same for the present, provided they will consider themselves good citizens, and are willing to take the oath of allegiance to the United States.

The United States hereby absolve all persons residing within the boundaries of New Mexico from any further allegiance to the republic of Mexico, and hereby claim them as citizens of the United States. Those who remain quiet and peaceable will be considered good citizens, and receive protection—those who are found in arms, or instigating others against the United States, will be considered as traitors, and treated accordingly.

Don Manuel Armijo, the late governor of this department, has fled from it : the undersigned has taken possession of it without firing a gun, or spilling a single drop of blood, in which he most truly rejoices, and, for the present, will be considered as governor of the territory.

Given at Santa Fé, the capital of the territory of New Mexico, this 22d day of August, 1846, and in the 71st year of the Independence of the United States.   S. W. KEARNY,

Brigadier-general U. S. Army.

By the Governor, JUAN BAUTISTA VIGIL Y ALAND.

And on the day after, the following letter was addressed to Gen. Roger Jones :

Head-quarters, Army of the West,
Santa Fé, New Mexico, August 24, 1846.

Sir :—I have to report, that on the 18th instant, the army under my command marched into this city, the capital of New Mexico, having met with no armed resistance ; the Mexican troops, numbering about 4000, which had been collected on the road under Governor Armijo to oppose us, having dispersed on our approaching them, and the governor himself having fled with a troop of his dragoons, towards Chihuahua. On the 22d, I issued a proclamation, claiming the whole of New Mexico, with its then boundaries, as a territory of the United States of America, and taking it under our protection. I send, herewith, copies of all official papers on the subject. The people of the territory are now perfectly tranquil, and can easily be kept so. The intelligent portion know the advantages they are to derive from the change of government, and express their satisfaction at it.

In a few days, I shall march down the Del Norte, and visit some of the principal cities below, for the purpose of seeing the people and explaining to them personally our intentions relating to the territory. On my return (which will be in two or three weeks) a civil government shall be organized, and the officers appointed for it ; after which, I will be ready to start for Upper California, which I hope may be by the latter end of next month ; and in such case, I shall expect to have possession of that department by the close of November.

I have not heard from or of Colonel Price and his command, which he was to raise and bring here, and have received but vague rumours of Captain Allen and the Mormons. I suppose, however, they will all be here in a few weeks. Captain Allen's command will accompany me to the Pacific, and the number of efficient men he brings will determine the additional number I must take from here. After deciding upon that, and upon the number which will be necessary to hold this territory, I shall send the surplus to Chihuahua, to report to Brigadier-general Wool. I enclose a copy of my communication to him of the 22d instant.

On the 15th instant, I received yours of 2d and 3d July, the former enclosing a copy of a letter to Captain Tompkins, Third Artillery, from the general-in-chief—the latter enclosing for me a commission of brigadier-general, which I hereby accept of, and for which I offer to the President and Senate my acknowledgment and thanks for the honour they have conferred on me.

Very respectfully, your obedient servant,

S. W. KEARNY,

Brigadier-general R. Jones,   *Brigadier-general.*
Adjutant-general U. S. A. Washington.

In a word, the expedition of Gen. Kearny with the "*Army of the West*," had—without firing a gun, or spilling a drop of blood, and after a march of 873 miles in forty-nine days,—resulted, thus far, in the most successful triumph which even the most sanguine could have imagined.

On the other hand, it is necessary to state, that the "orders or instructions" relating to the "occupation of Mexican territory," together with the substance, intent, and meaning, &c., of the proclamations, laws, &c., promulgated by military and naval commanders, in New Mexico and in California, became a subject of discussion in the Congress of 1846-7.

In answer to a call from the House of Representatives, of December 15, 1846, to communicate all "orders or instructions" to any military, naval, or other officers of the government, "in relation to the establishment or organization of civil government in any portion of the territory of Mexico which has or might be taken possession of by the army or navy of the United States," the President, on the 22d of that month, replied:

"These orders and instructions were given to regulate the exercise of the rights of a belligerent, engaged in actual war, over such portions of the territory of our enemy as, by military conquest, might be 'taken possession of' and be occupied by our armed forces—rights necessarily resulting from a state of war, and clearly recognised by the laws of nations. This was all the authority which could be delegated to our military and naval commanders, and its exercise was indispensable to the secure occupation and possession of territory of the enemy which might be conquered. The regulations authorized were temporary, and dependent on the rights acquired by conquest. They were authorized as belligerent rights, and were to be carried into effect by military or naval officers. They were but the amelioration of martial law, which modern civilization requires, and were due as well to the security of the conquest, as to the inhabitants of the conquered territory.

"Among the documents accompanying the report of the Secretary of War, will be found (see Ex. Doc. No. 19, House of Reps. 2d sess. 29th Cong., from which these extracts are made) a 'form of government,' 'established and organized' by the military commander who conquered and occupied, with his forces, the territory of New Mexico. This document was received at the Wár Department in the latter part of the last month, and as will be perceived by the report of the Secretary of War, was not, for the reasons stated by that officer, brought to my notice until after my annual message of the 8th instant was communicated to Congress.

"It is declared on its face to be a 'temporary government of the said territory;' but there are portions of it which purport to 'establish and organize' a permanent territorial government of the United States over the territory, and to impart to its inhabitants political rights which, under the Constitution of the United States, can be enjoyed permanently only by citizens of the United States. These have not been 'approved and recognised' by me. Such organized regulations as have been established in any of the conquered territories for the security of our conquest, for the preservation of order, for the protection of the rights of the inhabitants, and for depriving the enemy of the advantages of these territories while the military possession of them by the forces of the United States continue, will be recognised and approved.

"It will be apparent, from the reports of the officers who have been required by the success which has crowned their arms to exercise the powers of temporary government over the conquered territories, that if any excess of power has been exercised, the departure has been the offspring of a patriotic desire to give to the inhabitants the privileges and immunities so cherished by the peo-

F

ple of our own country, and which they believed calculated to improve their condition and promote their prosperity. Any such excess has resulted in no practical injury, but can and will be early corrected, in a manner to alienate as little as possible the good feelings of the inhabitants of the conquered territory."

Accompanying the reply of the President, was the report of the Secretary of War, above alluded to, which is here given entire:

WAR DEPARTMENT, *December* 21, 1846.

SIR : In compliance with your request to be furnished with all the information in the War Department in regard to the objects of inquiry embraced in the resolution of the House of Representatives of the 15th instant, I have the honour to report that the accompanying papers, numbered from 1 to 24, contain all the orders and instructions which have issued from this department to any officer of the army " in relation to the establishment or organization of civil government in any portion of the territory of Mexico, which has been or might be taken possession of by the army or navy of the United States." They also furnish all the information in this department in relation to any form of government which any such officer has established or organized, and also in relation to any approval or recognition of such government.

As the information called for by the resolution of the House of Representatives is contained in various despatches which relate principally to military operations, I have preferred, in most instances, to give the whole document, though parts of it have little or no direct relation to the matters embraced in that resolution. What is omitted does not relate to any branch of the inquiry, but chiefly to the plans of the campaign, and contemplated military movements, which it would not be proper to make public.

You will perceive that I stated, in my letter of the 3d of June last, to Gen. Kearny, that a proclamation in the Spanish language would be furnished to him for the purpose of being distributed among the Mexican people. A few copies of the proclamation prepared for Gen. Taylor were sent to Gen. Kearny ; but, owing to the different circumstances in which the two generals might be placed, it was afterwards deemed proper to instruct Gen. Kearny not to use them, and I am not aware that he did so in any instance. My letter to him on this subject, dated the 6th of June, is one of the papers herewith transmitted.

Among the accompanying documents you will find two proclamations issued by Gen. Kearny, but neither the form nor substance of them was furnished from this department.

In relation to the annexed paper, No. 24, called the "Organic Law of the Territory of New Mexico," it is proper that I should state that it was received at the Adjutant-general's office on the 23d of November, and thence sent to me. As the document was voluminous, and my whole time was required for the indispensable current business of the department, then unusually pressing, and for preparing my annual report to accompany your message to Congress, I did not, at that time, nor until a few days since, examine it; and it was not laid before you to receive your directions in regard to it.

I have the honour to be, very respectfully, your obedient servant,

W. L. MARCY.

To the PRESIDENT.

Of the "accompanying papers," it is believed that all of importance to our subject are either given here in the narrative, or in the Appendix, with the exception of the "Organic Law of the Territory of New Mexico," which is too voluminous for our publication. And it may be proper to add, that the executive action above detailed, applies to any "organization of civil government," if such there be, that may come to be spoken of in this work.

On the 27th, Gen. Kearny issued an order regulating licenses for stores, &c., duties on wagons, &c.; and, on the 29th, the use of stamped paper, previously required by Mexican law, was abolished.

On the 1st of September, he writes the Adjutant-general of the United States: "I am now endeavouring to raise from the inhabitants of the territory a company of infantry (volunteers for one year). I have appointed a Mexican the captain, and an American the first lieutenant of it. I think much good will result from it."

About this time rumours reached Santa Fé that Armijo, with Col. Ugarte, was rallying the south, and advancing on the capital. To quiet the minds of the people, Gen. Kearny, on the 2d September, marched out of Santa Fé with 700 men, principally of Col. Doniphan's regiment and Major Clark's artillery. Their route lay for some 100 miles down the Rio Grande, as far as the village of Tomé, but they were met by friendly rather than hostile demonstrations.

On his return, a fortnight from the last date, arrangements were made for the civil government, and on the 22d Gen. Kearny writes as follows:

> HEAD-QUARTERS, ARMY OF THE WEST,
> *Santa Fé, New Mexico, Sept. 22, 1846.*

SIR: I inclose herewith a copy of the laws prepared for the government of the territory of New Mexico, and a list of appointments to civil offices in the territory—both of which I have this day signed and published.

I take great pleasure in stating that I am entirely indebted for these laws to Col. A. W. Doniphan, of the 1st regiment of Missouri mounted volunteers, who received much assistance from private Willard P. Hall, of his regiment.

These laws are taken, part from the laws of Mexico—retained as in the original—a part with such modifications as our laws and constitution made necessary: a part are from the laws of the Missouri Territory: a part from the laws of Texas, and also of Texas and Coahuila; a part from the statutes of Missouri; and the remainder from the Livingston code.

The organic law is taken from the organic law of Missouri Territory. (See act of Congress, June 4th, 1842.)

> Very respectfully, your obedient servant,
> S. W. KEARNY,
> *Brigadier-general, U. S. A.*

The ADJUTANT-GENERAL, *U. S. A., Washington.*

[Received at the War Department, November 23d.]

Appointment, by Gen. Kearny, of civil officers.

Being duly authorized by the President of the United States of America, I hereby make the following appointments for the government of New Mexico, a territory of the United States. The officers thus appointed will be obeyed and respected accordingly.

Charles Bent to be governor.

Donaisano Vigil, to be secretary of the territory.

Richard Dallam, to be marshal.

Francis P. Blair, to be United States district attorney.

Charles Blumner, to be treasurer.

Eugene Leitzendorfer, to be auditor of public accounts.

Joab Houghton, Antonio José Otero, Charles Beaubian, to be judges of the superior court.

Given at Santa Fé, the capital of the Territory of New Mexico, this 22d day of September, 1846, and in the 71st year of the Independence of the United States.

S. W. KEARNY,

Brigadier-general, U. S. A.

On the 16th of September, Gen. Kearny had written to the department, through the Adjutant-general:

"As this territory is now perfectly quiet, I have determined (knowing the wishes of the Executive) to leave here for Upper California as soon as possible, and have fixed upon the 25th as the day of departure. As I am ignorant when to expect Capt. Allen and his command, I have determined upon taking with me Major Sumner and the efficient men (about 300) of the First Dragoons. Orders will be left for Capt. Allen to follow on our trail. From the most reliable information yet received as to the best route, we have determined upon marching about 200 miles down the Del Norte; then to the Gila; down that river near to its mouth; leaving which we cross the Colorado; and then, keeping near the Pacific, up to Monterey. This route will carry us not far from and along the southern boundary of New Mexico and Upper California; and we hope to reach the Pacific by the end of November No exertions will be wanting on the part of any

F 2   5

one attached to this expedition in insuring to it full and entire success.

"I have now respectfully to ask, that, in the event of our getting possession of Upper California—of establishing a civil government there—securing peace, quiet, and order among the inhabitants, and precluding the possibility of the Mexicans again having control there, I may be permitted to leave there next summer with the First Dragoons, and march them back to Fort Leavenworth, on the Missouri; and I would respectfully suggest that troops, to remain in California and Oregon, should be raised expressly for the purpose—say for three years—to be discharged at the expiration of that time; each man, from the colonel to the private, receiving a number of acres of land in proportion to his rank. Regiments could easily be raised on such terms; and when discharged, military colonies would thus be established by them."

Information came of the approach of the Mormons and of the regiment from Missouri, under Col. Price, and, assuming their arrival as now certain, Gen. Kearny made the following distribution of the forces under his command, in preparation for his long and arduous march to California.

The squadrons of First United States Dragoons, numbering about three hundred, with two howitzers, under Major Sumner, were ordered to prepare for the march on California, to be followed by Capt. Hudson's company and the Mormon battalion, enlisted under a promise of being discharged in California. Major Clark's battalion of artillery, embracing Captains Fischer and Weightman's companies, from St. Louis, to remain at Santa Fé, with the battalion of infantry under Captains Angney and Murphy. The regiment of Col. Doniphan to be stationed about forty miles south of Albuquerque, with two of its companies at Tomé. Upon the arrival of Col. Price's regiment, the last-mentioned companies to be relieved by two companies from that regiment, and Col. Doniphan to march to Chihuahua and report to Gen. Wool. Col. Price to station the main body of his regiment at Taos, and two companies thereof on the frontier, to hold the Indians in constant dread.

The various tribes of savages of New Mexico had been met in council, and with the Navahoes and Pueblo Indians treaties were formed.

Lieutenants Peck and Abert, of the topographical corps, having suffered much from sickness, and still too weak to accompany the California expedition, were ordered to remain, and make surveys of the country, which they are understood to have done with great ability, and to published results of which the public may look with interest.   On the 25th September, 1846, all arrangements completed, Gen. Kearny departed on his difficult and dreary journey of over 1000 miles, a great portion of which was a desert.

CHAPTER V.

Combination of forces employed in the Conquest of California and New Mexico, Military and Naval—Reinforcement of a Regiment and of a Battalion of Mounted Volunteers, under Col. Price, to "Army of the West"—Mormon Battalion—Nauvoo difficulties and emigrants—New York Regiment under Col. J. D. Stevenson—Capt. C. Q. Tompkin's Company of Third Artillery—Orders and instructions—Co-operation with the Naval forces—Col. Mason—Departures and Arrivals—Unexpected Co-operation.

THE combination of forces employed in the conquest of California and New Mexico were of various organization, both military and naval, and were launched forth, by sea and by land, at different periods. The points of their distinct embodiment were almost as many thousand miles apart as were their destined points of concentration on the soil of Mexico. It will therefore be impossible, in the circumscribed limits of this work, to follow each detachment in their separate marches, voyages and exploits. Nor do these magnificent distances, in connection with events so recent, admit of the receipt of that full information requisite to ample and accurate detail of much that was well and nobly done.

It will be seen Gen. Kearny had been advised by the Secretary of War, that 1000 additional volunteers from Missouri would be sent as a reinforcement, and to augment his disposable force for California; and that he was authorized to muster into service a battalion of Mormon emigrants, but that they had not joined him when he departed from Santa Fé for that country.

This requisition on Missouri for volunteers was composed of fourteen companies, amounting in the aggregate to near 1300 men —ten companies formed a regiment, of which Sterling Price was colonel, D. D. Mitchell, lieutenant-colonel, and Edmonson, major—the four remaining companies constituted a battalion under command of Col. Willock, all mounted and armed, either with rifles, carbines or muskets. By the 23d August, 1846, this force had all taken up their line of march to Santa Fé from Fort Leavenworth. An immense number of wagons with stores and baggage, with some nine or ten thousand mules and oxen, and teamsters, &c. in proportion, accompanied these troops on their long and arduous journey. On the 18th July preceding, an additional requisition for a regiment of infantry issued on the Governor of Missouri, but they were not mustered into service from the belief of the Executive of the United States that they would not be needed, and from the difficulty of passing them over the route at so late a period in the season with the requisite quantity of supplies, &c. Capt. James Allen of First Dragoons had enrolled the 500 Mormons, and formed them into a battalion of infantry, of which he was elected lieutenant-colonel. They had arrived at a high state of discipline, when, on 23d August, 1846, in about a fortnight after their departure from Fort Leavenworth, the service lost a most efficient, estimable, and gallant officer, by his death.

Capt. Philip St. George Cooke, of First Dragoons, was subsequently placed in command, and, under his orders, the Mormon battalion, in good condition, marched, after their arrival at Santa Fé, through the province of Sonora, to La Plagas and San Bernardino—arrived at the banks of the Rio San Pedro, and, following that river to the Gila and Gulf of California, proceeded thence to the capital of California, where the American flag had waved in triumph for some time previous.

It may be here appropriate to note, that, simultaneously with this array of armed bands, hosts of emigrants, each man "good at the rifle," mingled with the tide of war. "The Nauvoo difficulties" is a familiar, perhaps painful subject. The peculiar fanaticism of these people rendered their residence within the States incompatible with the habits of their fellow citizens. They almost in a body—men, women and children—dared the "Deserts of the Dead," the savages, and the horrors of a winter in the Rocky Mountains, to seek a home in California. Others of them sought its distant western shore by water, and, after a long and tempestuous voyage, arrived at Yerba Buena, in the Bay of San Francisco. Most of these settled on the San Joaquin, and immediately busied themselves in putting in crops to sustain their emigrant brethren when they should arrive by the over-land route—the bones of many of whom were then whitening the Sierras and plains of that route.

Emigrants from Missouri, under ex-Gov. Boggs of that state, arrived in comparative safety, but the thrilling accounts of the sufferings of others are still reaching the east, as well as west. The want of proper organization and prudent preparation is said to be much the cause of this. The Mormon chief represents the country and climate as not having disappointed their expectations, though much exaggerated.

On the 12th September, 1846, the Secretary of War wrote to Gen. Kearny, that a volunteer regiment raised in the State of New York—to serve during the war—to be discharged wherever they were at its termination, if in a territory of the United States, was about to embark from New York for California; that it was to be a part of his command; but, as it might reach its destination before Gen. Kearny was in a condition to subject it to his orders, the colonel, J. D. Stevenson, had been furnished with instructions for his conduct in the mean time. A copy of these, with the instructions of the Navy Department to the commander of the naval squadron in the Pacific; a copy of a letter to Gen. Taylor, with a circular from the Treasury Department; a copy of a letter from Gen. Scott to Capt. Tompkins; and a copy of general regulations relative to the respective rank of naval and army officers, Gen. Kearny was informed were sent him, and he was directed to look upon these, "so far as applicable," "in the light of instructions" to himself.*

Gen. Kearny having left Santa Fé on the 25th, this communication of the Secretary of War did not reach him.

The copy of Gen. Scott's letter, dated 20th June, 1846, to Capt. Tompkins, would have informed him of First Lieutenant (afterwards Captain) C. Q. Tompkin's destination with a company of Third Artillery for California, and of the probable nature of the service to which he was assigned. A subsequent letter, dated 3d November, 1846, from Gen. Scott to Gen. Kearny, tells him that

---

* See Appendix, Nos. 2, 3, and 4, &c.

he will find an engineer officer (Lieut. Halleck) at Monterey, or the bay of San Francisco, and that the company of artillery, aided by other troops under his command, " ought promptly to be employed in erecting and garrisoning durable defences for holding the bays of Monterey and San Francisco, together with such other important points in the same province as he may deem necessary to occupy."

That intrenching tools, ordnance and ordnance stores, went out in the ship Lexington, with Capt. Tompkins, and that further ordnance supplies might soon be expected.

Col. Stevenson's regiment, (familiarly known as the " California regiment,") numbered 800 men, with the same number of percussion muskets, and flint muskets, with 200 rifles, and six pieces of artillery. They carried out machinery for saw and grist mills, mechanic's tools, &c. &c. A large number of them were mechanics, and two of their principal officers belonged to the Third Artillery; one to the company commanded by Capt. Tompkins. The letter of the Secretary of War to Col. Stevenson, dated Sept. 11, 1846, informs him that his regiment was destined to the Pacific, to co-operate with the naval commander in carrying out his plans, (with a copy of whose instructions Col. Stevenson was furnished,) so far as the land forces might be needed for that purpose: he is told, " There are three points deemed to be worthy of particular attention." These were San Francisco, Monterey, and San Diego, and that it was " important to have possession of the bay of San Francisco, and the country in that vicinity." That "a fortification, such as the means at his command may enable him to construct, will be erected, and that the heavy guns heretofore sent out, and those taken by the transports, to the extent needed, will be used for its armament," &c. The Secretary of War adds, " The regiment under your command, as well as the company of Capt. Tompkins, which has preceded it, is a part of Gen. Kearny's command ; but it may be that he will not be in a situation to reach you by his orders, immediately on your debarkation. Until that is the case, yours will be an independent command, except when engaged in joint operations with the naval force ;" and Col. Stevenson was directed to show his instructions to the commander of the squadron, and told, " Where a place is taken by the joint action of the naval and land force, the naval officer, if superior in rank to yourself, will be entitled to make arrangements for the civil government of it, while it is held by the co-operation of both branches of the military force ;" and that all his powers would, "of course," devolve on Gen. Kearny, when he arrived, &c.*

Gen. Scott's letter of 3d November, 1846, concluded as follows :—

" As a guide to the civil governor of Upper California, in our hands, see the letter of June the 3d (last), addressed to you by the Secretary of War. You will not, however, formally declare the province to be annexed. Permanent incorporation of the territory must depend on the government of the United States.

" After occupying with our forces all necessary points in Upper California, and establishing a temporary civil government therein, as well as assuring yourself of its internal tranquillity, and the absence of any danger of reconquest on the part of Mexico, you may charge Col. Mason, United States First Dragoons, the bearer of this open letter, or land officer next in rank to your own, with your several duties, and return yourself, with a sufficient escort of troops, to St. Louis, Missouri ; but the body of the United States Dragoons that accompanied you to California, will remain there until further orders.

" It is not known what portion of the Missouri Volunteers, if any, marched with you from Santa Fé to the Pacific. If any, it is necessary to provide for their return to their homes and honourable discharge ; and, on the same supposition, they may serve you as a sufficient escort to Missouri.

" It is known that Lieut. Col. Fremont, of the United States rifle regiment, was, in July last, with a party of men in the service of the United States Topographical Engineers, in the neighbourhood of San Francisco or Monterey bay, engaged in joint

---

* See Appendix.

operations against Mexico with the United States squadron on that coast. Should you find him there, it is desired that you do not detain him, against his wishes, a moment longer than the necessities of the service may require.

"I need scarcely enjoin deference, and the utmost cordiality, on the part of our land forces towards those of our navy, in the joint service on the distant coast of California. Reciprocity may be cordially expected; and towards that end, frequent conferences between commanders of the two arms are recommended. Harmony in co-operation, and success cannot but follow.

" Measures have been taken to supply the disbursing officers, who have preceded, and who may accompany you, with all necessary funds. Of those measures you will be informed by Col. Mason."

Col. Mason left Washington city on the 7th of November, 1846, for New York, whence he embarked for Chagres, to cross the isthmus of Panama, and thus reached Monterey, on the Pacific.

Col. Price, with the Missouri Volunteers, and their heavy trains, reached Santa Fé, and relieved Col. Doniphan, who, we have seen, was awaiting his arrival to commence the " Chihuahua expedition," which proved so glorious.

The company of the Third regiment Artillery embarked at New York for Monterey, California, July 14th, and the New York regiment of Volunteers, for the same destination, embarked the 25th of September, 1846, and arrived in due time as designated :— " But, (says the Secretary of War,) before these forces had reached their destination, and even before their departure from the United States, the Mexican authority in the whole province of the Californias had been subverted."

Of the "series of events which led to the overthrow of the Mexican power in that extensive country, and its occupation as a conquest of the United States,"*—of the distinguished actors— and, especially, of the unexpected co-operation which " a party of

---

* Secretary of War.

G

men in the service of the United States Topographical Engineers," under their young and gallant leader, brought, without
"orders" or "instructions," in aid of these results,—of Fremont,
Sloat, Stockton, Kearny, Doniphan, Price, &c., we have, in other
chapters, much to tell—"reflecting the highest credit alike upon
officers and soldiers, who participated in these memorable actions."

CHAPTER VI.

THE march of the Missouri volunteers under Col. A. W. Doniphan—the citizen commander of citizen soldiers—down the valley
of the Rio Grande, through New Mexico, and the states of Chihuahua, Durango, New Leon and Tamaulipas—passing over many
a dreary desert and through deep snows, penetrating a thickly
settled country of the enemy where they were cut off from all
supplies unless drawn from the theatre of action, and entirely from all
reinforcements, yet still fearlessly marching on against every obstacle,
until they met the enemy and overcame him in two pitched battles,
and with flying colours entered Chihuahua, his largest town in the
north, and there established their order and law—comprises achievements worthy of no stinted applause. The more, when this bold
and fearless band are found thus, full two thousand miles from
their homes—without pay—almost naked, and destitute of nearly
all the absolute necessaries of life, resuming their weary march,
and pressing to the relief of their brethren in arms, who, they
hear, are nine hundred miles off, surrounded by the enemy and in
peril.

To these displays of courage and of fortitude no commendation
can be applied more appropriate than through the eloquent words
addressed to these Missouri volunteers, at St. Louis, on their return
to their homes, by Senator Benton—whose language is here quoted
entire, as not only justly eulogizing their exploits, but as giving a

historical summary of transactions, to which some few details are alone necessary to be first added for our purposes here.

It will have been seen in a preceding chapter, that Col. Doniphan's regiment had been mustered into service, at Fort Leavenworth, on the 6th June, 1846—that, as part of the "Army of the West," it had marched victoriously into Santa Fé, on the 18th of August, and that, on the departure of Gen. Kearny for California, 25th September, his orders were, for Col. Doniphan, on the arrival of Col. Price at Santa Fé, to march his regiment to Chihuahua and report to General Wool.* Previous, however, to General Kearny's departure from Santa Fé, he ordered Col. Doniphan to make a campaign against the Navaho Indians, which was accomplished in the dead of winter, without supplies, tents, &c. The district of country inhabited by this tribe lies in the Rocky Mountains, and partly on the Pacific slope, and was invaded by several detachments of troops, headed respectively by Major Gilpin, Capt. Reid, Lieut. Col. Jackson, and Col. Doniphan in person. He succeeded in forming a treaty with these troublesome Indians, represented as more warlike than the New Mexicans, to whom they were a great source of dread and injury, on the 22d of November, 1846.

On the 17th of December, Col. Doniphan, with his regiment, and Lieut. Col. D. D. Mitchell's escort, composed of 100 picked men from the army at Santa Fé, commenced the march from Valverde against the state of Chihuahua. Col. Price was left at Santa Fé, in command of his own regiment, Lieut. Col. Willock's battalion, Major Clark's artillery, and Capt. Angney's battalion of infantry, all Missourians. Col. Doniphan's whole force numbered 924 men.

Their march lay along the Rio Grande to Fra Christobal, and from thence they had proceeded down to within about twenty-five miles of the Paso de Norte, when, at Brazito, the first battle of the "Army of the West" occurred. This, however, is all so well told by Lieut. C. H. Kribben, of the Missouri Light Artillery, universally represented as a gallant officer, and highly intelligent gentleman, that his letter is here cheerfully adopted, in the absence

---

* See Appendix, No. 5.

of any official account, as giving a correct and accurate narrative
of the *Battle of Brazito*, on 25th December, 1846.

DETACHMENT OF MO. LIGHT ARTILLERY,
Camp below Brazito, Rio Grande, Dec. 26, 1846.

DEAR SIR: I can only write to you a few lines, being on the
point of breaking up camp. One detachment at Fra Cristobal
overtook Col. Doniphan's command. Major Gilpin, with 250
men, had previously left for El Paso, and Col. Jackson was following him with 200 men. Col. Doniphan had but 150 men
with him, the remainder of his regiment being sick, attending on
the sick, and scattered about the country. From Fra Cristobal
one detachment marched with Col. Doniphan south, when, at the
Laguna of the Jornada del Muerto, news reached us through an
express sent by Major Gilpin, that the Mexicans had determined
to resist at the El Paso, and had collected a considerable number
of troops, intending to give us battle. An express had been sent
to Santa Fé for part of the artillery under Major Clark, but no
news had, as yet, reached us from there, so that the detachment
of thirty men from the three companies of our corps are all that
are here from the battalion. At the southern end of the Jornada,
ten miles north of Donaha, the traders had encamped. Contra-
dictory rumors of the enemy's approach reached us daily. Yesterday, (Christmas day,) when we had just arrived in camp here,
with about five hundred men, had unsaddled our animals, and most
of the men were engaged in carrying wood and water, the news
was brought into camp of the enemy's being in sight and advancing.
It was about 2 o'clock, P. M., and the day was very pleasant. Our
horses grazing some distance from camp at the time, we formed
a single line, and determined to meet the enemy as infantry. Their
attack being evidently designed on the left flank, near which was
our wagon train, one detachment was ordered from the extreme
right to the left, where we soon took up our position. One piece
of artillery, 500 regular lancers and cavalry, and one hundred
regular infantry, besides some five hundred militia troops from El
Paso, composed the enemy's force, according to the best informa-

G 2

tion I can obtain. The enemy ranged themselves on the east, within half a mile of our line, the mountains in their rear. In our rear was the river, with a little brushwood on its banks.

Previous to the encounter, a lieutenant from their ranks came forward, waving a black flag in his hand, but halted when within a hundred steps of our line. Thomas Caldwell, our interpreter, rode out to meet him. The messenger, with the black flag of defiance, demanded that the commander should come into their camp and speak to their general. The reply was, "If your general wants to see our commander, let him come here." "We shall break your ranks, then, and take him there;" was the retort of the Mexican. "Come and take him," said our interpreter; unwittingly using the phrase of the Spartan at Thermopylæ. "A curse on you, prepare for a charge," cried the Mexican. "We give no quarter and ask none," and, waving his black flag gracefully over his head, galloped back towards the enemy's line. Their charge was made by the dragoons from the right, directed upon our left flank, bringing one detachment into the closest fire—their infantry, with one howitzer with them, at the same time attacking our right flank.

Their charge was a handsome one, but was too well and too coolly met to break our line. After their fire had been spent, their front column being at about a hundred steps from the front of our flank, our line poured a volley into them, which being a few times repeated, created such a havoc in their columns, that their forces wheeled to the left, retreating from our fire, and, in their flight, made an attack on the provision train. Here they met a very warm reception, and were soon compelled to fly in all directions, and in the utmost confusion. Their infantry had been put to flight even before, and the Howard county company, under the command of Lieut. N. Wright, taking advantage of their position, on the route of the enemy, charged upon them and took their cannon from them: this was soon manned by the artillery detachment in Col. Mitchell's escort. The enemy had by this time fled, leaving their arms, provisions, and other stores on the field of battle.

A small body of mounted men under the command of Capt. Reid had by this time gathered together in a line and charged upon the enemy, pursuing them into the mountains where they sought refuge.

The number of their dead is said to be thirty—that of their wounded was slight, as far as ascertained.

We lost not a single man, and had but seven slightly wounded; we took eight prisoners, six of whom died last night. Thus ended the battle of the Brazito, the first battle of the army of the west, and as bravely fought by our men as ever men fought at any engagement.

We have every reason to believe that there is more in store for us.   C. H. KRIBBEN.

One piece of cannon was taken, and, opportunely, such store of provisions, bread and wine, as enabled the victors to spend a merry Christmas night.

El Paso, near which the battle took place, is a town in Chihuahua of some 3000 inhabitants, and is on the high road from New Mexico to the city of Chihuahua, distant nearly 300 miles. Twelve miles north of the town, the road narrows so as to form a pass, which a few determined men might successfully defend against any large force. But it appears the Mexicans were so dispirited after their defeat, that they made no effort to retain possession of the pass, but retreated over 100 miles north. The town of El Paso was thus occupied on the 27th of December, without a struggle.

Here Col. Doniphan was reinforced by Major M. L. Clark's artillery. The march by which this small force joined the main column, is so entirely characteristic of the endurance and indomitable energy of this portion of the "Army of the West," that a condensed account—less than the merit of the act—is here attempted to be given. An express reached Major Clark, at Santa Fé, requesting him to come, if possible; but at all events, to send Capt. Richard H. Weightman, with the battery, and thirty or forty men, if no more could be spared.

Major Clark promptly ordered Capt. Weightman to take sixty-five men of his company—being all that were able to endure the fatigues of a forced march of 350 miles, in the dead of winter—together with forty-five Lacled Rangers to man his battery of six pieces, and to proceed forthwith to join Col. Doniphan. Major Clark and his staff set out a few days after Capt. Weightman and his command, who had departed on the 10th of January. Major Clark overtook the command near Tomé, and, passing them, arrived at El Paso about the 25th. Here he found that a night attack was expected from the Mexicans, and sent expresses, with twenty-eight fresh mules, and orders for Capt. Weightman to push on with all speed, as it was believed the Mexicans would attack on the night of the 31st of January.

Capt. Weightman had started from San Diego, a point of the Rio Grande, on the southern extremity of the Jornada del Muerto—a desert of ninety-three miles in extent, when, after proceeding about eight miles, he was met by the express. Replacing his most exhausted mules by those sent him, he proceeded rapidly to Doña Ana, twenty-two miles from San Diego, and there informed his command of the prospect before them, and of his intention to leave, at that place, all baggage whatever—tents, cooking utensils, &c., every thing, except their arms, ammunition, and such provisions as each man could carry ready cooked, and to march as fast as the mules would endure, until they reached El Paso. By 12 o'clock at night, the food prepared and the mules fed, they pushed forward with all speed until, at one o'clock on the night of the 31st, they reached El Paso, making the distance from San Diego, eighty or ninety miles, in thirty-eight consecutive hours.

This command was met four miles from El Paso by their gallant and noble-hearted comrades, Capt. John W. Reid, and Lieut. John Hinton, escorting a wagon load of supper, and a barrel of wine, to comfort these weary victims of a false alarm. So cold was the weather at this time, that, while marching by night through the Jornada del Muerto, and on the nights of the 30th and 31st, it was found necessary to make fires every four or five miles, at which a few men at a time, and by turns, warmed them-

selves, hastening up afterwards to overtake the battery, which
constantly moved on.   On this march from Santa Fé to El Paso,
the Rio Grande was forded three times by the artillery.   On one
occasion, the river being frozen over, except near the middle, down
which masses of floating ice were being whirled, the guns, cais-
sons, &c., were in imminent danger from the ice, but more from
quicksands.   It became instantly necessary to order a large detail
into the deep and struggling waters to extricate the artillery.   The
orderlies produced their books, and were about to name the men
subject to this duty, when they all cried out, "No—no—we are
volunteers," and instantly rushed to the hard duty.

Capt. Weightman's command had the high gratification of receiving from Col. Doniphan, Major Clark, and their comrades, well
merited compliments for the spirited march of the 30th and 31st.

Col. Doniphan, thus reinforced by Major Clark's artillery, commenced his march upon the city of Chihuahua, on the 8th of
February, 1847, and, on the 28th of that month, fought the *Battle
of Sacramento*, of which, and of the occupation of Chihuahua,
the following is Col. Doniphan's report :—

Battle of Sacramento—Capture of Chihuahua.

HEAD-QUARTERS OF THE ARMY IN CHIHUAHUA,
City of Chihuahua, March 4, 1847.

I have the honour to report to you the movements of the army
under my command, since my last official report.

On the evening of the 8th of February, 1847, we left the town
of El Paso del Norte, escorting the merchant train or caravan of
about 315 wagons for the city of Chihuahua.   Our force consisted
of 924 effective men ; 117 officers and privates of the Artillery ;
93 of Lieut. Col. Mitchell's escort, and the remainder the First
regiment Missouri mounted Volunteers.   We progressed in the
direction of this place until the 25th, when we were informed by
our spies that the enemy, to the number of 1500 men, were at
Inseneas, the country-seat of Gov. Trias, about twenty-five miles
in advance.

When we arrived, on the evening of the 26th, near that point,
we found that the force had retreated in the direction of that city.

6

On the evening of the 27th, we arrived at Sans, and learned from our spies that the enemy, in great force, had fortified the pass of the Sacramento river, about fifteen miles in advance, and about the same distance from this city. We were also informed that there was no water between the point we were at, and that occupied by the enemy; we therefore determined to halt until morning. At sunrise on the 28th, the last day of February, we took up the line of march and formed the whole train, consisting of 315 heavy traders' wagons and our commissary and company wagons, into four columns, thus shortening our line so as to make it more easily protected. We placed the artillery and all the command, except 200 cavalry proper, in the intervals between the columns of wagons. We thus fully concealed our force and its position, by masking our force with the cavalry. When we arrived within three miles of the enemy, we made a reconnoissance of his position and the arrangement of his forces. This we could easily do—the road leading through an open prairie valley, between the sterile mountains. The pass of the Sacramento is formed by a point of the mountains on our right, their left extending into the valley or plain, so as to narrow the valley to about one and a half miles. On our left was a deep dry sandy channel of a creek, and between these points the plain rises to sixty feet abruptly. This rise is in the form of a crescent, the convex part being to the north of our forces. On the right, from the point of mountains, a narrow part of the plain extends north one and a half miles further than on the left. The main road passes down the centre of the valley and across the crescent, near the left or dry branch. The Sacramento rises in the mountains on the right, and the road falls on to it about one mile below the battle-field or intrenchment of the enemy. We ascertained that the enemy had one battery of four guns, two nine and six-pounders, on the point of the mountain, (their left,) at a good elevation to sweep the plain, and at the point where the mountain extended farthest into the plain. On our left (their right) they had another battery, on an elevation commanding the road, and three intrenchments of two six-pounders, and on the brow of the crescent near the centre, another of two six and two four and six culverins, or rampart pieces, mounted on carriages; and on the crest of the hill or ascent between the batteries, and the right and left, they had twenty-seven redoubts dug and thrown up, extending at short intervals across the whole ground. In these their infantry were placed, and were entirely protected. Their cavalry was drawn up in front of the redoubts, four deep, and in rear of the redoubts two deep, so as to mask them as far as practicable.

When we had arrived within $1\frac{1}{4}$ miles of the intrenchments along the main road, we advanced the cavalry still further, and suddenly diverged with the columns to the right, so as to gain the narrow part of the ascent on our right, which the enemy discovering endeavoured to prevent by moving forward with 1000 cavalry and four pieces of cannon in their rear, masked by them. Our movements were so rapid that we gained the elevation with our forces and the advance of our wagons in time to form before they arrived within reach of our guns. The enemy halted, and we advanced the head of our column within 1200 yards of them, so as to let our wagons attain the high lands and form as before.

We now commenced the action by a brisk fire from our battery, and the enemy unmasked and commenced also; our fires proved effective at this distance, killing fifteen men, wounding and disabling one of the enemy's guns. We had two men slightly wounded, and several horses and mules killed. The enemy then slowly retreated behind their works in some confusion, and we resumed our march in our former order, still diverging more to the right to avoid their battery on our left, (their right,) and their strongest redoubts, which were on the left near where the road passes. After marching as far as we safely could, without coming within range of their heavy battery on our right, Capt. Weightman, of the artillery, was ordered to charge with the two 12-pound howitzers, to be supported by the cavalry, under Capts. Reid, Parsons, and Hudson. The howitzers charged at speed, and were gallantly sustained by Capt. Reid ; but by some misunderstanding, my order was not given to the other two companies. Capt. Hudson, anticipating my order, charged in time to give ample support to the howitzers. Capt. Parsons, at the same moment, came to me and asked permission for his company to charge the redoubts immediately to the left of Capt. Weightman, which he did very gallantly.

The remainder of the two battalions of the First Regiment were dismounted during the cavalry charge, and following rapidly on foot, and Maj. Clark advancing as fast as practicable with the remainder of the battery, we charged their redoubts from right to left, with a brisk and deadly fire of riflemen, while Maj. Clark opened a rapid and well-directed fire on a column of cavalry attempting to pass to our left so as to attack the wagons and our rear. The fire was so well directed as to force them to fall back ; and our riflemen, with their cavalry and howitzers, cleared it after an obstinate resistance. Our forces advanced to the very brink of their redoubts, and attacked them with their sabres. When the redoubts were cleared, and the batteries in the centre and our left were silenced, the main battery on our right still continued to pour in a constant and heavy fire, as it had done during the heat of the engagement ; but as the whole fate of the battle depended upon carrying the redoubts and centre battery, this one on the right remained unattacked, and the enemy had rallied there five hundred strong.

Maj. Clark was directed to commence a heavy fire upon it, while Lieuts. Col. Mitchell and Jackson, commanding the First Battalion, were ordered to remount and charge the battery on the left, while Maj. Gilpin was directed to pass the Second Battalion on foot up the rough ascent of the mountain on the opposite side. The fire of our battery was so effective as to completely silence theirs, and the rapid advance of our column put them to flight over the mountains in great confusion.

Capt. Thompson, of the First Dragoons, acted as my aid and adviser on the field during the whole engagement, and was of the most essential service to me. Also, Lieut. Wooster, of the United States army, who acted very coolly and gallantly. Maj. Campbell, of Springfield, Missouri, also acted as a volunteer aid during part of the time, but left me and joined Capt. Reid in his gallant charge. Thus ended the battle of Sacramento. The force of the enemy was 1200 cavalry from Durango and Chihuahua, 300 artillerists, and 1420 rancheros, badly armed with lassos, lances, and machetoes, or corn-knives, ten pieces of artillery, two nine, two eight, four six, and two four-pounders, and six culverins, or rampart pieces. Their forces were commanded by Major-general Heredia, general of Durango, Chihuahua, Sonora, and New Mexico. Brigadier-general Justimani, Brigadier-general Garcia Conde, formerly minister of war for the republic of Mexico, who is a scientific man, planned this whole field of defence; Gen. Uguarte, and Gov. Trias, who acted as brigadier-generals on the field, and colonels and other officers without number.

Our force was 924 effective men; at least one hundred of whom were engaged in holding horses and driving teams.

The loss of the enemy was his entire artillery, ten wagons, masses of beans and pinola, and other Mexican provisions, about three hundred killed, and about the same number wounded, many of whom have since died, and forty prisoners.

The field was literally covered with the dead and wounded from our artillery and the unerring fire of our riflemen. Night put a stop to the carnage, the battle having commenced about three o'clock. Our loss was one killed, one mortally wounded, and seven so wounded as to recover without any loss of limbs. I cannot speak too highly of the coolness, gallantry, and bravery of the officers and men under my command.

I was ably sustained by the field-officers, Lieutenant-colonels Mitchell and Jackson, of the First Battalion, and Maj. Gilpin, of the Second Battalion; and Maj. Clark and his artillery acted nobly, and did the most effective service in every part of the field. It is abundantly shown, in the charge made by Capt. Weightman with the section of howitzers, that they can be used in any charge of calvary with great effect. Much has been said, and justly said, of the gallantry of our artillery, unlimbering within 250 yards of the enemy at Palo Alto; but how much more daring was the charge of Capt. Weightman, when he unlimbered within fifty yards of the redoubts of the enemy.

On the 1st day of March, we took formal possession of the capi-

H

tal of Chihuahua, in the name of our government. We were ordered by Gen. Kearny to report to Gen. Wool at this place : since our arrival we hear he is at Saltillo, surrounded by the enemy. Our present purpose is either to force our way to him, or return by Bexar, as our term of service expires on the last of May next.

I have the honour to be, your obedient servant,

A. W. DONIPHAN,
Col. First Regiment Missouri Volunteers.

Brigadier-general R. JONES, *Adjutant-general, U. S. A.*

The American flag was thus planted on the walls of Chihuahua. Here Col. Doniphan remained about three weeks, resting his tired forces—made an excursion to disperse an assemblage at Parral, organized as a kind of temporary government, &c., and stipulated with the authorities for safety to the persons and property of the United States traders, and threatening to return with vengeance if infracted.

Many of these traders were gentlemen of wealth, intelligence, and enterprise, and had large capitals, as well as their lives, at issue in the observance of this treaty, when Col. Doniphan should have withdrawn.

Among this class was Mr. Magoffin of Missouri, who had very recently borne a young, rich, and lovely bride, of the noblest blood of Kentucky, to this mart of his commerce. Perhaps he feared to trust her safety to the slightest chance of danger, or that he dreaded insult or inconvenience to her, and, therefore persuaded her to avoid the possibility of either. She, the granddaughter of *Shelby*, as also the grand-daughter, on the maternal side, of *Hart*, had it not in her nature to know fear, and would not that her husband should thus act against his interests from any anxiety on her account. Mr. Magoffin, however, determined to take advantage of the march of the troops, and to withdraw his dauntless lady and property from this danger, which in reality was imminent and great. Through all the alarms of the camp— the toils of the march, and the privations of the army, this lady was found cheerful, and the charms of the social circle of the encampment in hours of ease, and of danger, brave as the bravest. Nor was her courage untried, for it happened that her carriage, getting off the line of march of the army, and under a small escort which had lagged behind, was suddenly ridden up to by a squad of guerillas, whose further proceedings were instantly and timely stopped by the sight of a pair of pistols presented at them by a lovely woman, and by the shouts of her escort rapidly galloping up to her rescue. Such was the intrepidity of a lady in the Chihuahua column of the "Army of the West."

Col. Doniphan, on the 23d of April, received orders from Gen. Wool to march his command forthwith to Saltillo. On the 25th, he directed his course thither, taking, in his way, the towns of San Pablo, Santa Cruz, Soucillo, Santa Rosalia, and Guaguquilla in the state of Chihuahua.

"While Col. Doniphan's column was on its march from Chihuahua to Saltillo, a small advance party, under Capt. Reid, of about thirty rank and file, arrived at El Paso, (twenty-five miles above Parras,) very early on the morning of the 13th of May. About 9 o'clock, A. M., a party of Indians were seen emerging from a gap of the mountains, distant about five miles, and making direct for the rancho. Our troops went out at full gallop nearly half a mile to meet them. When within thirty or forty steps of each other, the Indians discharged a few arrows, when the Americans fired their entire volley at them. Immediately, the Indians raised the yell and rushed in on them, discharging their arrows with astonishing rapidity. Our men were forced to retreat about 100 yards to load, when they, in their turn, charged the enemy and forced him to retreat. Thus alternately did they charge, keeping up the contest for two hours with much spirit, our troops gaining inch by inch of the ground by dint of hard fighting, while the Indians held it with much tenacity, and yielding it only with their lives. The Indians numbered between fifty and sixty, and their superior horsemanship gave them much advantage; notwithstanding which, they were forced to fall back before the noble daring of Capt. Reid and his little band.

"Capt. Reid, who was ably assisted by Lieutenants Gordon, Sproule, and Winston, was the only American wounded. He had the satisfaction of driving the Indians entirely off the ground, carrying with them all their wounded and some dead, yet leaving fifteen on the field. Nine Mexican prisoners were taken from them and restored to liberty, and about 1000 head of horses and mules, which, as far as practicable, were returned to the Mexicans from whom they had been taken.

"Captain Reid had the gratification of receiving an official document from the citizens of Parras, through the prefect of the city, expressive of their admiration and gratitude for his noble conduct, and sympathy for his wounds."

Such is an excellent account of one of the many very gallant achievements of Capt. Reid.

Upon Col. Doniphan's approach to the confines of Durango, Governor Ochoa prepared to surrender the capital without a struggle, for the army had already fled or dispersed; but Col. Doniphan's route lay further to the north, through the cities of Mapimi, San Sabastian, San Lorenzo, and in the state of Coahuila, through Parras, Castannella, the Hacienda de Patos, and thence, by Encantada, to Saltillo, where he reported to Gen. Wool, on the 22d of May, and to Gen. Taylor at Monterey, on the 27th of May, and thence to Matamoras, a distance of 900 miles from Chihuahua, they marched in forty-five days, carrying with them seventeen pieces of artillery, as trophies, which Gen. Taylor permitted them to bring home, in consideration, as assigned in the "Order," of their gallantry and noble bearing. About the 16th of June, they arrived at New Orleans, thence they sped their way to St. Louis, and home. There a most cordial and hearty welcome greeted them, on the 2d of July, 1847, after their twelve months' arduous expedition.

Their reception was enthusiastic beyond description. The whole city turned out to bid welcome to the band who had achieved so much honour for their state. Flags were flung to the breeze, and the bells rung a merry peal of joy. Judge Bowlin, on the part of the citizens, bade them welcome. A banquet was spread before

them, and Col. Benton, United States senator from Missouri, addressed the volunteers and the immense crowd of citizens, as follows:—

"COL. DONIPHAN, AND OFFICERS AND MEN:—I have been appointed to an honourable and a pleasant duty—that of making you
the congratulations of your fellow-citizens of St. Louis, on your
happy return from your long and almost fabulous expedition.
You have indeed marched far, and done much, and suffered
much, and well entitled yourselves to the applauses of your fellow-citizens, as well as the rewards and thanks of your government. A year ago you left home. Going out from the western
border of your state, you re-enter it on the east, having made a
circuit equal to a fourth of a circumference of the globe, provid-
ing for yourselves as you went, and returning with trophies taken
from fields, the names of which were unknown to yourselves and
your country, until revealed by your enterprise, illustrated by
your valour, and immortalized by your deeds. History has but
few such expeditions to record; and when they occur, it is as
honourable and useful as it is just and wise to celebrate and commemorate the events which entitle them to renown.

"Your march and exploits have been among the most wonderful
of the age. At the call of your country you marched a thousand
miles to the conquest of New Mexico, as part of the force under
Gen. Kearny, and achieved that conquest, without the loss of a
man, or the fire of a gun. That work finished, and New Mexico,
itself so distant, and so lately the *Ultima Thule*—the outside boundary of speculation and enterprise—so lately a distant point to be
attained, becomes itself a point of departure—a beginning point
for new and far more extended expeditions. You look across the
long and lofty chain—the Cordilleras of North America—which
divide the Atlantic from the Pacific waters; and you see beyond
that ridge a savage tribe which had been long in the habit of de-
predating upon the province which had just become an American
conquest. You, a part only of the subsequent Chihuahua column
under Jackson and Gilpin, march upon them—bring them to
terms—and they sign a treaty with Col. Doniphan, in which they
H 2

bind themselves to cease their depredations on the Mexicans, and to become the friends of the United States. A novel treaty, that! signed on the western confines of New Mexico, between parties who had hardly ever heard each other's names before, and to give peace and protection to Mexicans, who were hostile to both. This was the meeting, and this the parting of the Missouri volunteers, with the numerous and savage tribe of the Navaho Indians, living on the waters of the Gulf of California, and so long the terror and scourge of Sonora, Sinaloa, and New Mexico.

"This object accomplished, and impatient of inactivity, and without orders, (Gen. Kearny having departed for California,) you cast about to carve out some new work for yourselves. Chihuahua, a rich and populous city of near 30,000 souls, the seat of government of the State of that name, and formerly the residence of the captains-general of the internal provinces, under the vice-regal government of New Spain, was the captivating object which fixed your attention. It was a far-distant city—about as far from St. Louis as Moscow is from Paris; and towns and enemies, and a large river, and defiles and mountains, and the desert, whose ominous name portending death to travellers—*el jornada de los muertos*—the journey of the dead—all lay between you. It was a perilous enterprise, and a discouraging one, for a thousand men, badly equipped, to contemplate. No matter. Danger and hardship lent it a charm: the adventurous march was resolved on, and the execution commenced. First, the ominous desert was passed, its character vindicating its title to its mournful appellation—an arid plain of ninety miles, strewed with the bones of animals perished of hunger and thirst—little hillocks of stone, and the solitary cross, erected by pious hands, marking the spot where some Christian had fallen, victim of the savage, of the robber, or of the desert itself—no water—no animal life—no sign of habitation. There the Texan prisoners, driven by the cruel Salazar, had met their direst sufferings, unrelieved, as in other parts of their march in the settled parts of the country, by the compassionate ministrations (for where is it that *woman* is not compassionate?) of the pitying women. The desert was passed, and the place for crossing the

river approached. A little arm of the river, Bracito, (in Spanish,)
made out from its side. There the enemy in superior numbers,
and confident in cavalry and artillery, undertook to bar the way.
Vain pretension! Their discovery, attack, and rout, were about
simultaneous operations. A few minutes did the work! And in
this way our Missouri volunteers of the Chihuahua column spent
their Christmas day of the year 1846.

"The victory of the Bracito opened the way to the crossing of
the river Del Norte, and to admission into the beautiful little town
of the Paso del Norte, where a neat cultivation, a comfortable people, fields, orchards, and vineyards, and a hospitable reception,
offered the rest and refreshment which toils, and dangers, and victory had won. You rested there till artillery was brought down
from Santa Fé; but the pretty town of the Paso del Norte, with
all its enjoyments, and they were many, and the greater for the
place in which they were found, was not a *Capau* to the men of
Missouri. It did not detain, and enervate them. You moved forward in February, and the battle of the Sacramento, one of the
military marvels of the age, cleared the road to Chihuahua, which
was entered without further resistance. It had been entered once
before by a detachment of American troops; but under circumstances how different! In the year 1807, Lieut. Pike and his
thirty brave men, taken prisoners on the head of the Rio del Norte,
had been marched captives into Chihuahua; in the year 1847,
Doniphan and his men entered it as conquerors. The paltry triumph of a captain-general over a lieutenant, was effaced in a
triumphal entrance of a thousand Missourians into the grand and
ancient capital of all the INTERNAL PROVINCES! and old men still
alive, could remark the grandeur of the American spirit under
both events—the proud and lofty bearing of the captive thirty—
the mildness and moderation of the conquering thousand.

"Chihuahua was taken, and responsible duties, more delicate
than those of arms, were to be performed. Many American citizens were there, engaged in trade; much American property was
there. All this was to be protected, both lives and property, and
by peaceful arrangement; for the command was too small to admit

of division, and of leaving a garrison. Conciliation and negotiation were resorted to, and successfully. Every American interest was provided for, and placed under the safeguard, *first*, of good will, and *next*, of guarantees not to be violated with impunity.

"Chihuahua gained, it became, like Santa Fé, not the terminating point of a long expedition, but the beginning point of a new one. Gen. Taylor was somewhere—no one knew exactly where—but some seven or eight hundred miles towards the other side of Mexico. You had heard that he had been defeated—that Buena Vista had not been a *good prospect* to him. Like good Americans, you did not believe a word of it; but, like good soldiers, you thought it best to go and see. A volunteer party of fourteen, headed by Collins, of Boonville, undertake to penetrate to Saltillo, and to bring you information of his condition. They set out. Amidst innumerable dangers they accomplish their purpose; and return. You march. A vanguard of 100 men, led by Lieut. Col. Mitchell, led the way. Then came the main body, (if the name is not a burlesque on such a handful,) commanded by Col. Doniphan himself.

"The whole table-land of Mexico, in all its breadth, from west to east, was to be traversed. A numerous and hostile population in towns—treacherous Cumanches in the mountains—were to be passed. Every thing was to be self-provided—provisions, transportation, fresh horses for remounts, and even the means of victory—and all without a military chest, or even an empty box, in which government gold had ever reposed. All was accomplished. Mexican towns were passed, in order and quiet; plundering Cumanches were punished; means were obtained from traders to liquidate indispensable contributions; and the wants that could not be supplied were endured like soldiers of veteran service.

"I say the Cumanches were punished. And here presents an episode of a novel, extraordinary, and romantic kind—Americans chastising savages for plundering people who they themselves came to conquer, and forcing the restitution of captives and plundered property. A strange story this to tell in Europe, where backwoods character, western character, is not yet completely known. But to

the facts. In the mosquit forest of the Bolson de Mapimi, and in
the sierras around the beautiful town and fertile district of Parras,
and in all the open country for hundreds of miles round about, the
savage Cumanches have held dominion ever since the usurper
Santa Anna disarmed the people ; and sally forth from their fast-
nesses to slaughter men, plunder cattle, and carry off women and children. An exploit of this kind had just been performed on the line
of the Missourians' march, not far from Parras, and an advanced
party chanced to be in that town at the time the news of the
depredation arrived there. It was only fifteen strong. Moved by
gratitude for the kind attentions of the people, especially the
women, to the sick of Gen. Wool's command, necessarily left in
Parras, and unwilling to be outdone by enemies in generosity, the
heroic fifteen, upon the spot, volunteered to go back thirty miles,
hunt out the depredators and punish them, without regard to numbers. A grateful Mexican became their guide. On their way,
they fell in with fifteen more of their comrades ; and, in a short
time, seventeen Cumanches killed out of sixty-five, eighteen captives restored to their families, and three hundred and fifty head of
cattle recovered for their owners, was the fruit of this sudden and
romantic episode.

  " Such noble conduct was not without its effect on the minds of
the astonished Mexicans. An official document from the prefect of
the place to Capt. Reid, leader of this detachment, attests the verity
of the fact, and the gratitude of the Mexicans ; and constitutes a
trophy of a new kind in the annals of war. Here it is in the
original Spanish, and I will read it off in English.

  "It is officially dated from the Prefecture of the Department of
Parras, signed by the prefect, Jose Ignacio Arrabe, and addressed
to Capt. Reid, the 18th of May, and says :

  " 'At the first notice that the barbarians, after killing many, and
taking captives, were returning to their haunts, you generously
and bravely offered, with fifteen of your subordinates, to fight
them on their crossing by the pass of the Pozo, executing this
enterprise with celerity, address and bravery worthy of all eulogy,
and worthy of the brilliant issue which all celebrate. You re-

covered many animals and much plundered property, and eighteen captives were restored to liberty and to social enjoyments, their souls overflowing with a lively sentiment of joy and gratitude, which all the inhabitants of this town equally breathe, in favour of their generous deliverers and their valiant chief. The half of the Indians killed in the combat, and those which fly wounded, do not calm the pain which all feel for the wound which your excellency received defending Christians and civilized beings against the rage and brutality of savages. All desire the speedy re-establishment of your health ; and although they know that in your own noble soul will be found the best reward of your conduct, they desire also to address you the expression of their gratitude and high esteem. I am honoured in being the organ of public sentiment, and pray you to accept it, with the assurance of my most distinguished esteem.

"'God and Liberty !'

"This is a trophy of a new kind in war, won by thirty Missourians, and worthy to be held up to the admiration of Christendom.

"The long march from Chihuahua to Monterey, was made more in the character of protection and deliverance than of conquest and invasion. Armed enemies were not met, and peaceful people were not disturbed. You arrived in the month of May in General Taylor's camp, and about in a condition to vindicate, each of you for himself, your lawful title to the double *soubriquet* of the general, with the addition to it which the colonel of the expedition has supplied—ragged—as well as rough and ready. No doubt you all showed title, at that time, to that third *soubriquet ;* but to see you now, so gayly attired, so sprucely equipped, one might suppose that you had never, for an instant, been a stranger to the virtues of soap and water, or the magic ministrations of the *blanchisseuse,* and the elegant transformations of the fashionable tailor. Thanks, perhaps, to the difference between pay in the lump, at the end of service, and driblets along in the course of it.

"You arrived in Gen. Taylor's camp ragged and rough, as we can well conceive, and ready, as I can quickly show. You re-

ported for duty! you asked for service!—such as a march upon
San Luis de Potosi, Zacatecas, or the ' halls of the Montezumas ;'
or any thing in that way that the general should have a mind to.
If he was going upon any excursion of that kind, all right. No
matter about fatigues that were passed, or expirations of service
that might accrue : you came to go, and only asked the privilege.
That is what I call ready. Unhappily the conqueror of Palo Alto,
Resaca de la Palma, Monterey and Buena Vista, was not exactly
in the condition that the lieutenant-general, that might have been,
intended him to be. He was not at the head of 20,000 men ! he
was not at the head of any thousands that would enable him to
march ! and had to decline the proffered service. Thus the long
marched and well-fought volunteers : the rough, the ready, and
the ragged : had to turn their faces towards home, still more than
two thousand miles distant. But this being mostly by water, you
hardly count it in the recital of your march. But this is an unjust
omission, and against the precedents as well as unjust. 'The
Ten Thousand' counted the voyage on the Black Sea as well as
the march from Babylon ; and twenty centuries admit the validity
of the count. The present age, and posterity, will include in ' the
going out and coming in,' of the Missouri Chihuahua Volunteers,
the water voyage as well as the land march ; and then the expedition of the One Thousand will exceed that of the Ten by some
two thousand miles.

"The last nine hundred miles of your land march, from Chihuahua to Matamoras, you made in forty-five days, bringing seventeen
pieces of artillery, eleven of which were taken from the Sacramento
and the Bracito. Your horses, travelling the whole distance without
the United States provender, were astonished to find themselves
regaled, on their arrival on the Rio Grande frontier, with hay, corn
and oats from the States. You marched further than the farthest,
fought as well as the best, left order and quiet in your train, and
cost less money than any.

"You arrive here to-day, absent one year, marching and fighting
all the time, bringing trophies of cannon and standards from fields
whose names were unknown to you before you set out, and only

grieving that you could not have gone further. Ten pieces of
cannon rolled out of Chihuahua to arrest your march, now roll
through the streets of St. Louis, to grace your triumphal return.
Many standards, all pierced with bullets while waving over the
heads of the enemy at the Sacramento, now wave at the head
of your column. The black flag, brought to the Bracito, to
indicate the refusal of that quarter which its bearers so soon
needed and received, now takes its place among your nobler
trophies, and hangs drooping in their presence. To crown the
whole, to make public and private happiness go together, to spare
the cypress where the laurel hangs in clusters: this long and
perilous march, with all its accidents of field and camp, presents
an incredibly small list of comrades lost. Almost all return!
and the joy of families resounds intermingled with the applauses
of the State.

"I have said that you made your long expedition without
government orders; and so indeed you did. You received no
orders from your government, but, without knowing it, you were
fulfilling its orders—orders which never reached you. Happy the
soldier who executes the command of his government; happier
still he who anticipates command, and does what is wanted before
he is bid. This is your case. You did the right thing, at the
right time, and what the government intended you to do, and without knowing its intention. The facts are these: Early in the
month of November last, the President asked my opinion on the
manner of conducting the war. I submitted a plan to him, which,
in addition to other things, required all the disposable troops in
New Mexico, and all the Americans in that quarter who could be
engaged for a dashing expedition, to move down through Chihuahua and the State of Durango, and if necessary to Zacatecas, and
get into communication with General Taylor's right as early as
possible in the month of March. In fact, the disposable Missourians in New Mexico were to be one of three columns destined for
a combined movement on the city of Mexico, all to be on the table-
land, and ready for the movement in the month of March. The
President approved the plan, and the Missourians being most dis-

tant, orders were despatched to New Mexico, to put them in motion. Mr. Solomon Sublette carried the order, and delivered it to
the commanding officer, at Santa Fé, Col. Price, on the 23d day
of February—just five days before you fought the marvellous
battle of Sacramento.

" I well remember what passed between the President and myself, at the time he resolved to give this order. It awakened his
solicitude for your safety It was to send a small body of men a
great distance, into the heart of a hostile country, and upon the
contingency of uniting in a combined movement, the means for
which had not yet been obtained from Congress. The President
made it a question, and very properly, whether it was safe, or prudent, to start the small Missouri column before the movement of
the left and of the centre was assured. I answered, that my own
rule in public affairs was to do what I thought was right, and
leave it with others to do what they thought was right; and that
I believed it the proper course for him to follow on the present
occasion. On this view he acted. He gave the order to go, without waiting to see whether Congress would furnish the means of
executing the combined plan; and, for his consolation, I undertook to guaranty your safety. Let the worst come to the worst, I
promised him, that you would take care of yourselves. Though
the other parts of the plan should fail—though you should become
far involved in the advance, and deeply compromised in the enemy's country, and without support—still I relied on your courage,
skill, and enterprise to extricate yourselves from every danger—
to make daylight through all the Mexicans that should stand before you—cut your way out—and make good your retreat to
Taylor's camp. This is what I promised the President in November last, and what you have so manfully fulfilled. And here
is a little manuscript volume, (the duplicate is in the hands of the
President,) from which I will read you a page, to show you are
the happy soldiers who have done the will of the government,
without knowing its will.

" ' THE RIGHT WING.—To be composed of all the disposable
troops in New Mexico—to advance rapidly towards Zacatecas, and

I   7

to attain a position about on a line with Gen. Taylor in the month of March, and be ready for a push on the capital. This column to move light—to have no rear—to keep itself mounted from horses in the country—and to join the centre column, or cut its way out if the main object fails.'

"This is what was proposed for you in the month of November last, and what I pledged myself to the President that you would perform; and nobly have you redeemed the pledge.

"But this was not the first, or the only time that I pledged myself for you. As far back as June, 1846, when a separate expedition to Chihuahua was first projected, I told the President that it was unnecessary—that the Missouri troops under Gen. Kearny would take that place, in addition to the conquest of New Mexico —and that he might order the column under Gen. Wool to deflect to the left, and join Gen. Taylor as soon as he pleased. Again: when I received a letter from Lieut. Col. Mitchell, dated in November last, and informing me that he was leaving Santa Fé with one hundred men, to open a communication with Gen. Wool, I read that letter to the President, and told him that they would do it. And again: when we heard that Col. Doniphan, with a thousand men, after curbing the Navahoes, was turning down towards the south, and threatening the ancient capital of the captains-general of the Internal Provinces, I told him they would take it. In short, my confidence in Missouri enterprise, courage and skill, was boundless. And now let boundless honour and joy salute, as it does, your return to the soil of your state, and to the bosoms of your families."

Col. Doniphan's reply was very eloquent, but, as he himself said, Col. Benton anticipated much. The gallant Missourian thus commenced his address :—

"FELLOW-CITIZENS,—I return you, on behalf of my command, our most heartfelt thanks for the distinguished reception which we have this day received at your hands. Such a reception entitles you to our warmest gratitude, and is deeply felt by those to whom it is extended. The honour conferred is greatly enhanced by the consideration of the medium through which it is presented. No selfish considerations could, we are satisfied, have induced the honourable senator to have passed this flattering eulogy upon us. The part which he has taken here to-day can add nothing to *his* fame. From an early day, his history has been identified with the history of the state of Missouri, and a feeling of state pride has induced him to give a favourable consideration to the services rendered by the volunteers of Missouri. To him, and yourselves, I again return our warmest thanks. The minute description given by the orator of scenes through which we have passed has excited our wonder. Indeed, so correct and minute are his details, that they resemble history, and I might almost say that they have become a part of history.

"The few brief remarks which I shall make to you, fellow-citizens, will of necessity be disconnected. Man seldom speaks of himself, without vanity ; and it is a habit which I do not often indulge. Officers of the Regular army, whose lives are devoted to their country, may, by their prowess—by their long continuance in the service—obtain promotion. The ladder of fame is before them ; and, by their deeds of chivalry, they may at length reach the topmost round. Not so with volunteers. They only enlist for a limited period, at the call of their country in her emergency ; and then return to mingle with their friends. The only reward that awaits a volunteer, is the gratitude and warm reception, and honour of his fellow-citizens. If our services have merited honour, then we have been more than repaid.

" Upon returning from our arduous campaign, and when entering upon the bosom of that noble stream that washes the borders of your city—when, in passing the magnificent country seats, bright eyes and smiling faces greeted us, and white handkerchiefs were waved in honour of the returning volunteers, we felt that we were sufficiently rewarded for all our toils. When we arrived at the great city of New Orleans, we were all unknown. That city is the thoroughfare through which have passed the heroes of Palo Alto, Resaca de la Palma, Monterey, Buena Vista, and Cerro Gordo —indeed the heroes of all the brilliant victories achieved in Mexico —and it was to be supposed that they would have been wearied long ago.   Yet their patriotism, their regard for their country, is unceasing.   There was not a volunteer in this corps who was not proffered a welcome hand.   The hospitalities of the city were extended to all.   Men who arrived there in rags, were clothed—the wealthiest merchants, who had never seen them, proffered them every thing they wished for their comfort, and on credit.

"FELLOW-CITIZENS : It has been said of Republics, which have existed heretofore, that they have been ungrateful.   However true the charge may be with regard to former republics, it is not true of our own.   Patriotism, talent, and virtue, have ever been remembered in this government, and they ever will be."

More eloquent words were uttered by Col. Doniphan, and happy as glowing were those addressed to his comrades in arms ; and warm and feeling were his adieus to the conquerors of Chihuahua.

His gallant officers then present, Col. Mitchell, Major Clark, Capt. Weightman, Capt. Hudson, and Capt. Reid, all eloquently bade farewell to men who must ever live in their memories, as they deserve to be proudly remembered by their countrymen of this wide Union.

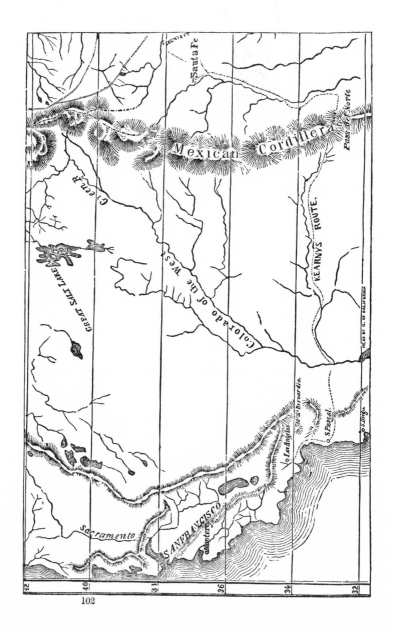

CHAPTER VII.

Pacific Squadron—Com. Sloat—Any Emergency—Distance and Difficulty of Communication—Orders and Instructions—Operations commenced—Bay of Monterey occupied—Proclamation—Bay of San Francisco—Capt. Fremont— Enrolment of Militia—British Man of War—Company of Dragoons—Com. Sloat returns to the United States—Com. Stockton—Operations and Despatches—Proclamation—Tariff and Civil Government—Newspaper established—Com. Stockton and Fremont—Despatch—Fremont Governor— Insurrection—Los Angeles—Santa Barbara—Battle—Military and Naval Operations—Settlements and Towns—Com. Stockton's Despatches—Gen. Kearny and Battles of Los Angeles—Fremont and Capitulation—Com. Stockton—Gen. Kearny and Col. Fremont meet at Los Angeles and separate —Com. Shubrick arrives—Capt. Tompkins' Artillery, and Col. Stevenson's Regiment—Com. Shubrick, Gen. Kearny and Joint-Circular—Col. Mason, of First Dragoons, Governor and Commander-in-chief of the Land Forces— Gen. Kearny, Com. Stockton, and Col. Fremont returns—American flag waves over California.

Of the combination of forces employed in the conquest of California and New Mexico, the Pacific Squadron had been early prepared to perform an active and efficient part.

On the 24th of June, 1845, Com. John D. Sloat, commanding the United States naval forces in the Pacific,* was instructed by a "secret and confidential" order of the Navy Department, "as soon as he ascertained with certainty that Mexico had declared war against the United States," at once to possess himself of the port of San Francisco, and to blockade or occupy such ports as his force might permit." In fact, he was required "to exercise all the belligerent rights which belonged to him on the declaration of war, or the commencement of hostilities."

Com. Sloat lost no time in preparing to meet any emergency that might arise, having, at that time, and on that distant coast, to contemplate not only the probability as to Mexico, but the possibility of a war with England. At the commencement of the year 1846, the largest American fleet ever collected in that quarter,

---

* Appendix, No. 6.

were on the west coast of Mexico. The Pacific squadron was
then composed of the frigates Savannah of 52 guns ; (the Constitution 50, and the Congress 52 guns under orders to join,) the
sloops of war Portsmouth, Levant and Cyane, each of 22 guns,
with the Warren of 24,—in all 244 guns and 2210 officers and
men. This gallant force anxiously awaited the arrival of the
President's message, to learn his views in regard to our Oregon
and Mexican relations, especially in reference to the latter. In
the confidential instructions, Com. Sloat's attention had been particularly called to the then aspect of the relations between this
country and Mexico—that it was "the earnest desire of the President to pursue the policy of peace," &c.—"should Mexico,
however, be resolutely bent on hostilities," he was required "to
protect the persons and interests of citizens of the United States
near his station ; and should he ascertain, beyond a doubt, that
the Mexican government had declared war" against the United
States, he was "at once to employ the forces under his command
to the best advantage." The then Secretary of the Navy, Mr.
Bancroft, added, "The great distance of your squadron, and the
difficulty of communicating with you, is the cause of issuing this
order."

The line of conduct prescribed by these instructions was observed by this officer "with such intelligence and fidelity, that no
complaint has ever been. made of any unauthorized aggression on
his part."*

On the 13th of May, 1846, the Secretary of the Navy wrote to
inform Commodore Sloat that "the state of things alluded to in his
letter of June 24, 1845," had occurred ; that he should be governed
by the instructions therein contained, and should "carry into effect
the orders then communicated, with energy and promptitude."

Two days thereafter, the Secretary again wrote him, and transmitted through Midshipman McRae, sent express, a file of papers
containing the President's message, proceedings of Congress, and
the President's proclamation of war, &c.

---

* Report of Secretary Mason, of December 5, 1846.

On the 8th of June following, Com. Sloat was told by the Secretary of the Navy, "it is rumoured the province of California is well disposed to accede to friendly relations with the United States;" that he should "encourage the people of that region to enter into relations of amity with our country;" and that, "in taking possession of their harbours," he should "if possible, endeavour to establish the supremacy of the American flag without any strife with the people of California," &c.*

The order, now given entire, contains the substance† of the two mentioned above, with other details:

UNITED STATES NAVY DEPARTMENT,
Washington, July 12, 1846.

COMMODORE : Previous instructions have informed you of the intention of this government, pending the war with Mexico, to take and hold possession of California. For this end a company of artillery, with cannon, mortars, and munitions of war, is sent to you in the Lexington, for the purpose of co-operating with you, according to the best of your judgment, and of occupying, under your direction, such post or posts as you may deem expedient in the bay of Monterey, or in the bay of San Francisco, or in both. In the absence of a military officer higher than captain, the selection of the first American post or posts on the waters of the Pacific, in California, is left to your discretion.

The object of the United States is, under its rights as a belligerent nation, to possess itself entirely of Upper California.

When San Francisco and Monterey are secured, you will, if possible, send a small vessel of war to take and hold possession of the port of San Diego; and it would be well to ascertain the views of the inhabitants of Pueblo de los Angeles, who, according to information received here, may be counted upon as desirous of coming under the jurisdiction of the United States. If you can take possession of it, you should do so.

---

* The letters from which quotations are here made, may be found in Ex. Doc. No. 19, of House of Reps. of U. S., 2d sess. 29th Cong., which embraces all the orders as yet promulgated, and are here *seriatim* noticed or given in full.

† Appendix, Nos. 7, 8, and 9.

The object of the United States has reference to ultimate peace with Mexico ; and if, at that peace, the basis of the *uti possidetis* shall be established, the government expects, through your forces, to be found in actual possession of Upper California.

This will bring with it the necessity of a civil administration. Such a government shall be established under your protection ; and, in selecting persons to hold office, due respect should be had to the wishes of the people of California, as well as to the actual possessors of authority in that province. It may be proper to require an oath of allegiance to the United States from those who are intrusted with authority. You will also assure the people of California of the protection of the United States.

In reference to commercial regulations in the ports of which you are in actual possession, ships and produce of the United States should come and go free of duty.

For your further instruction, I enclose to you a copy of confidential instructions from the War Department to Brig.-Gen. S. W. Kearny, who is ordered, overland, to California. You will also communicate your instructions to him, and inform him that they have the sanction of the President.

The government relies on the land and naval forces to co-operate with each other in the most friendly and effective manner.

After you shall have secured Upper California, if your force is sufficient, you will take possession, and keep the harbours on the Gulf of California as far down, at least, as Guaymas. But this is not to interfere with the permanent occupation of Upper California.

A regiment of volunteers from the state of New York, to serve during the war, have been called for by the government, and are expected to sail from the 1st to the 10th of August. This regiment will, in the first instance, report to the naval commander on your station, but will ultimately be under the command of Gen. Kearny, who is appointed to conduct the expedition by land.

The term of three years having nearly expired since you have been in command of the Pacific squadron, Com. Shubrick will soon be sent out in the Independence to relieve you. The department

confidently hopes that all Upper California will be in our hands
before the relief shall arrive.

Very respectfully,

GEORGE BANCROFT.

Com. JOHN D. SLOAT,
  Commanding U. S. Naval Forces in the Pacific ocean.

This was followed by the order of August 13, given entire
below :

UNITED STATES NAVY DEPARTMENT,

Washington, August 13, 1846.

SIR : The United States being in a state of war by the action of
Mexico, it is desired, by the prosecution of hostilities, to hasten the
return of peace, and to secure it on advantageous conditions. For
this purpose orders have been given to the squadron in the Pacific
to take and keep possession of Upper California, especially of the
ports of San Francisco, of Monterey, and of San Diego; and also,
if opportunity offer, and the people favour, to take possession, by
an inland expedition, of San Pueblo de los Angeles, near San
Diego.

Your first duty will be to ascertain if these orders have been
carried into effect. If not, you will take immediate possession of
Upper California, especially of the three ports of San Francisco,
Monterey, and San Diego, so that if the treaty of peace shall be
made on the basis of the *uti possidetis,* it may leave California to
the United States.

The relations to be maintained with the people of Upper California are to be as friendly as possible. The flag of the United
States must be raised; but under it the people are to be allowed
as much liberty of self-government as is consistent with the
general occupation of the country by the United States. You, as
commander-in-chief of the squadron, may exercise the right to
interdict the entrance of any vessel or articles, that would be unfavourable to our success in the war, into any of the enemy's ports
which you may occupy. With this exception, all United States
vessels and merchandise must be allowed, by the local authorities

of the ports of which you take possession, to come and go free of
duty ; but on foreign vessels and goods reasonable duties may be
imposed, collected, and disposed of by the local authorities, under
your general superintendence.

A military force has been directed by the Secretary of War to
proceed to the western coast of California for the purpose of co-
operation with the navy, in taking possession of and holding the
ports and positions which have been specified, and for otherwise
operating against Mexico.

A detachment of these troops, consisting of a company of artillery,
under command of Captain Tompkins, has sailed in the United
States ship Lexington. A regiment of volunteers, under Col.
Stevenson, will soon sail from New York ; and a body of troops
under Brigadier-general Kearny may reach the coast via Santa
Fé. Copies of so much of the instructions to Capt. Tompkins and
Gen. Kearny as relates to objects requiring co-operation are here-
with enclosed.*

By article 6 of the " General Regulations for the Army,"† edition
of 1825, which is held by the War Department to be still in force,
and of which I enclose you a copy, your commission [that is, the
commission of Commodore Biddle] places you in point of precedence, on occasions of ceremony or upon meetings for consultation,
in the class of major-general, but no officer of the army or navy,
whatever may be his rank, can assume any direct command, independent of consent, over an officer of the other service, excepting
only when land forces are specially embarked in vessels of war to
do the duty of marines.

The President expects and requires, however, the most cordial
and effectual co-operation between the officers of the two services,
in taking possession of and holding the ports and positions of the
enemy which are designated in the instructions to either or both
branches of the service, and will hold any commander of either
branch to a strict responsibility for any failure to preserve harmony
and secure the objects proposed.

---

* See Chapter 4, and Appendix.   † Appendix, No. 10.

The land forces which have been or will be sent to the Pacific may be dependent upon the vessels of your squadron for transportation from one point to another, and for shelter and protection in case of being compelled to abandon positions on the coast. It may be necessary also to furnish transportation for their supplies, or to furnish the supplies themselves, by the vessels under your direction.

In all such cases you will furnish all the assistance in your power which will not interfere with objects that, in your opinion, are of greater importance.

You will, taking care, however, to advise with any land officer of high rank—say of the rank of brigadier-general—who may be at hand, make the necessary regulations for the ports that may be occupied.

Having provided for the full possession of Upper California, the next point of importance is the Gulf of California. From the best judgment I can form, you should take possession of the port of Guaymas. The progress of our arms will probably be such that, in conjunction with land forces, you will be able to hold possession of Guaymas, and so to reduce all the country north of it on the gulf.

As to the ports south of it, especially Mazatlan and Acapulco, it is not possible to give you special instructions. Generally, you will take possession of, or blockade, according to your best judgment, all Mexican ports as far as your means allow; but south of Guaymas, if the provinces rise up against the central government, and manifest friendship towards the United States, you may, according to your discretion, enter into a temporary agreement of neutrality. But this must be done only on condition that our ships have free access to their ports, and equal commercial rights with those of other nations; that you are allowed to take in water and fuel, to purchase supplies, to go to and from shore without obstruction, as in time of peace; and that the provinces which are thus neutral shall absolutely abstain from contributing towards the continuance of the war by the central government of Mexico against the United States.

K

Generally you will exercise the rights of a belligerent; and bear in mind that the greater advantages you obtain, the more speedy and the more advantageous will be the peace.

The Savannah, the Warren, and the Levant ought soon to return. If you hear of peace between the United States and Mexico, you will at once send them home.

If war continues, you will send them home singly, or in company, at the earliest day they can be spared. The Savannah will go to New York, and the Warren and Levant to Norfolk.

Very respectfully, your obedient servant,

GEORGE BANCROFT.

To Com. JAMES BIDDLE, or
   Com. R. F. STOCKTON, or
   The SENIOR OFFICER *in command of the*
       United States Naval Forces in the Pacific ocean.

Four days after the date of the above, on the 17th of August, Mr. Bancroft addressed to "Commodore W. B. Shubrick, appointed to command the United States naval forces in the Pacific ocean," a letter of instructions* exactly similar, (with the omission of the words in brackets, "*that is the commission of Commodore Biddle,*) and with the insertion of the following:

"*Should Commodore Biddle be in the Pacific, off the shores of Mexico, at the time you arrive there, you will report yourself to him; and as long as he remains off the coast of Mexico, you will act under his direction in concert with him, communicating to him these instructions.*"

On the 1st of July, 1846, the naval forces under the command of Com. Sloat consisted of the frigate Savannah; sloops Portsmouth, Levant, Warren, and Cyane; schooners Shark, and store-ship Erie. They were reinforced by the frigate Congress, Commodore Stockton; the sloops Saratoga,* Dale, and Preble, and

---

* Appendix, No. 11.
† Saratoga, disabled by stress of weather, returned before reaching her destination.

by the razee Independence, under command of Com. W. Bradford Shubrick, who went out to relieve Com. Sloat, under orders issued in August, 1846.

The frigate Columbus, Com. James Biddle, had also been ordered on the 6th of January, 1846, from the China seas, to the north-west coast of America, and to assume the command, but could not reach the station till a later period.

The active operations of the Pacific squadron were commenced under the order of June, 1845, which required the commander of the naval forces "to exercise all the belligerent rights which belonged to him on the declaration of war, or the commencement of hostilities by Mexico against the United States."

On the 7th of June, 1846, Com. Sloat received, at Mazatlan, satisfactory information, through Mexico, "that the Mexican troops, six or seven thousand strong, had, by order of the Mexican government, invaded the territory of the United States, north of the Rio Grande, and had attacked the forces under Gen. Taylor, and that the squadron of the United States was blockading the ports of Mexico on the Gulf, and he properly considered these hostilities as justifying his commencing offensive operations on the west coast."*

Distance had precluded their knowledge of the order of the 13th of May, 1846; issued on the day when the American Congress recognised the fact that war existed—and, indeed, of all the subsequent instructions, until the Conquest of California had been almost consummated.

Thus had the time of action arrived, and right quickly did our gallant tars enter upon a series of achievements as glorious and important as they were novel and exciting.

On the day after the receipt of the war news, Com. Sloat, in the flag-ship Savannah, left Mazatlan, and, on the 2d of July, reached Monterey in Upper California. Here he found the Cyane and Levant, and learned that the Portsmouth was at San Francisco, as before arranged.

---

* Report of the Secretary of the Navy.

Having previously examined the defences, &c., of the town,
and made every arrangement, on the morning of the 7th, Capt.
Wm. Mervine, of the United States navy, was sent to demand its
immediate surrender.   By 9 o'clock A. M., the answer of the
Mexican commandant was received.   He stated that he was not
authorized to surrender the place, and referred Com. Sloat to
the commanding general of California, Don Jose Castro.   By
10 o'clock, the necessary force of 250 seamen and marines were
landed under the immediate command of Capt. Mervine, assisted
by Commander H. N. Page, as second, and were immediately
marched to the custom-house, where Com. Sloat's " proclamation
was read, the standard of the United States hoisted amid three
hearty cheers, by the troops and foreigners present, and a salute
of twenty-one guns fired by all the ships.   Immediately afterwards, the proclamation, both in English and Spanish, was posted
up about the town, and two justices of the peace appointed to
preserve order and punish delinquencies, the alcaldes declining to
serve."*

The following is the proclamation above alluded to :—

To the Inhabitants of California.

The central government of Mexico having commenced hostilities against the United States of America, by invading its territory,
and attacking the troops of the United States stationed on the
north side of the Rio Grande, and with a force of 7000 men under
the command of Gen. Arista, which army was totally destroyed,
and all their artillery, baggage, &c., captured on the 8th and 9th
of May last, by a force of 2300 men, under the command of Gen.
Taylor, and the city of Matamoras taken and occupied by the
forces of the United States, and the two nations being actually at
war by this transaction, I shall hoist the standard of the United
States at Monterey immediately, and shall carry it throughout California.

I declare to the inhabitants of California, that, although I come

---

* Com. Sloat's despatch, of 31st of July, 1846.

in arms with a powerful force, I do not come among them as an enemy to California : on the contrary, I come as their best friend, as henceforth California will be a portion of the United States, and its peaceable inhabitants will enjoy the same rights and privileges they now enjoy, together with the privilege of choosing their own magistrates and other officers for the administration of justice among themselves, and the same protection will be extended to them as to any other State in the Union.   They will also enjoy a permanent government, under which life, property, and the constitutional right and lawful security to worship the Creator in the way most congenial to each one's sense of duty, will be secured, which, unfortunately, the central government of Mexico cannot afford them, destroyed, as her resources are by internal factions, and corrupt officers, who create constant revolutions to promote their own interests and oppress the people. Under the flag of the United States, California will be free from all such troubles and expense ; consequently, the country will rapidly advance and improve both in agriculture and commerce, as, of course, the revenue laws will be the same in California as in all other parts of the United States, affording them all manufactures and produce of the United States, free of any duty, and all foreign goods at one quarter of the duty they now pay. A great increase in the value of real estate and the products of California may also be anticipated.

With the great interest and kind feelings I know the government and people of the United States possess towards the citizens of California, the country cannot but improve more rapidly than any other on the continent of America.

Such of the inhabitants of California, whether native or foreigners, as may not be disposed to accept the high privileges of citizenship, and to live peaceably under the government of the United States, will be allowed time to dispose of their property, and to remove out of the country, if they choose, without any restriction ; or remain in it, observing strict neutrality.

With full confidence in the honour and integrity of the inhabitants of the country, I invite the judges, alcaldes, and other civil

K 2   8

officers, to retain their offices, and to execute their functions as heretofore, that the public tranquillity may not be disturbed; at least, until the government of the territory can be more definitely arranged.

All persons holding titles to real estate, or in quiet possession of lands under a colour of right, shall have those titles and rights guarantied to them.

All churches, and the property they contain, in possession of the clergy of California, shall continue in the same rights and possessions they now enjoy.

All provisions and supplies of every kind furnished by the inhabitants for the use of the United States ships and soldiers will be paid for at fair rates; and no private property will be taken for public use without just compensation at the moment.

JOHN D. SLOAT,
Commander-in-chief of the United States
Naval Force in the Pacific ocean.

Previous to landing, Com. Sloat had an order read to the crews of all the ships, in the spirit of the proclamation, enforcing order, vigilance, &c., so that, from the moment of landing to that of departure, not the least depredation, or slightest injury, or irregularity, was committed.

Immediately after taking possession of Monterey, a courier was despatched to Don Jose Castro, with a copy of the proclamation, requiring him, in order to prevent the sacrifice of life and the horrors of war, to surrender every thing under his control and jurisdiction in California; and he was invited to meet Com. Sloat at Monterey, to enter into articles of capitulation, that he, with his officers and soldiers, together with the inhabitants of California, might receive assurance of perfect safety to themselves and posterity.

To which a reply, dated "Head-quarters, San Juan de Bautista, July 9," was received, stating, that in a matter of so much importance, he must consult the governor and assembly of the department; meanwhile, he should spare no sacrifice in the defence of the country under his charge, as long as he could reckon on a single individual to join him in the cause.

On the 9th, Com. Sloat despatched a letter, by courier, to Don Pio Pico, the governor at Santa Barbara, informing him of the summons to Gen. Castro to surrender the country—of the proclamation—assuring him that not the least impropriety had been committed in the town, its business and social intercourse remaining undisturbed, and invites Pico to come to Monterey to assure himself, &c., so that he may be satisfied, and through him the people of California, that "although he comes in arms with a powerful force, he comes as the best friend of California ;" concluding with the assurance that he had "already employed all the means in his power to stop the sacrifice of human life in the north," and of his belief that he shall succeed, "provided there is no further opposition." To this no answer is known to have been returned.

On the 6th of July, Com. Sloat wrote :

FLAG SHIP SAVANNAH,
Monterey, July 6, 1846.

SIR : Since I wrote you last evening, I have determined to hoist the flag of the United States at this place to-morrow, as I would prefer being sacrificed for doing too much than too little.

If you consider you have sufficient force, or if Fremont will join you, you will hoist the flag of the United States at Yerba Buena, or any other proper place, and take possession, in the name of the United States, of the fort, and that portion of the country.

I send you a copy of my summons to the military commandant of Monterey to surrender the place, and also my proclamation to the people of California, which you will have translated into Spanish, and promulgate many copies in both languages. I have sent a similar letter to Gen. Castro, with an addition of an invitation for him to meet me at this place to enter into a capitulation. I will send you a duplicate copy of these documents to-morrow, which I hope will reach you before the boat can get up. You will secure the bay of San Francisco as soon as possible, at all events. It is my intention to go up to San Francisco as soon as I can leave this, which I hope will not be many days.

Mr. Larkin advises that you should not send by courier any thing that would do harm to make public; and should you have any thing that you consider important for me to know, you can send the launch down again.

I am very anxious to know if Capt. Fremont will co-operate with us. Mr. Larkin is writing to him by the launch, and you will please put him in possession of his letter as soon as possible. I have not time to write more at present.

Very respectfully, your obedient servant, &c.,

JOHN D. SLOAT,
Commander-in-chief, &c.

To Commander J. B. MONTGOMERY,
U. S. ship Portsmouth, San Francisco.

A duplicate of this order, sent by land, was received by Commander Montgomery on the 8th, who, in a few hours after its receipt, despatched Lieut. Revere to Capt. John Grigsby, at Sonoura, with Com. Sloat's letter, and flags for him and Sutter's fort, on the Sacramento. At eight o'clock next morning, Com. Montgomery landed at Yerba Buena with seventy seamen and marines— hoisted the American flag in the public square, with twenty-one guns from the sloop of war Portsmouth, amid cheers from all quarters—addressed the people, and posted the proclamation on the flag-staff. The seamen and a few of the marines returned to the ship, without a man having left the ranks. Lieut. H. B. Watson, of the marine corps, remained with part of his guard, and was formally installed as military occupant of the post. The male residents of Yerba Buena were then called together, and a volunteer guard of thirty-two men at once enrolled, and electing their own officers, were fully organized for emergency, under the direction of Lieuts. Missroon, of the navy, and Watson. At one o'clock, Lieut. Missroon was, by order, on his way to the Presidio and fort, with an armed party of this volunteer guard to ascertain their condition, &c.; and that day promptly reported he had found the Presidio abandoned—the fort, about seven miles from the town, in a dilapidated condition, with three old Spanish pieces, made in **1623,**

1628, and 1693, besides three long iron forty-twos, and four smaller iron guns—all the iron guns lately spiked by Capt. Fremont, but that new vents might be drilled in the brass ones, &c.; and that he had displayed the flag of the United States upon its ramparts. On the same day, Commander Montgomery ordered Purser Watmough to proceed to Santa Clara, and to the Pueblo, if necessary, to intercept Capt. Fremont, then on his march from the Sacramento, and deliver a notification of the change in the political condition of California—of the official notification of the existence of the war, and of Com. Sloat's request to see him in Monterey— "with a view to future arrangements and co-operation, at as early a period as possible." On the same day, Commander Montgomery issued a proclamation, calling upon "all the residents of the district, agreeably to the laws of the United States of America, regulating the militia, to enrol themselves into a military company, appoint their own officers, &c.—for the maintenance of order, and protection of property in Yerba Buena and its immediate neighbourhood; and Henry B. Watson, Esq., was appointed military commandant *pro tem.* of all the marines and militia." On the 11th, Commander Montgomery informed Com. Sloat that the flag of the United States was then flying at Yerba Buena, at Sutter's fort, on the Sacramento, at Bodega, on the coast, and at Sonoura, and adds, "the protection of person and property which our flag promises to California and its inhabitants, seems to be generally hailed with satisfaction."

That day, says Commander Montgomery, the Juno, British 26 gun ship, arrived and anchored at Sausalita, &c. "On the appearance of that ship, the necessary preparation was made to defend our position, in the event of English opposition to our claims." It thus became necessary to withdraw the marines from the shore to the ship. Ashore the flag of the United States was committed, by Mr. Watson, to the care of the "Volunteer Guards of Yerba Buena, who "unanimously gave the strongest assurances that it should wave while a single man of the "Guards" lived to defend it.

A summons was sent, by Commander Montgomery, to the military commandant of that district, Don Francisco Sanchez, to deliver up arms, public property, &c., and to come in ; which he did, and stated that he possessed no public property, but indicated where several guns were buried.

Lieut. Missroon was ordered to the Mission of Dolores in search of arms, ammunition, &c., and the public documents of the district. No arms were found. A collection of public documents was made, carefully packed and sealed with the consulate seal, &c., and deposited in the custom-house at Yerba Buena.

The details of gallant exploits and achievements in this quarter of the war are abundantly full of interest ; it is not, however, permitted in the plan of this work to do otherwise than sketch their outlines, hence the most concise official reports must be followed, however unwillingly.

At their request, on the 13th July, Com. Sloat furnished a flag to the foreigners of the Pueblo of San Jose, about seventy miles interior from Monterey, and appointed a justice of the peace, the alcaldes declining to serve. On the 8th, Purser D. Fauntleroy, well qualified for such service, was ordered to organize a company of thirty-five dragoons, from volunteers from the ships and citizens, to reconnoitre the country, keep the communication open between Monterey and San Francisco, &c. Of this troop, passed Midshipman McLane was appointed first lieutenant. On the 17th, this command was ordered to reconnoitre as far as the mission of St. John's ; to take possession of that place, hoist the flag, and to recover ten brass guns, said to have been buried there when he retreated from that place. On his arrival there, Mr. Fauntleroy found the place had been taken possession of an hour or two previous by Capt. Fremont, with whom he returned to Monterey on the 19th. Subsequently Mr. Fauntleroy garrisoned the mission of St. Johns—dug up and mounted the guns, and recovered a large quantity of powder and shot secreted there, and kept open the communication between St. Johns, the Pueblo of San Jose, and San Francisco.

From the return of Capt. Fremont with Mr. Fauntleroy resulted the first interview between the former and Com. Sloat.

On the afternoon of the 15th, the frigate Congress arrived at Monterey, and Com. Stockton reported for duty.

On the 16th, the British admiral, Sir George Seymour, arrived in the Collingwood, 80. An officer was immediately sent to tender him the usual courtesies, &c., of the port. He was subsequently furnished with spars for his ship. On the 23d, Com. Stockton was ordered to the command on shore ; and on the 29th of July Com. Sloat found his infirm health so enfeebled by his arduous duties, that he determined to avail himself of a permission which had been given him, in his discretion, to assign the command to Com. Stockton, and sailed for Panama on his return home. "After encountering much peril and hardship, this gallant and meritorious officer arrived at the seat of government early in November, 1846." *

The operations of Com. Stockton are rapidly sketched, by himself, down to the 28th of August, in the following despatch :

Cuidad de los Angeles,
August 28, 1846.

Sir : You have already been informed of my having, on the 23d of July, assumed the command of the United States forces on the west coast of Mexico. I have now the honour to inform you that the flag of the United States is flying from every commanding position in the territory of California, and that this rich and beautiful country belongs to the United States, and is for ever free from Mexican dominion.

On the day after I took this command I organized the "California battalion of mounted riflemen," by the appointment of all the necessary officers, and received them as volunteers into the service of the United States. Capt. Fremont was appointed major, and Lieut. Gillespie captain of the battalion.

The next day they were embarked on board the sloop of war Cyane, Commander Dupont, and sailed from Monterey for San Diego, that they might be landed to the southward of the Mexican forces, amounting to 500 men, under Gen. Castro and Governor

---

* Secretary Mason's Report, 5th Dec. 1846.

Pico, and who were well fortified at the "Camp of the Mesa," three miles from this city.

A few days after the Cyane left, I sailed in the Congress for San Pedro, the port of entry for this department, and thirty miles from this place, where I landed with my gallant sailor army, and marched directly for the redoubtable "Camp of the Mesa."

But when we arrived within twelve miles of the camp, General Castro broke ground and run for the city of Mexico. The governor of the territory, and the other principal officers, separated in different parties, and ran away in different directions.

Unfortunately, the mounted riflemen did not get up in time to head them off. We have since, however, taken most of the principal officers: the rest will be permitted to remain quiet at home, under the restrictions contained in my proclamation of the 17th.

On the 13th of August, having been joined by Major Fremont with about eighty riflemen, and M. Larkin, late American consul, we entered this famous "City of the Angels," the capital of the Californias, and took unmolested possession of the government house.

Thus, in less than a month after I assumed the command of the United States force in California, we have chased the Mexican army more than three hundred miles along the coast; pursued them thirty miles in the interior of their own country; routed and dispersed them, and secured the territory to the United States; ended the war; restored peace and harmony among the people; and put a civil government into successful operation.

The Warren and Cyane sailed a few days since to blockade the west coast of Mexico, south of San Diego; and having almost finished my work here, I will sail in the Congress as soon as the store-ship arrives, and I can get supplied with provisions, on a cruise for the protection of our commerce; and dispose of the other vessels as most effectually to attain that object, and at the same time to keep the southern coast strictly blockaded.

When I leave the Territory, I will appoint Major Fremont to be governor, and Lieut. Gillespie to be secretary.

I enclose you several papers, marked from 1 to 14 inclusive, including this letter, and the first number of the "Californian," by which you will see what sort of a government I have established, and how I am proceeding.

I have not time to specify individual merit ; but I cannot omit to say, that I do not think that ardent patriotism and indomitable courage have ever been more evident than amongst the officers and men, 360 in number, from the frigate Congress, who accompanied me on this trying and hazardous march—a longer march, perhaps, than has ever been made in the interior of a country by sailors, after an enemy. I would likewise say, that the conduct of the officers and men of the whole squadron has been praiseworthy.

I have received your despatch of the 13th of May, and at the same time a Mexican account of the proceedings of Congress, and the President's proclamation, by the United States ship Warren, from Mazatlan.

Faithfully, your obedient servant,
R. F. STOCKTON.

To the Hon. GEORGE BANCROFT,
       Secretary of the Navy, Washington, D. C.

The despatch had been sent overland from Chagres, and arrived on the 19th of August. It will thus be seen, at what distant time the President's proclamation reached the distant scene, where victory had already crowned the arms of the republic. The instructions of a subsequent date were, of course, still on the way.

Meanwhile, the proclamation, indicated in the above letter, had been issued, as follows :—

TO THE PEOPLE OF CALIFORNIA !

On my approach to this place with the forces under my command, José Castro, the commandant-general of California, buried his artillery, and abandoned his fortified camp " of the Mesa," and fled, it is believed, towards Mexico.

With the sailors, the marines, and the California battalion of mounted Riflemen, we entered the "City of the Angels," the
L

capital of California, on the 13th of August, and hoisted the North American flag.

The flag of the United States is now flying from every commanding position in the territory, and California is entirely free from Mexican dominion.

The Territory of California now belongs to the United States, and will be governed, as soon as circumstances will permit, by officers and laws similar to those by which the other Territories of the United States are regulated and protected.

But, until the governor, the secretary, and council are appointed, and the various civil departments of the government are arranged, military law will prevail, and the commander-in-chief will be the governor and protector of the Territory.

In the mean time the people will be permitted, and are now requested, to meet in their several towns and departments, at such time and place as they may see fit, to elect civil officers to fill the places of those who decline to continue in office, and to administer the laws according to the former usages of the Territory. In all cases where the people fail to elect, the commander-in-chief and governor will make the appointments himself.

All persons of whatever religion or nation, who faithfully adhere to the new government, will be considered as citizens of the Territory, and will be zealously and thoroughly protected in the liberty of conscience, their persons, and property.

No persons will be permitted to remain in the Territory who do not agree to support the existing government; and all military men who desire to remain, are required to take an oath that they will not take up arms against it, or do or say any thing to disturb its peace.

Nor will any persons, come from where they may, be permitted to settle in the Territory, who do not pledge themselves to be, in all respects, obedient to the laws which may be from time to time enacted by the proper authorities of the Territory.

All persons who, without special permission, are found with arms outside of their own houses, will be considered as enemies, and will be shipped out of the country.

All thieves will be put to hard labour on the public works, and there kept until compensation is made for the property stolen.

The California battalion of mounted Riflemen will be kept in the service of the Territory, and constantly on duty, to prevent and punish any aggressions by the Indians, or any other persons, upon the property of individuals, or the peace of the Territory; and California shall hereafter be so governed and defended as to give security to the inhabitants, and to defy the power of Mexico.

All persons are required, as long as the Territory is under martial law, to be within their houses from ten o'clock at night, until sunrise in the morning.

R. F. STOCKTON,

Commander-in-chief and Governor of the Territory of California.

Cuidad de los Angeles, *August* 17, 1846.

The form of government established, was announced as follows :—

" I, Robert F. Stockton, commander-in-chief of the United States forces in the Pacific ocean, and governor of the Territory of California, and commander-in-chief of the army of the same, do hereby make known to all men, that, having by right of conquest taken possession of that territory known by the name of Upper and Lower California, do now declare it to be a Territory of the United States, under the name of the Territory of California.

" And I do by these presents further order and decree, that the government of the said Territory of California shall be, until altered by the proper authority of the United States, constituted in manner and form as follows ; that is to say :

" The executive power and authority in and over the said Territory shall be vested in a governor, who shall hold his office for four years, unless sooner removed by the President of the United States. The governor shall reside within the said Territory ; shall be commander-in-chief of the army thereof; shall perform the duties and receive the emoluments of superintendent of Indian affairs, and shall approve of all laws passed by the legislative council before they shall take effect. He may grant pardons for offences against the laws of the said Territory, and reprieves for offences against the laws of the United States, until the decision of the President can be made known thereon : he shall commission all officers who shall be appointed to office under the laws of the said Territory, and shall take care that the laws be faithfully executed.

"There shall be a secretary of the said Territory, who shall reside therein, and hold his office for four years, unless sooner removed by the President of the United States. He shall record and preserve all the laws and proceedings of the legislative council hereinafter constituted, and all the acts and proceedings of the governor in his executive department. He shall transmit one copy of the laws, and one copy of the executive proceedings, on or before the first Monday in December in each year, to the President of the United States; and, at the same time, two copies of the laws to the Speaker of the House of Representatives, for the use of Congress. And, in case of the death, removal, resignation, or necessary absence of the governor from the Territory, the secretary shall have, and he is hereby authorized and required to execute and perform all the powers and duties of the governor during such vacancy or necessary absence.

" The legislative power shall be vested in the governor and legislative council. The legislative council shall consist of seven persons, who shall be appointed by the governor for two years ; after which they shall be annually elected by the people.

"The power of the legislative council of the Territory shall extend to all rightful subjects of legislation; but no law shall be passed interfering with the primary disposal of the soil; no tax shall be imposed upon the property of the United States; nor shall the land or property of non-residents be taxed higher than the lands or other property of residents.

" All the laws of the legislative council shall be submitted to, and if disapproved by the governor, the same shall be null and of no effect.

" The municipal officers of cities, towns, departments, or districts, heretofore existing in the Territory, shall continue to exist, and all their proceedings be regulated and controlled by the laws of Mexico, until otherwise provided for by the governor and legislative council.

"All officers of cities, towns, departments, or districts, shall be elected every year by the people, in such a manner as may be provided by the governor and legislative council.

"The legislative council of the Territory of California shall hold its first session at such time and place in said territory as the governor thereof shall appoint and direct; and at said session, or as soon thereafter as may by them be deemed expedient, the said governor and legislative council shall proceed to locate and establish the seat of government for said territory, at such place as they may deem eligible; which place, however, shall thereafter be subject to be changed by the said governor and legislative council, and the time and place of the annual commencement of the session of the said legislative council thereafter shall be on such day and place as the governor and council may appoint."

On the 15th of August, 1846, Com. Stockton adopted a tariff of duties on all goods imported from foreign ports of fifteen per cent. ad valorem, and a tonnage duty of fifty cents per ton on all foreign vessels.

On the 22d of August, the elections were ordered to be held on the 15th of the following month, when Walter Colton, Esq., the chaplain of the frigate Congress, was declared duly elected Alcalde of Monterey. There were seven competitors for this office, and 338 votes, out of which Mr. Colton received sixty-eight. In San Juan, Mathew Felon was elected alcalde, and the councillors chosen were Messrs. Hartnall, Spence, Dias, &c.

Meanwhile, Messrs. Colton and Semple had established a newspaper, and on the 5th of August was published the first number of "The Californian."

In this situation of affairs was issued the following order:—

CUIDAD DE LOS ANGELES, *August* 24, 1846.

SIR:—By the Mexican newspapers, I see that war has been declared both by the United States and Mexico, and the most vigorous measures have been adopted by Congress to carry it to a speedy conclusion.

Privateers will, no doubt be fitted out to prey upon our commerce ; and the immense value of that commerce in the Pacific ocean, and the number of valuable men engaged in it, require immediately all the protection that can be given to them by the ships under my command.

I must, therefore, withdraw my forces from California as soon as it can be safely done, and as soon as you can enlist men enough to garrison this city, Monterey, San Francisco, Santa Barbara, and San Diego, and to have a sufficient force besides to watch the Indians and other enemies.

For these purposes, you are authorized and required to increase your present force to 300 men.

Fifty for San Francisco, fifty for Monterey, twenty-five for Santa Barbara, fifty for this city, and twenty-five for San Diego, and 100 to be kept together, with whom, those in the several garrisons can, at a short notice, be called upon at any time, in case of necessity, to act.

I propose, before I leave the territory, to appoint you to be the governor, and Captain Gillespie the secretary thereof; and to appoint also the council of state, and all the necessary officers.

You will, therefore, proceed without delay to do all you can to further my views and intentions thus frankly manifested. Supposing that by the 25th of October, you will have accomplished your part of these preparations, I will meet you at San Francisco on that day, to complete the whole arrangement, and to place you as governor over California.

You will dispose of your present force in the following manner, which may be hereafter altered as occasion may require:—

Capt. Gillespie to be stationed at this city, with fifty men and officers in the neighbourhood ; twenty-five men, with an officer, at Santa Barbara ; fifty men and officers at Monterey, and fifty at San Francisco.

If this be done at once, I can, at any time, safely withdraw my forces as I proceed up the coast to San Francisco, and be ready, after our meeting, on the 25th of October, to leave the desk and the camp, and take to the ship and to the sea.

Faithfully, your obedient servant,

R. F. STOCKTON,

Commander-in-chief, and Governor of the

To Major Fremont, *Territory of California.*

California Battalion, Cuidad de los Angeles.

At all the points occupied, defensive works were being erected, particularly at Monterey and San Francisco. At Yerba Buena, settlers were establishing themselves, and all things wore the aspect of a prosperous settlement.

On the 28th of August, Com. Stockton and Col. Fremont were at Los Angeles, whence, early in September, Col. Fremont went north with only forty men, intending to recruit and return immediately. Com. Stockton withdrew all his forces and proceeded with the squadron to San Francisco.

Capt. Gillespie was left in command of the Pueblo de los Angeles, with about thirty riflemen, and Lieut. Talbot in command at Santa Barbara, with only nine men.

Scarcely had Com. Stockton arrived at San Francisco, when he received information that all the country below Monterey was in arms, and the Mexican flag again hoisted.

Our limits do not permit of other than a brief sketch of this contest. Briefly, the Californians rebelled and invested, on the 23d of September, the "City of the Angels," where Capt. Gillespie, finding himself and his very few men overpowered by full 300 Californians, capitulated on the 30th following. He thence retired with all the foreigners, aboard the sloop of war, &c., lying at San Pedro, and sailed to Monterey.

Manual Gaspar then marched to Santa Barbara, and summoned Lieut. Talbot to surrender; this he refused, but marched out with his nine men, arms in hand. (As belonging to Col. Fremont's command, Lieut. Talbot is deservedly mentioned in another chapter.)

Com. Stockton sent down, from San Francisco, the frigate Savannah to relieve the Pueblo de los Angeles, but she arrived a few days after the above events. Our eager tars lost no time, however, and her crew, numbering 320 men, were landed to march to Los Angeles. They met the Californians on a plain near Domingo's Rancho—about half-way from San Pedro and Los Angeles—distant about fifteen miles from the ship. The enemy, mounted on fine horses and with artillery, had every advantage over our brave sailors, who, on foot, and with small arms alone, were forced to retreat with the loss of five killed, and six wounded.

Com. Stockton himself came down in the Congress to San Pedro, whence he took up his march for the "City of the Angels," dragging up, by hand, six of the ship's guns, (for the Californians had driven off every animal.) At the Rancho Sepulvida, they met a large force of the enemy; when, sending 100 men in advance to receive the fire of the Californians, and to fall back on the main body without returning it, Com. Stockton thus decoyed the enemy close up to the main body, formed in a triangle, with the guns hid by the men, and loaded with grape and canister, when the wings were extended, and a most deadly fire opened, by which more than 100 were killed, and more than that number wounded, and the enemy routed, leaving about 100 prisoners, many of whom, thus captured, were at the time on parol, and had before signed an obligation not to take up arms during the war. Their subsequent disposition will be seen elsewhere.

As rapidly as possible, Com. Stockton mounted his men and organized his forces for operations on shore. All the horses were thus taken by one party or the other from the purposes of agriculture; in fact, the emigrants were all more or less enrolled and engaged in the contest which was waged in series of skirmishes until January, 1847, when the war was put an end to by a decisive action.

Of the efficient and gallant co-operation of Col. Fremont in almost all these, and other important events, we have had to tell elsewhere.

Meanwhile, individual feats of gallantry, a characteristic courage, activity, and ardour, strongly marked all the operations of our sailors in their novel position ashore.

The fleet had cruised actively along the whole western coast of Mexico, blockading all her ports. Guayamas had been taken by bombardment. Commander Dupont, in the Cyane, had taken fourteen prizes, &c., and had captured, at San Blas, many guns. Lieut. Radford, in command of the boats of the Warren, had gallantly cut out of the harbour of Mazatlan, the Mexican vessel of war Malek-Abdel, and various other achievements had signalized their efficiency.

Busy settlements were being formed by emigrants, of whom numbers arrived, and who, marching in arms through the country, acquired, at least, a knowledge of its real value and resources.

On the bay of San Francisco, several towns were located. Yerba Buena, in rivalry with Monterey, was rapidly becoming an important place ; lots, squares, &c., were laid out, and a newspaper established by the leader of the Mormon emigrants, S. Brannon, Esq., entitled "The California Star."

It is to be remembered that our gallant tars carried on this contest up to this time, almost entirely without the means of transportation, whereby they could "meet the enemy," while the Californians were mounted on fine horses, and the best riders in the world, and could thus choose their own time, place, and distance of attack.

This warfare was kept up, principally, south of Monterey, and continued until the arrival of Gen. Kearny, when the brilliant events which led to the final conquest of California took place, and are thus described by Com. Stockton :

HEAD-QUARTERS, CUIDAD DE LOS ANGELES,
January 11, 1847.

SIR : I have the honour to inform you that it has pleased God to crown our poor efforts to put down the rebellion, and to retrieve the credit of our arms, with the most complete success. The insurgents determined, with their whole force, to meet us on our march from San Diego to this place, and to decide the fate of the territory by a general battle.

Having made the best preparation I could, in the face of a boasting and vigilant enemy, we left San Diego on the 29th day of December, (that portion of the insurgent army who had been watching and annoying us, having left to join the main body,) with about six hundred fighting men, composed of detachments from the ships Congress, Savannah, Portsmouth, and Cyane, aided by Gen. Kearny, with a detachment of sixty men on foot, from the First Regiment of United States Dragoons, and by Capt. Gillespie, with sixty mounted riflemen.

We marched nearly one hundred and forty miles in ten days, and found the rebels, on the 8th day of January, in a strong position, on the high bank of the "Rio San Gabriel," with six hundred mounted men and four pieces of artillery, prepared to dispute our passage across the river.

We waded through the water dragging our guns after us against the galling fire of the enemy, without exchanging a shot until we reached the opposite shore, when the fight became general, and our troops having repelled a charge of the enemy, charged up the bank in a most gallant manner, and gained a complete victory over the insurgent army.

The next day, on our march across the plains of the "Mesa" to this place, the insurgents made another desperate effort to save the capital and their own necks ; they were concealed with their artillery in a ravine until we came within gun-shot, when they opened a brisk fire from their field-pieces on our right flank, and at the same time charged both on our front and rear. We soon silenced their guns, and repelled the charge, when they fled, and permitted us the next morning to march into town without any further opposition.

We have rescued the country from the hands of the insurgents, but I fear that the absence of Col. Fremont's battalion of mounted riflemen will enable most of the Mexican officers, who have broken their parole, to escape to Sonora.

I am happy to say that our loss in killed and wounded does not exceed twenty, whilst we are informed that the enemy has lost between seventy and eighty.

This despatch must go immediately, and I will wait another

opportunity to furnish you with the details of these two battles, and the gallant conduct of the officers and men under my command, with their names.

Faithfully, your obedient servant,

R. F. STOCKTON, *Commodore, &c.*

To the Hon. GEORGE BANCROFT,

Secretary of the Navy, Washington, D. C.

P. S. Enclosed I have the honour to send to you a translation of the letter handed to me by the commissioners mentioned in another part of this despatch, sent by Jose Ma. Flores, to negotiate peace honourable to both nations. The verbal answer, stated in another page of this letter, was sent to this renowned general and commander-in-chief. He had violated his honour, and I would not treat with him nor write to him.

Gen. Flores' letter is here given:

[Translation.]

Civil and Military government of the department of California.

The undersigned, governor and commandant-general of the department and commander-in-chief of the national troops, has the honour to address himself to the commander-in-chief of the naval and land forces of the United States of North America, to say that he has been informed by persons worthy of credit, that it is probable at this time the differences which have altered the relations of friendship between the Mexican republic and that of the United States of North America have ceased, and that you looked for the news of the arrangement between the two governments by the schooner Shark, expected every moment on this coast.

A number of days have elapsed since the undersigned was invited by several foreign gentlemen settled in the country, to enter into a communication with you, they acting as mediators, to obtain an honourable adjustment for both forces, in consequence of the evils which all feel are caused by the unjust war you wage; but the duty of the undersigned prohibited him from doing so, and if to-day he steps beyond the limits marked out by it, it is with the confidence inspired by the hope there exists a definitive arrangement

between the two nations; for the undersigned being animated with
the strongest wishes for the return of peace, it would be most painful to him not to have taken the means to avoid the useless effu-
sion of human blood and its terrible consequences, during moments
when the general peace might have been secured.

The undersigned flatters himself with this hope, and for that
reason has thought it opportune to direct to you this note, which
will be placed in your hands by Messrs. Julian Workman and
Charles Fluge, who have voluntarily offered themselves to act as
mediators. But if, unfortunately, the mentioned news should prove
untrue, and you should not be disposed to grant a truce, to the
evils under which this unfortunate country suffers, of which you
alone are the cause, may the terrible consequences of your want
of consideration fall on your head. The citizens, all of whom
compose the national forces of this department, are decided firmly
to bury themselves under the ruins of their country, combating to
the last moment before consenting to the tyranny and ominous
discretionary power of the agents of the government of the United
States of North America.

This is no problem; different deeds of arms prove that they
know how to defend their rights on the field of battle.

The undersigned still confides you will give a satisfactory solu-
tion to this affair, and in the mean time has the honour of offering
to you the assurance of his consideration and private esteem.

God and Liberty !   JOSE MA. FLORES.
    HEAD-QUARTERS AT THE ANGELES, *Jan.* 1, 1847.

General Order.

HEAD-QUARTERS, CUIDAD DE LOS ANGELES,
                                Jan. 11, 1847.

The commander-in-chief congratulates the officers and men of
the southern division of the United States forces in California on
the brilliant victories obtained by them over the enemy on the 8th
and 9th inst., and on once more taking possession of the "Cuidad
de los Angeles."

He takes the earliest moment to commend their gallantry and

good conduct both in the battle fought on the 8th, on the banks of the "Rio San Gabriel," and on the 9th inst. on the plains of the "Mesa."

The steady courage of the troops in forcing their passage across the "Rio San Gabriel," where officers and men were alike employed in dragging the guns through the water against the galling fire of the enemy, without exchanging a shot, and their gallant charge up the banks against the enemy's cavalry, has perhaps never been surpassed ; and the cool determination with which, in the battle of the 9th, they repulsed the charge of cavalry made by the enemy at the same time on their front and rear, has extorted the admiration of the enemy, and deserves the best thanks of their countrymen. R. F. STOCKTON,

Governor and commander-in-chief of the territory of California.

On the 14th, Col. Fremont had arrived, and Com. Stockton wrote as follows :

HEAD-QUARTERS, CUIDAD DE LOS ANGELES, *Jan.* 15, 1847

SIR : Referring to my letter of the 11th, I have the honour to inform you of the arrival of Lieutenant-colonel Fremont at this place, with 400 men—that some of the insurgents have made their escape to Sonora, and that the rest have surrendered to our arms.

Immediately after the battles of the 8th and 9th, they began to disperse ; and I am sorry to say that their leader, José Ma. Flores, made his escape, and that the others have been pardoned by a capitulation agreed upon by Lieutenant-colonel Fremont.

José Ma. Flores, the commander of the insurgent forces, two or three days previous to the 8th, sent two commissioners with a flag of truce to my camp, to make "a treaty of peace." I informed the commissioners that I could not recognise José Ma. Flores, who had broken his parole, as an honourable man, or as one having any rightful authority, or worthy to be treated with—that he was a rebel in arms, and if I caught him I would have him shot. It seems that not being able to negotiate with me, and having lost the battles of the 8th and 9th, they met Col. Fremont on the 12th

M

instant, on his way here, who, not knowing what had occurred, he entered into the capitulation with them, which I now send to you; and, although I refused to do it myself, still I have thought it best to approve it.

The territory of California is again tranquil, and the civil government formed by me is again in operation in the places where it was interrupted by the insurgents.

Col. Fremont has 500 men in his battalion, which will be quite sufficient to preserve the peace of the territory; and I will immediately withdraw my sailors and marines, and sail as soon as possible for the coast of Mexico, where I hope they will give a good account of themselves,

Faithfully, your obedient servant,   R. F. STOCKTON,
Commodore, &c.

To the Hon. GEORGE BANCROFT,
  Secretary of the Navy, Washington, D. C.

A more detailed narrative of Col. Fremont's action in the matter of the capitulation given below, will be found in the chapter which separately relates his gallant enterprises.

To all to whom these presents shall come, greeting :

Know ye that, in consequence of propositions of peace or cessation of hostilities being submitted to me as commandant of the California battalion of United States forces, which has so far been acceded to by me, as to cause me to appoint a board of commissioners to consult with a similar board appointed by the Californians ; and it requiring a little time to close the negotiations, it is agreed upon and ordered by me, that an entire cessation of hostilities shall take place until to-morrow afternoon, (January 13th,) and that the said Californians be permitted to bring in their wounded to the mission of San Fernandez, where also, if they choose, they can remove their camp, to facilitate said negotiations.

Given under my hand and seal, this 12th day of January, 1847.

J. C. FREMONT,
  Lieut. Col. U. S. A., and Military Commandant, California.

The Capitulation.

Articles of capitulation made and entered into at the Ranch of Cowanga, this thirteenth day of January, anno Domini eighteen hundred and forty-seven, between P. B. Reading, major, Louis McLane, jr., commanding artillery, Wm. H. Russell, ordinance officer, commissioners appointed by J. C. Fremont, lieutenant-colonel United States army, and military commandant of the Territory of California, and Jose Antonio Carrillo, commandant Esquadron, Agustine Olvera, deputado, commissioners appointed by Don Andres Pico, commander-in-chief of the Californian forces under the Mexican flag:

Art. 1. The commissioners on the part of the Californians agree that their entire force shall, on presentation of themselves to Lieut. Col. Fremont, deliver up their artillery and public arms, and that they shall return peaceably to their homes, conforming to the laws and regulations of the United States, and not again take up arms during the war between the United States and Mexico, but will assist and aid in placing the country in a state of peace and tranquillity.

Art. 2. The commissioners on the part of Lieut. Col. Fremont agree and bind themselves on the fulfilment of the 1st article by the Californians, that they shall be guarantied protection of life and property whether on parol or otherwise.

Art. 3. That until a treaty of peace be made and signed between the United States of North America and the republic of Mexico, no Californian or other Mexican citizen shall be bound to take the oath of allegiance.

Art. 4. That any Californian or other citizen of Mexico desiring, is permitted by this capitulation to leave the country without let or hindrance.

Art. 5. That in virtue of the aforesaid articles, equal rights and privileges are vouchsafed to every citizen of California as are enjoyed by the citizens of the United States of North America.

Art. 6. All officers, citizens, foreigners, or others, shall receive the protection guarantied by the 2d article.

Art. 7. This capitulation is intended to be no bar in effecting such arrangements as may in future be in justice required by both parties.

P. B. READING,
Major California Battalion.
WM. H. RUSSELL,
Ord. officer of California Bat.
LOUIS McLANE, Jr.
Commd'g Art., Cailfornia Bat.
JOSE ANTO. CARRILLO,
Commandante de Escuadron.
AGUSTINE OLVERA,
Deputado.

Approved :   J. C. FREMONT,
Lt. Col. U. S. A., and Mil. Com. of California.
Aprobado :   ANDRES PICO,
Com. de Escuadron en géfe de las fuerzas nacionales en Californias.

Additional Article.

That the paroles of all officers, citizens, and others of the United States, and of naturalized citizens of Mexico, are by this foregoing capitulation cancelled, and every condition of said paroles from and after this date are of no farther force and effect, and all prisoners of both parties are hereby released.

Cuidad de los Angeles, *Jan.* 16, 1847.

P. B. READING,
Major California Battalion.
LOUIS McLANE, Jr.
Commd'g Art. California Bat.
WM. H. RUSSELL,
Ord. officer of California Bat.
JOSE ANTO. CARRILLO,
Commandante de Escuadron.
AGUSTINE OLVERA,
Deputado.

H

Approved: J. C. FREMONT,
       Lt. Col. U. S. A., and Mil. Com. of California.
Aprobado: ANDRES PICO.
       Com. de Escuadron en géfe de las fuerzas nacionales
       en Californias.

It was here, at the meeting of Com. Stockton and Gen. Kearny, and of Fremont, that misunderstandings as to prerogatives arose.

Gen. Flores fled to Sonora, with some of his officers, and violent measures were not used towards the rest.

On the 23d of January, 1847, the Independence, Com. W. B. Shubrick, arrived at Monterey, when,* in virtue of his rank, he took command of all the naval forces, and on the 1st of February issued the following " general order :"

" The commander-in-chief has great satisfaction in announcing to the inhabitants of Monterey, that from information received from various sources, he has reason to believe that the disorders which have recently disturbed the territory of California are at an end, and that peace and security are restored to this district certainly, and he hopes to the whole territory.

" The improved state of affairs in the district, and the arrival of a company of United States artillery under Capt. Tompkins, has enabled the commander-in-chief to dispense with the services of the company of mounted volunteers, under Lieut. Maddox of the marine corps. The patriotic settlers who composed this company, nobly stepped forward in time of danger, and stood between the flag of the United States, and the defenceless women and children of Monterey on the one hand, and the bands of lawless disturbers of the peace on the other.

" For such disinterested conduct, the company of mounted volunteers, under Lieut. Maddox, of the marine corps, (acting as captain,) is tendered the thanks of the commander-in-chief, and will, without doubt, receive commendation and due recompense from the general government.

---

* Appendix, No. 12.

M 2

"Given on board the United States ship Independence, Harbour of Monterey,

"**W. BRANDFORD SHUBRICK,**
Commander-in-chief."

February 1, 1847.

The Lexington, loaded with twenty-four-pounders, mortars, &c., had arrived, and three other transports, with Col. Stevenson's regiment, were shortly expected, at the time of this order.

On the 8th of February, the United States sloop of war, Cyane, arrived in port, and fired the appropriate salute for Com. Shubrick, and, Gen. Kearny being on board, the Cyane received a salute from the Independence.

On the 11th, the following was issued :

General Order.

To all whom it may concern :—The undersigned, commander-in-chief of the naval forces of the United States in the Pacific ocean, in virtue of the authority vested in him by the President of the United States, and taking into consideration the injury caused to the agricultural pursuits of the inhabitants of California, by the late unsettled state of the country, the great demand at present for all articles of provisions, and the probable increase of that demand, directs that for the space of six months from the first of March next, viz. : from the 1st of said month of March, to the 1st of the month of September next, the following articles of provisions shall be admitted into the ports of California, free of all charge of duty, viz. : beef, pork, bread, flour, butter, cheese, sugar and rice.

Done, &c., 11th of February, 1847.

W. BRANDFORD SHUBRICK,
Commander-in-chief.

About the 1st of March, 1847, Com. Biddle arrived in the United States frigate Columbus, from the China seas, and became, in virtue of his rank, commander-in-chief.

The squadron had, as before, been actively engaged in enforcing rigid blockades. The Portsmouth had been employed in taking possession of the towns in Lower California, on the Gulf, but at no place was there the means of making resistance to our flag.

On the arrival of Com. Biddle, it became known that Com. Shubrick would retain command of the northern Pacific squadron, and Com. Biddle to come home in July, and that Gen. Kearny would become the governor of California.

The assignment of their respective duties will be seen by the following joint announcement :—

General Order.

To all whom it may concern, be it known—That the President of the United States, desirous to give and secure to the people of California a share of the good government and happy civil organization enjoyed by the people of the United States, and to protect them at the same time from the attacks of foreign foes, and from internal commotions, has invested the undersigned with separate and distinct powers, civil and military ; a cordial co-operation in the exercise of which, it is hoped and believed, will have the happy results desired.

To the commander-in-chief of the naval forces, the President has assigned the regulation of the import trade, with conditions on which vessels of all nations (our own as well as foreign) may be admitted into the ports of the territory, and the establishment of all port regulations.

To the commanding military officer, the President has assigned the direction of the operations on land, and has invested him with administrative functions of government over the people and territory occupied by the forces of the United States.

Done at Monterey, capital of California, this 1st day of March, A. D. 1847.

W. BRANDFORD SHUBRICK,
Commander-in-chief of the Naval Forces.
S. W. KEARNY,
Brig. Gen. U. S. A. and Governor of California.

Monterey was fixed upon by Gen. Kearny and Com. Shubrick as the temporary seat of government.

On the 19th of Dec. 1846, John Y. Mason, then Secretary of the Navy, wrote as follows :—

" In my despatch of November 5th last, Com. Stockton was required to relinquish the conduct of operations on land, and the control of such measures of civil government as the military occupation of the country conquered might devolve on the conqueror, until a definitive treaty of peace should settle the right of possession to the officer in command of the land forces of the United States, who, in company with the bearer of my despatch, proceeded to the west coast to assume the command.

" There has been no approval or recognition of any organized or established form of civil government for the Californias, or any other Mexican territory in the occupation of the naval forces, through this department. The instructions have been confined to the acknowledged rights, under the laws of nations, resulting from conquest and occupation ; and the corresponding duties which the conqueror owed temporarily to the inhabitants have been performed in a spirit of kindness and conciliation, and in the only particulars embraced by the instructions from this department, of liberality to the commercial interests of citizens of the United States and of neutrals."

Col. Richard B. Mason, of the First regiment of Dragoons, was the officer alluded to. It will be seen in another chapter, that he left the seat of government on the 7th of November, 1846, for Upper California, by way of Chagres and Panama. On the 1st of June, 1847, he was acting as " governor and commander-in-chief of the land forces in California, at Monterey ;" Gen. Kearny having left that place on the 31st preceding, for the United States, reached Washington city, after a short visit to his family at St. Louis, on the 10th of September, 1847.

Col. Fremont accompanied Gen. Kearny as far as Fort Leavenworth. Com. Stockton was to leave California for the United States, about the 17th of July, and Com. Ap. C. Jones relieves Com. Shubrick.

Our flag again, by the united efforts of our soldiers and of our sailors, now covers the " farthest west," from 32 to 49 degrees of

north latitude ; and if there has been any differences among commanders as to rank and command, it is idle (and certainly no part
of the plan of this compilation) to discuss the glory of this or that
branch of the service—or of this or that commanding officer. To
use the language of the official organ of the government—"They
have all been distinguished—our troops and our sailors have all
proved themselves, in whatever position they were placed, worthy
of upholding the eagles of the republic."

CHAPTER VIII.

Unexpected and gallant movement—J. Charles Fremont—Scientific explora-
tion—Gen. Castro threatens—American flag hoisted—United States Consul,
T. O. Larkin, Esq.—Correspondence—Fremont's note—Withdraws—The
country raised—Attacked by Tlamath Indians—Determination—Capture of
Castro's horses—Sonoma surprised and taken—Prisoners—Fights de la Torre
—Men cut to pieces alive—Mexicans shot—Declaration of Independence and
War—Com. Sloat—Pursues Castro—Ordered to Monterey—Com. Stockton
in command—Major of California Mounted Riflemen—Embarks for San
Diego—Joins Com. Stockton's forces—Occupation of " City of the Angels"—
Again pursues Castro—Capt. Gillespie—Com. Stockton appoints Fremont
Governor—Lieut. Talbot—Com. Stockton officially announces the capture
of California—Californians revolt—Los Angeles and Santa Barbara evacu-
ated—Fremont—March on Los Angeles—Captures and pardons Don J. Pico
—Capitulation—Previous Battles of Gen. Kearny and Com. Stockton—Com.
Stockton's Despatches—Meeting of Fremont, Stockton and Kearny—Separate—Fremont Governor and Commander-in-chief—His Circular—Kit Carson—Interviews with Com. Shubrick, and Gen. Kearny—Adheres to his position—Fremont returns to the United States.

CONTEMPORANEOUS with the military combinations already detailed, a movement, as remarkable and unexpected as prompt and
gallant, mingled with the concentration of forces directed against
California, and, in some measure, anticipated their results.

There was a young and talented officer of United States Topographical Engineers who had served as principal assistant, before
entering the army, to the celebrated Nicollet, (pre-eminent as an
astronomer, mathematician and man of science, and whom rivalry
with the illustrious Arago had driven from France to become a
citizen of the United States,) in his explorations, by order of the
government, of the wild west and Rocky Mountains—who had
been commissioned, in 1838, a lieutenant while in the wilderness,
thus occupied, and suffering the utmost hardships and privations,
and who, when this country and the scientific world sustained a
heavy loss by the death of Nicollet in 1843, had been deemed
worthy to continue these important explorations.

Young, ambitious, and, though not robust in appearance, yet of vigorous health, John Charles Fremont had, in command of two scientific expeditions—to the Rocky Mountains in 1842, and to Oregon and North California in 1843-4—accomplished a reputation seldom acquired at his years. As an evidence of the estimate which the government had placed upon his services and labours, the commission of brevet-captain was conferred on him by the President, by and with the advice and consent of the Senate, thus advancing him two grades at the same time—an unusual and rare, but deserved compliment.

Capt. Fremont (on the organization of the Mounted Rifle Regiment, 27th May, 1846, made lieutenant-colonel thereof) once more left the seat of government to pursue his explorations in the regions beyond the Rocky Mountains. The orders of the War Department, and the objects of this service were, as before, of a scientific character, without any view whatever to military occupation. No officer or soldier of the United States army accompanied him; and his whole force consisted of 62 men, engaged by himself as security against Indians, and to procure subsistence in the wilderness through which he was to pass. One of the objects in view was to discover a new and shorter route from the western base of the Rocky Mountains to the mouth of the Columbia river. This search would carry him, for a part of the distance, through the unsettled, and afterwards through a corner of the settled part of California. With a full knowledge of the political as well as the personal difficulties of the enterprise, Capt. Fremont's private views and feelings were in unison with his ostensible mission—the dominant passion of his soul being the pursuit of science, he looked with dread and aversion upon any possible collision with either Indians, Mexicans, or British.

At the time of his departure from the United States, he knew well our difficulties with Mexico and Great Britain, and that jealousy would attach to his movements in going through the territories of the one, and the settlements of the other; he was perfectly determined, therefore, to use the utmost circumspection in all his conduct, confining himself wholly to his scientific pursuits, and carefully avoiding as well the appearance as the reality of either a political or military mission.

He approached these settlements in the winter of 1845–6, and, that he might give no cause of offence to the authorities of California, with commendable and pre-determined prudence, he left his men upon the frontier, a hundred miles from Monterey, and went alone to that city to explain, to the Commandant-general of Upper California, Don José Castro, his objects and wishes in person. This he did in the most formal and respectful manner, in company with the United States Consul, T. O. Larkin, Esq., and received from Gov. Castro leave to winter in the valley of the San Joaquin, where there was game for his men, and grass for his horses ; yet scarcely had he reached the spot desired for refreshment and repose, before he received information from the American settlements, and by expresses from the United States Consul at Monterey, that Gen. Castro was preparing to attack him with a comparatively large force of artillery, cavalry and infantry, upon the pretext that, under cover of a scientific mission, he was exciting the American settlers to revolt. In view of this danger, and to be in a condition to repel an assault, he took a position on a mountain overlooking Monterey, at a distance of about thirty miles, intrenched it, raised the flag of the United States, and with his own men, sixty-two in number, awaited the approach of the commandant-general.

Of the events of these days, no official despatches from Capt. Fremont have been published, yet they are well supplied by the official communications from the American consul at Monterey, to our Secretary of State, and by Capt. Fremont's brief note to the consul, while expecting the attack of Gov. Castro.

Of these our limits will preclude our giving but a portion. On the 9th of March, 1846, T. O. Larkin, United States consul at Monterey, writes the Secretary of State : " In the month of February, Capt. Fremont, in my company, visited the general, prefecto, and alcalde of this place, and informed them of his business ; and there was no objection made. Within twenty days, the general says he has received direct and specific orders from Mexico not to allow Capt. Fremont to enter California; which, *perhaps,* accounts for the change of feelings with the people."

While the latest and most graphic are the following:

CONSULATE OF THE UNITED STATES OF AMERICA,
Monterey, March 27, 1846.

SIR:—Capt. J. C. Fremont, of the United States army, arrived at this United States consular-house in Monterey, on the 27th of January, 1846. Being very anxious to join his party of fifty men at the second place of rendezvous, without the settlement, they having missed the first place by mistake, he remained but two days, in which time, with myself, he visited the commandant-general, prefecto, alcalde, and Col. Alvarado, informing them that he was surveying the nearest route from the United States to the Pacific ocean. This information, and that his men were not United States soldiers, was also, by myself, officially given to the prefecto. Having obtained funds and supplies from myself, he returned to his camp; it being well known in Monterey, that he was to return when he collected his men. Some fifteen or twenty days after this, Capt. Fremont, with his party, encamped at a vacant rancho belonging to Capt. Fisher, (about ninety miles from here,) to recruit his men and animals. From there, he proceeded towards Santa Cruz, making short journeys. On the 3d of March, he encamped on the rancho of Mr. E. P. Hartwell, where he received letters from the general and prefecto, ordering him out of the country, and to obey the order without any pretext whatever, or immediate measures would be taken to compel him to do so. This, not corresponding with assurances received at Monterey, it was not answered, and he gave orders to hoist the United States flag the next morning as the only protection his men was to look to. From the 7th to the 10th of March, they fortified their camp with a breastwork of logs. Encamped on a high hill, which commanded a view of the surrounding country, they could see (with the use of spy-glasses) the general and his troops, numbering about two hundred men, at their camp, in the mission of St. John's, preparing their cannon. On the 9th instant, I sent duplicate letters—one by an American, who lost his papers, and the other by

N   10

a Californian, to Capt. Fremont, informing him of the movements of the Californians. The California courier returned to the consulate in about nine or ten hours, bringing a letter from Capt. Fremont, having travelled in that time sixty miles. He reported being well treated by Capt. Fremont and his men; and that two thousand of his countrymen would not be sufficient to compel him to leave the country, although his party was so small. At the earnest request of the alcalde, for a translation of Capt. Fremont's letter, it was given, and immediately despatched to the general at St. John's; and one also to the governor of the Puebla of los Angeles. The general informed the alcalde on the night of the 10th instant, that Capt. Fremont had left his encampment, and that he (the general) should pursue and attack him the first opportunity, and chastise him for hoisting a foreign flag in California. In the postscript of the same letter, the general stated that Capt. Fremont had crossed a small river, and was then about three miles distant from them; but the general made no preparation to follow him. On the morning of the 11th, Gen. Castro sent John Gilroy, an Englishman, long resident in this country, to make offers of arrangement to Capt. Fremont. On his arrival at the camp-ground, he found Capt. Fremont had left with his party that morning; the camp fires were still burning. He found in the camp the staff used for the flag, tent poles, (cut on the spot,) some old clothes, and two old and useless pack-saddles, which the Californians have magnified into munitions of war. Gen. Castro informed his party that he had received various messages from the camp of Capt. Fremont, threatening to exterminate the Californians, &c., (but will hardly name his messengers, nor did they put any confidence in it themselves.) From the 11th to the 13th, the natives had returned to their respective homes, to resume their customary occupations. A few people that were ordered to march from San Francisco to join the general at his camp, returned to their homes. On the 12th, a proclamation was put up by the general, in the billiard-room, (not the usual place,) informing the inhabitants that a band of highwaymen, ("*bandoleros*") under Capt. Fremont, of the United States army, had come within the towns of this department; and that he, with two hundred patriots, had driven them out, and sent them into the back country. Some of the officers of the two hundred patriots (and more were expected to join them) arrived in Monterey, and reported that the cowards had run, and that they had driven them to the Sacramento river; some added that they drove them into the bulrushes, on the plains of the Sacramento; and that, in their haste, they had left some of their best horses behind. The horses proved to be those belonging to the Californians themselves, and had strayed into Capt. Fremont's band, (being an every-day occurrence in California;) and, on raising camp, they were turned out and left behind. Instead of the Americans being driven out of the country, they travelled less distance, for three or four days, than the natives did in returning to Monterey—moving from four to six miles per day, in order to recruit. One of the complaints made by the general was, that three men, when drinking, went to the house of Angel Castro (an uncle of the general) to purchase some beef for the camp, and insulted his family. On the 7th, I personally called upon Don Angel, for the truth of the story, and was informed by him (the father himself) that he was frightened by one of the Americans insisting on his daughter drinking with him. On ordering him to leave the house, he resisted, but was put out by his own companions, he drawing a pistol while they were putting him out. Don Angel mounted a horse, and rode off to Capt. Fremont's, about one mile distant, who, on hearing the case, came to the house immediately, and called up the family to inquire into the affair. On the examination, he asked the father what he should do with the men. He requested them to be punished, which was promised; and was told, if he would send a boy, a fine of five dollars should be sent to him, (he being alcalde.) The boy returned with ten dollars from the camp, which settled the business, although there had been nothing of consequence transacted; yet Capt. Fremont was anxious not to let the people of the country have any cause of complaint against him.

The undersigned has the honour to subscribe himself, your most obedient servant,   THOMAS O. LARKIN.

To the Hon. SECRETARY OF STATE, *City of Washington.*

SIR: In giving my first information to the department respecting Capt. Fremont's arrival in California, I did not anticipate such an extensive correspondence as it has now reached. Capt. Fremont was well received in this place, and to the last day we heard of him, by the natives individually, who sold him provisions, and liked his presence. During his encampment, thirty or forty miles from here, despatches were received by the commandant, Gen. José Castro, (a native of Monterey,) from Mexico, ordering him to drive Capt. Fremont out of this department; which order, with one hundred and seventy or two hundred men present, and over one hundred more daily expected, he pretended to execute. Capt. Fremont left his camp a few hours after he received the undersigned's letter of the 9th of March, (not from fright of Gen. Castro,) as he had been preparing the week before to travel. It is supposed he has gone to St. Barbara, where an American was sent by the undersigned, in February, with funds and provisions for his use. From there he proceeds on his journey, according to his instructions from his department in Washington. Although from the correspondence it may appear that in the centre of a strange country, among a whole people, with real or apparent hostile intentions towards him, Capt. Fremont was in much danger, it can be believed that he was only annoyed. Whether he will visit Monterey, after this unexpected affair, or not, is uncertain.

The undersigned has not supposed, during the whole affair, that Gen. Castro wished to go after Capt. Fremont; and was very confident that, with all California, he would not have attacked him, even had he been sure of destroying the whole party, as five times their number could have taken their place before the expected battle. Capt. Fremont received verbal applications from English and Americans to join his party, and could have mustered as many men as the natives. He was careful not to do so. Although he discharged five or six of his men, he took no others in their place. On the return of Gen. Castro, he published a flaming proclamation to the citizens, informing them that a band of bandoleros, (highwaymen or freebooters,) under Capt. Fremont of the United States army, had come into this district ; but with the company of two hundred patriots he had driven them away, and exhorted his companions and countrymen to be always ready to repel others of the same class.   This proclamation was missing from the place where it was put up on the third day.

The undersigned has written to the general for a copy.   To this day there has been no answer received.   Duplicate copies of consular letters to Capt. Fremont, are in the hands of Gen. Castro, he having taken them from one of the consular's couriers, promising to forward them as directed.   These copies he promised to return, but has not done so.   This government is about sending a commissioner to Mexico, (as the undersigned believes,) to report the country in danger of revolution from the Americans.   By this we understand in California, (foreigners,) that some Americans (who left Capt. Fremont) are joining the Indians to attack the farms, and others were about to take possession of a town in the upper part of the bay of San Francisco ; and that Sen. W. Hastings (author of the History of California) is laying off a town at New Helvetia, for the Mormons.   None of this information, (in the opinion of the undersigned can be relied upon,) is to be given to the President to urge upon him the necessity of giving Gen. Castro two hundred men, (he prefers not many men, nor any Mexican general,) with sufficient funds to protect the country.   As a general thing, Hastings's book is very untrue and absurd.   He brought a number to this country, which do his countrymen no good, and perhaps injure them.   No general English reader will read one quarter of the book.   The arrival of Capt. Fremont has revived the excitement in California respecting the emigration, and the fears of the Californians losing their country.   The undersigned believes that if a new flag was respectfully planted, it would receive the good will of much of the wealth and respectability of the country.   Those who live by office, and the absence of law, would faintly struggle against a change.   Many natives and foreigners of wealth and pursuits, are already calculating on the hopes, fears, and expectations

N 2

from the apparent coming change now before them, from the great influx of strangers.

In the mean time, the undersigned has the pleasure of saying that, with every department of office in this country, he is on the best terms of friendship, as far as appearances are before him.

With the highest respect and esteem,

I am your obedient servant,

THOMAS O. LARKIN.

To the Hon. SECRETARY OF STATE, *City of Washington.*

It will be seen, in Gov. Castro's despatch, that Capt. Fremont took a military position, intrenched it, and raised the American flag; but these events were the *consequence* and not the *cause* of Gov. Castro's movement against him; and this is fully shown in the following brief spirited note, written in pencil, in answer to the consul's warning, and after refusing the aid of the American settlers:

Note in pencil from Capt. Fremont to the consul Larkin, from his intrenched camp at the Alisal on the Sierra, thirty miles from Monterey, March 10, 1846.

MY DEAR SIR: I this moment received your letters, and without waiting to read them, acknowledge the receipt which the courier requires immediately. I am making myself as strong as possible, in the intention that if we are unjustly attacked we will fight to extremity and refuse quarter, trusting to our country to avenge our death. No one has reached our camp, and from the heights we are able to see troops (with the glass) mustering at St. John's and preparing cannon. I thank you for your kindness and good wishes, and would write more at length as to my intentions, did I not fear that my letter would be intercepted. We have in no wise done wrong to the people or the authorities of the country, and if we are hemmed in and assaulted here, we will die, every man of us, under the flag of our country.

Very truly, yours,

J. C. FREMONT.

P. S. I am encamped on the top of the Sierra, at the head-

waters of a stream which strikes the road to Monterey, at the house
of Don Joaquin Gomez.   J. C. F.

THOMAS O. LARKIN, Esq.,
        Consul for the United States, Monterey.

" The first letter" (and all the detail the public yet have) "that
we (says Senator Benton) received from Capt. Fremont, after his
withdrawal from the Sierra, and from the valley of the San Juan,
is dated the first day of April, in latitude 40, on the Sacramento
river; and though written merely to inform Mrs. Fremont of his
personal concerns, becomes important in a public point of view on
account of subsequent events in June and July, by showing that
on the first of April he was on his way to Oregon—that he had
abandoned all intention of returning through any part of California
—would cross the Rocky Mountains through the Northern Pass,
on the line between the Upper, or Kettle Falls of the Columbia,
and the Great Falls of the Missouri—and be in the United States
in September. This shows that he had, at that time, no idea of
the events in which he was subsequently involved, and that he had
abandoned the cherished field of his intended scientific researches
for the express purpose of avoiding all offence to the Mexican
authorities. Of the events in the valley of the San Joaquin and
the camp on the Sierra, he speaks a few words, without detail, but
descriptive of his condition, characteristic of his prudence in not
compromising his country, and worthy to be repeated in his own
language. He says: 'The Spaniards were somewhat rude and
inhospitable below, and ordered me out of the country after having
given me permission to winter there. My sense of duty did not
permit me to fight them, but we retired slowly and growlingly
before a force of three or four hundred men, and three pieces of
artillery. Without the shadow of a cause, the governor suddenly
raised the whole country against me, issuing a false and scandalous
proclamation. Of course, I did not dare to compromise the United
States, against which appearances would have been strong; but
though it was in my power to increase my party by Americans, I
refrained from committing a solitary act of hostility or impropriety.'

His next letter is dated the 14th of May, and informs me that, in his progress to Oregon, he found himself and party unexpectedly attacked by the Tlamath Indians—the most warlike of that quarter—had lost five men in killed and wounded—and still expected to be in the United States in the month of September."

All the information in continuance of the narrative, is contained in a letter from Capt. Fremont to Senator Benton, dated "Mission of Carmel, July 25, 1846." (The Mission of Carmel is three miles south of Monterey, Upper California.) The substance is given by Senator Benton, thus :—

"At the middle of May, Capt. Fremont, in pursuance of his design to reach Oregon, and return by the Columbia and Missouri through the Northern Pass in the Rocky Mountains, had arrived at the great Tlamath Lake, in the edge of the Oregon Territory, when he found his further progress completely barred by the double obstacle of hostile Indians, which Castro had excited against him, and the lofty mountains, covered with deep and falling snows, which made the middle of May in that elevated region the same as the middle of winter. These were the difficulties and dangers in front. Behind, and on the north bank of the San Francisco Bay, at the military post of Sonoma, was Gen. Castro assembling troops with the avowed intention of attacking both Fremont's party, and all the American settlers, against whom the Indians had been already excited. Thus, his passage barred in front by impassable snows and mountains—hemmed in by savage Indians, who were thinning the ranks of his little party—menaced by a general at the head of tenfold forces of all arms—the American settlers in California marked out for destruction on a false accusation of meditating a revolt under his instigation—his men and horses suffering from fatigue, cold, and famine—and after the most anxious deliberation upon all the dangers of his position, and upon all the responsibilities of his conduct, Capt. Fremont determined to turn upon his pursuers and fight them instantly, without regard to numbers, and seek safety for his party and the American settlers, by overturning the Mexican government in California. It was on the 6th day of June that he came to this determination ;

and, the resolution being once taken, all half-way measures were discarded, and a rapid execution of the plan was commenced. On the 11th of June, a supply of 200 horses for Castro's troops on the way to his camp, conducted by an officer and fourteen men, were surprised at daylight, and the whole captured—the men and officer being released, and the horses retained for American use. On the 15th, at daybreak, the military post of Sonoma, (the point of rendezvous, and intended head-quarters) was surprised and taken, with nine pieces of brass cannon, 250 stand of muskets, other arms and ammunition, with several superior officers, Gen. Vallejo, (Val-ya-ho,) his brother, Capt. Vallejo, Col. Greuxdon, and others; all of whom were detained and confined as prisoners. Capt. Fremont then repaired to the American settlements on the Rio de los Americanos to obtain assistance; and receiving an express from his little garrison of fourteen, in Sonoma, that Gen. Castro was preparing to cross the Bay of San Francisco, and attack him with a large force, he set out in the afternoon of the 23d of June, with ninety mounted riflemen, and, travelling day and night, arrived at 2 o'clock in the morning of the 25th, at Sonoma—eighty miles' distance. The vanguard of Castro's force had crossed the bay—a squadron of seventy dragoons, commanded by De la Torre—which was attacked and defeated by twenty Americans, with a loss of two killed and some wounded on the part of the Mexicans, and no injury to themselves—De la Torre barely escaping, with the loss of his transport boats, and spiking six pieces of artillery. In the mean time, two of Capt. Fremont's men, going as an express, were captured by De la Torre's men, and, being bound to trees, were cut to pieces, alive, with knives! in return for which, three of De la Torre's men being taken were instantly shot. The north side of the Bay of San Francisco was now cleared of the enemy, and on the 4th day of July, Capt. Fremont called the Americans together at Sonoma, addressed them upon the dangers of their situation, and recommended a declaration of independence, and war upon Castro and his troops, as the only means of safety. The independence was immediately declared, and the war proclaimed. A few days afterwards, an officer from

Com. Sloat brought intelligence that the American flag was hoisted at Monterey—an example which was immediately followed wherever the news flew. The pursuit and defeat of Castro was then the only remaining enterprise. He had fled south, towards the numerous Mexican towns and settlements beyond Monterey, with his four or five hundred men; and Capt. Fremont, leaving some fifty men in garrisons, set out with 160 mounted riflemen in the pursuit, when he received instructions from Com. Sloat to march upon Monterey. He did so, and found Com. Stockton in command, approving the pursuit of Castro, and aiding it by all the means in his power. The sloop of war Cyane was put at his service. Capt. Fremont, with 160 American riflemen and 70 marines, embarked on that vessel, and sailed down the coast, on the 26th of July, to San Diego, 400 miles south of Monterey, and 100 south of Pueblo de los Angeles, where Castro was understood to be, with an increasing force of 500 men. The descent of the coast as far as San Diego was with a view to get ahead of Castro, and to be in a position either to intercept him if he fled south to Mexico, or to Lower California, or to turn back upon him if he remained in Pueblo de los Angeles, or any of the numerous towns in its neighbourhood."

Com. Sloat had assigned the command of the Pacific squadron to Com. R. F. Stockton, about the 19th of July, 1846. On the day that the latter took the command as "Commander-in-chief, and Governor of the Territory of California," he organized the "California Mounted Riflemen," with the men whom Fremont had brought, and received them as Volunteers into the service of the United States, appointing Capt. Fremont major, and Lieut. Gillespie, of the Marine Corps, captain of the battalion.

The orders under which Capt. Fremont embarked for San Diego were as follows :—

UNITED STATES FRIGATE CONGRESS,
Monterey Bay, July 23, 1846.

SIR: You will please to embark on board the United States ship Cyane, with the detachment of troops under your command, on Saturday afternoon.

The ship, at daylight, on Sunday morning, will sail for San Diego, where you will disembark your troops and procure horses for them, and will make every necessary preparation to march through the country at a moment's notice from me.

You will endeavour to encamp so near San Diego as to have a daily communication with the Cyane, which will remain at anchor there until you receive orders to march.

The object of this movement is to take, or get between the Colorado and Gen. Castro.

I will leave Monterey in this ship for San Pedro, so as to arrive there about the time that you may be expected to have arrived at San Diego.

I will despatch a courier to you from San Pedro, to inform you of my movements.

Faithfully, your obedient servant,

R. F. STOCKTON,

Commodore, &c.

Captain FREMONT,
United States Army.

On the 29th he arrived at San Diego, where he was detained by the difficulty of finding horses, the Californians having driven off, and secreted, as far as possible, all their animals.   Thus Capt. Fremont was unable to move until the 8th of August, when he started in pursuit of Castro who had fled from Com. Stockton's forces at the "Camp of the Mesa."   On the 13th both commanders united their forces and entered the City of the Angels, of which they took unmolested possession.

On the 16th, Fremont again set off in pursuit of Castro, who it soon was found had succeeded in making his escape out of the country, his principal officers separating in different parties. These were most of them taken, and brought to the "City of the Angels," whither Fremont returned by the 28th.

Early in September, 1846, Com. Stockton, having determined to keep the California battalion of mounted riflemen in the service of the territory, and constantly on duty to prevent and punish any aggressions of the Indians, or any other persons, upon the property of individuals or the peace of the territory, withdrew all his forces and proceeded with the squadron to San Francisco. Captain Gillespie was left in command of the "City of the Angels" with about thirty riflemen.

Fremont left the city, for the purpose of recruiting his forces as fully instructed by the order already given on page 125.

Fremont had but forty men with him ; of these he left nine with Lieut. Talbot to garrison Santa Barbara, and from thence, on the 16th, continued his way north.

It was at this time that Com. Stockton had announced to the Secretary of the Navy, Mr. Bancroft, that the war was ended,* through his letter of the 28th of August, 1846.

On the 23d of September, the Californians invested the "City of the Angels," and on the 30th Capt. Gillespie was forced by overwhelming numbers to capitulate and to retire to San Pedro, and thence to embark for Monterey.

Manuel Gaspar, the Californian chief, then marched on San Barbara. Here was stationed a young officer, Theodore Talbot, (son of the late Isham Talbot, a very distinguished senator from Kentucky,) and who, though a mere boy, had won the entire confidence and esteem of Fremont, whom he had accompanied in his expeditions for scientific purposes to the Rocky Mountains, Oregon and California—and they had "*some rough ones,*" as Lieut. Talbot truly says, in the interesting letter which well describes the incidents at Santa Barbara, and affords a familiar and authentic insight of others.

Extract from a letter of Lieut. Theodore Talbot, dated

CITY OF THE ANGELS, CALIFORNIA,
January 15, 1847.

"Since last I wrote you I have had an active life. Col. Fremont left the City of the Angels in September under command of Capt. A. H. Gillespie with thirty-odd riflemen, the commodore having

---

* See his letter, Chapter 7.

entirely withdrawn his forces and proceeded with his squadron to San Francisco. We moved to the north, the colonel having with him only some forty men, (his old party,) the rest of the force having in part preceded us, and part been disbanded, with the exception of two small parties stationed south of the City of the Angels. I was left as military commandant of the town and jurisdiction of Santa Barbara, a pretty place lying on the ocean one hundred miles north of the City of the Angels, and the principal town between that place and Monterey. There were only nine men left with me, it being the colonel's intention to recruit at the north, and return immediately. The prefect, the principal civil authority of the southern department, resided there, and I was left for the purpose of supporting him. My position was a very pleasant one; Santa Barbara being the residence of some of the stateliest Dons and prettiest Señoras in all California. I had been here, however, but a few days when I received a *correo*, post-haste from Capt. Gillespie, bringing news of a rebellion in the south—the City of the Angels being surrounded by 500 of the Californians under arms. The courier had barely escaped with his life, and brought me Gillespie's motto seal, concealed in a cigarita, to vouch for the truth of what he told. Having warned me, he hurried on to the north, to give this news to the colonel and commodore. I spent several anxious days—every moment expecting to be attacked in my barracks; hearing only through the women, who, noble and disinterested always in the hour of need, would give me such little information as they could obtain with regard to the motions of the insurgents.

"Here let me remark, that nothing has surprised me so much, in my little intercourse with the Mexicans, as the humanity and charity of the women, as compared with the almost brutal ferocity of the men. You will recollect that Kendall sustains the same opinion with reference to the Santa Fé expedition.

"Although my position was very precarious, I kept a firm upper lip, in order to keep down the people of Santa Barbara, which has some 70 fighting men, and several resident Mexican officers, until aid could be received from the north. I succeeded in this until the

o

City of the Angels was taken, and Gillespie forced to capitulate. Manuel Garpis, the commander, then marched with two hundred men on Santa Barbara. They surrounded the town, and sent in a letter demanding my surrender, and guarantying our lives, &c., &c. They gave us two hours to deliberate. We had all determined not to surrender our arms ; and, finding the place we then occupied untenable, with so small a force, we determined to push for the hills, (our best ground for fighting,) or die in the attempt. I accordingly marshalled my little force and marched out of the town without opposition—those who lay on the road retreating to the main force which was on the lower side of the town. The few foreigners living in the town dared not assist me ; and the Californians, all of course, took arms against us. Having so unexpectedly been allowed to pass their force, I camped in the hills overlooking the town, and determined to remain there a few days, and co-operate with any force which might be landed at Santa Barbara. I remained here eight days, when the Californians having discovered my whereabouts, finally determined to rout me out. Not knowing my exact position, they had divided into two or three parties; and one of them, consisting of. some forty men, happened to strike upon the very spot where I was. I was aware of their coming, and had given my men orders not to fire until they were in among us. But my men were so eager to get a shot, that two of them who were posted in the arroy, or ravine, nearest the enemy, forgetting my instructions, fired just as they came marching in on us. They had fired too far for their own shots even to be effective, killing only the horse of one, and wounding the horse and grazing the hip of another of the enemy. But the Californians fled, nor would they again come within reach of our rifles, pouring a fire from their long carbines from the neighbouring hills. They sent a foreigner to me, offering to allow me to retain my arms and freedom, giving my parole of honour not to interfere farther in the war about to be waged.

"I sent the man back with word that I preferred to fight. Finding I would not give up, they put fire in all round me, and succeeded in burning me out. I eluded them, however, and after

lingering another day, in hopes that a force would arrive, I determined to push for Monterey.   I came down on a rancho, called
San Marco, where we got something to eat, for we had been
starving for several days.   We were also so fortunate as to find
an old soldier of Gen. Micheltorena, who was naturally inimical
to the Californians.   He piloted us across the coast mountain,
which is here ninety miles wide, and very rugged, into the head
of the Tulare valley to the Lake of Buena Vista.   Here I was
familiar with the country, and after a month's travel, coming some
500 miles, mostly afoot, enduring much hardship and suffering,
we at length effected a junction with Col. Fremont at Monterey.

"They were all very glad to see us, for they certainly thought
we were all killed.   In fact, the Californians had circulated that
report.   You must excuse me for dwelling on my little adventure;
for the fact is, I suffered more from downright starvation, cold,
nakedness, and every sort of privation, than in any trip I have yet
had to make, and I have had some rough ones.   Col. Fremont
had started from San Francisco in the ship Sterling; but after
being out twenty days, and much bad weather, he was compelled
to put into Monterey.   I found him recruiting more men from the
new emigrants, and preparing to go by land to the south.   A day
or two after I arrived, a part of two companies, under command
of Capts. Burrows and Thompson, were attacked by the Californians, 80 in number, the Americans having 57; they fought—4
Americans were killed, and 3 Californians.   Capt. Burrows was
among the killed.   We marched to their assistance, to the mission
of St. John's, from which place they were afraid to move, as they
had a cavallada of 400 head of horses.   We left St. John's for the
south the 26th of November, and arrived at San Fernando on the
11th of January.

"This place is twenty-five miles from the City of the Angels,
which we heard the commodore and Gen. Kearny, with 700 men,
were in possession of.   The commander of the Californians, Don
Andres Pico, finding it impolitic to wage the war further, sent a
deputation of his officers offering to surrender to Col. Fremont.
Their surrender was accepted, and we marched into the city the

14th of January. The volunteer force was soon disbanded, and I will have a chance of returning home, I hope."

Col. Fremont had, without money or men, and, in a country where the first was not to be seen, and the latter, few and widely scattered, set about raising in the north a force sufficient for the occasion, from the emigrants and strangers. With untiring energy, and in a very short time, he had succeeded in organizing about 450 men, well mounted, and supplied with every equipment of war, including four pieces of artillery. The troops constituting Col. Fremont's command, gathered up hastily as they were, and from the midst of a population so few and scattered, were perhaps, taken as a whole, the most strange and discordant that ever marched under any one banner. They were representatives from almost every nation on earth, including many tribes of North American Indians, and speaking all manner of tongues. Yet this motley crew had been disciplined into a very efficient corps.

Col. Fremont then embarked in the ship Sterling from San Francisco for the south, the more immediate scene of action ; but after having been out at sea for twenty days, he was forced by bad weather to disembark at Monterey. Here it was that Col. Fremont made his successful excursion to the Mission of St. John's, of which Lieut. Talbot speaks.

(It is to be remembered that, on the 27th of May, 1846, Capt. Fremont had been appointed, in his absence, by the President of the United States, the lieutenant-colonel of the new regiment of "Mounted Riflemen." Of this, distance had precluded hitherto any knowledge in California.—Henceforth, Fremont will be spoken of under his proper title as an officer of the United States army.)

From the Mission of St. John's, Col. Fremont commenced, about the 26th of November, his march on the "City of the Angels." On this march of nearly 400 miles, the Californians hovered around its flanks, watching for some false move or decline of vigilance. Our limits preclude details to any great extent. On the 14th of December, Don Jesu Pico, with several others, was taken prisoners, at Wilson's Rancho, and the next day he was tried by a court-martial, and condemned to be shot the day

after, at 12 o'clock. The incident of Pico's pardon is too well
told to seek other language than Lieut. Talbot's, who thus describes
the scene :—

"There was no time to lose ; the hour of twelve next day was
fixed for the execution. It was 11 o'clock, and I chanced to be
in the colonel's room, when a lady with a group of children, followed by many other ladies, burst into the room, throwing themselves upon their knees, and crying for mercy for the father and
husband. It was the wife and children and friends of Pico.
Never did I hear such accents of grief. Never did I witness
such an agonizing scene. I turned away my eyes, for I could not
look at it, and soon heard from Col. Fremont (whose heart was
never formed to resist such a scene) the heavenly words of pardon. Then the tumult of feeling took a different turn. Joy and
gratitude broke out, filled the room with benedictions, and spread
to those without. To finish the scene, the condemned man was
brought in, and then I saw the whole impulsiveness and fire of
the Spanish character, when excited by some powerful emotion.
He had been calm, composed, quiet, and almost silent, under his
trial and condemnation ; but at the word pardon, a storm of impe-
tuous feeling burst forth, and, throwing himself at the feet of
Col. Fremont, he swore to him an eternal fidelity ; and demanded
the privilege of going with him and dying for him.

"But it was not yet all over with Col. Fremont. His own men
required the death of Pico—he had done us much harm, and, in
fact, was the head of the insurrection in that district, and had
broken his parole. The colonel went among them and calmed
the ferment in his own camp. He quieted his own men ; but
others, who were not there, have since cried out for the execution
of Pico, and made his pardon an accusation against Col. Fremont.
The pacified state of the country will answer the accusation, and
show that it was a case in which policy and humanity went together."

On the 27th, Col. Fremont arrived at Santa Barbara, where he
caused the American flag to be hoisted, with much ceremony, by
Lieut. Talbot and the nine men who had before refused to sur-

o 2   11

render at that place, the principal authorities of the town being required to be present.

This march, in mid-winter, was one of very great hardship. Both men and horses suffered exceedingly. On Christmas day, the battalion lost, in crossing the Santa Barbara mountains, from a hundred and fifty to two hundred horses. The artillery was brought over by hand, engaging at one time over 100 men at the ropes.

From Santa Barbara, Col. Fremont again pressed on towards the "City of the Angels," when, on the 12th of January, 1847, at the Ranch of Couenga, near the point of their destination, the California forces, under Don Andres Pico, were met, in advance of the position where Col. Fremont had expected to have encountered them in deadly strife.

Such, however, was not the result. The Californians sent forward a flag of truce—propositions of peace or of cessation of hostilities were submitted to the commandant of the California battalion of United States forces, which Col. Fremont so far acceded to as to appoint a board of commissioners to consult with a similar board appointed by the Californians, and to agree to an entire cessation of hostilities until the next afternoon, by which time the negotiations were to close. The American commissioners were P. B. Reading, major of the California battalion, Wm. H. Russel, ordnance officer, and Louis McLane, Jr., commanding artillery, of the California battalion. The Californian commissioners were José Anto. Carrillo, commandant de Escuadron, and Augustine Olvera, deputado—who, on the 13th, agreed on the terms of capitulation, whereby the Californian forces delivered up their artillery and public arms, and disbanded themselves, which was approved of on the same day, by Col. Fremont, as "Military Commandant of California," and by Andres Pico, who signed as "Commandante de Escuadron en géf de las fuerzas nacionales en California."

These terms did not treat the Californians as rebels or citizens of the United States, and did not exact oaths of allegiance, but postponed it for a definitive treaty of peace, requiring nothing but present obedience to the American authorities, and forgetfulness of the past.

It will be seen in another chapter devoted to the operations of the Pacific squadron, and their co-operation in the conquest of California, that the official details there given of the capitulation, &c., accompanied the official despatches of Com. Stockton, to whom, as his presumed superior in authority, they were given by Col. Fremont, after his arrival at the "City of the Angels." On his arrival, (the 13th,) he found Gen. Kearny and Com. Stockton, and reported, that day, his battalion to Gen. Kearny.

It will be seen that Com. Stockton, in his despatch of the next day to Mr. Bancroft, Secretary of the Navy, speaks thus of these occurrences:—"I have the honour to inform you of the arrival of Lieutenant-colonel Fremont at this place, with four hundred men— that some of the insurgents have made their escape to Sonora, and that the rest have surrendered to our arms."

"Immediately after the battles of the 8th and 9th, they began to disperse; and I am sorry to say, that their leader, José Ma. Flores, made his escape, and that the others have been pardoned by a capitulation agreed upon by Lieut. Col. Fremont.

"José Ma. Flores, the commander of the insurgent forces, two or three days previous to the 8th, sent two commissioners with a flag of truce to my camp, to make '*a treaty of peace.*' I informed the commissioners that I could not recognise José Ma. Flores, who had broken his parole, as an honourable man, or as one having any rightful authority, or worthy to be treated with—that he was a rebel in arms, and if I caught him, I would have him shot. It seems, that not being able to negotiate with me, and having lost the battles of the 8th and 9th, they met Col. Fremont on the 12th instant, on his way here, who, not knowing what had occurred, entered into the capitulation with them, which I now send to you; and, although I refused to do it myself, still I have thought it best to approve it. The territory of California is again tranquil, and the civil government formed by me is again in operation in the places where it was interrupted by the insurgents.

"Col. Fremont has five hundred men in his battalion, which will be quite sufficient to preserve the peace of the territory; and I will immediately withdraw my sailors and marines, and sail as soon as possible for the coast of Mexico, where I hope they will give a good account of themselves."

It was here, at this meeting of Col. Fremont with Com. Stockton and Gen. Kearny, that a misunderstanding arose as to their relative prerogatives.

In a few days after, Gen. Kearny withdrew to San Diego. Com. Stockton also departed "immediately," as he had declared his intention, leaving Col. Fremont to occupy, with his battalion, the "City of the Angels," whence he issued, on the 22d, the following circular:

"The peace of the country being restored, and future tranquillity vouchsafed by a treaty made and entered into by commissioners respectively appointed by the properly authorized California officers on the one hand, and by myself as military commandant of the United States forces in the district of California on the other, by which a civil government is to take place of the military, an exchange of all prisoners, &c., &c., forthwith ensure to the end that order, and a wholesome civil police should obtain throughout the land—a copy of which said treaty will be immediately published in the Californian newspaper, published at Monterey.

"Therefore, in virtue of the aforesaid treaty, as well as the functions that in me rest as civil governor of California, I do hereby proclaim order and peace restored to the country, and require the immediate release of all prisoners, the return of the civil officers to their appropriate duties, and as strict an obedience of the military to the civil authority, as is consistent with the security of peace, and the maintenance of good order when troops are garrisoned.

"Done at the capital of the Territory of California, temporarily seated at the Cuidad de los Angeles, this 22d day of January, 1847.   "J. C. FREMONT,

"Governor and Commander-in-chief of California.

"Witness: W. H. RUSSELL, Secretary of State."

Col. Fremont discharged a portion of his battalion, and sent the residue to San Gabriel, a Catholic mission, seven miles distant from Cuidad de los Angeles, (or the "City of the Angels,") residing thus without military protection in a city of about 7000 Califor nians, until the latter part of March, when he learned that which we have already related in another chapter—the arrival of Com. Shubrick at Monterey, and of the joint circular of the commodore, as "Commander-in-chief of the naval forces," and of Brig. Gen. Kearny, as "Governor of California."

About the 25th of February, Col. Fremont sent despatches to the United States government, through passed Midshipman Beale, Lieut. Talbot, and a personage who has often figured in these sketches, and whose memoir, from very competent hands, is here inserted—not alone in justice to him, but that it fills up details, perhaps, wanting in this narrative,—KIT CARSON.

"Under this name, within a few years, has become quite familiar to the public, mainly through his connection with the expeditions of Fremont, one of the best of those noble and original characters that have from time to time sprung up on and beyond our frontier, retreating with it to the west, and drawing from association with uncultivated nature, not the rudeness and sensualism of the savage, but genuine simplicity and truthfulness of disposition, and generosity, bravery, and single-heartedness to a degree rarely found in society. Although Kit has only become known to the reading people of 'the States' and of Europe through Fremont's reports, he was long ago famous in a world as extended, if not as populous; famous for excelling in all the qualities that life in the trackless and vast west requires and developes. He has been celebrated (though now aged only about thirty-seven years) as a hunter, trapper, guide or pilot of the prairies, and Indian fighter, uniting to the necessary characteristics of that adventurous and sturdy class, a kindness of heart, and gentleness of manner that relieves it of any possible harshness or asperity. He is now in 'the States,' having recently arrived with despatches from California; and I have taken the opportunity to extract from him a few incidents of his eventful life. He is worthy of an honourable and more extended memoir; and were his adventures fully written out,

they would possess an interest equal to any personal narrative
whatever.

" Christopher Carson was born in Kentucky, in the year 1810,
or 1811, his father having been one of the early settlers, and also
a noted hunter and Indian fighter.   In the year following Kit's
birth, the family removed, for the sake of more elbow-room than
the advancing population of Kentucky left them, to the territory
of Missouri.   On this frontier, bred to border life, Kit remained to
the age of fifteen, when he joined a trading party to Santa Fé.
This was his introduction to those vast plains that stretch beyond
the state of Missouri.   Instead of returning home, Kit found his
way, by various adventures, south, through New Mexico, to the
copper-mines of Chihuahua, where he was employed some months
as a teamster.

" When about seventeen years old, he made his first expedition
as a trapper.   This was with a party which had been induced by
favourable accounts of fresh trapping grounds on the Rio Colorado
of California, to an adventure thither; so that Kit's first exploits
were in the same remote and romantic region where, during the
last year, he and all his comrades, with their commander, have
earned imperishable honour.   The enterprise was successful, and
Kit relates many interesting anecdotes of the hardships of the
wilderness, and of the encounters of his party with the Indians.
The Mexican authorities and settlers in California were even at
that time jealous of the Americans, and threatened to seize even
this inoffensive and roving party of beaver-catchers.   They made
good their return, however, to Taos, in New Mexico; whence,
soon after, Kit joined a trapping party to the head-waters of the
Arkansas, (likewise a region embraced, since the last published
Expedition, in the surveys of Col. Fremont.)   Without recrossing
the prairies, Kit went northward to the region of the Rocky Mountains that gives rise to the Missouri and Columbia rivers, and there
remained near eight years, engaged in the then important occupation of trapping.   The great demand for the beaver, and the consequent high prices at that time paid for the peltries, gave an additional stimulus to the adventurous spirit of the young men of the

west, and drew nearly all who preferred the excitements and hazards of life in the wilderness to quieter pursuits, into the recesses of the Rocky Mountains. Here a peculiar class was formed; the elements, the sturdy, enterprising, and uncurbed character of the frontier; the circumstances that influenced and formed it, nature in her wildest, roughest, and grandest aspects—savages, both as associates and foes, of every cast, from the wretched Root-diggers to the vindictive Blackfeet, and the courageous and warlike Crows —and a vocation of constant labour, privation, and peril in every shape, yet of gains of a nature and degree to give it somewhat of the characteristics of gambling. The decrease of the beaver before a pursuit of the poor animal so ruthless as was thus stimulated, and the substitution of other commodities for the beaver fur, have left trapping scarcely worth following as a vocation; and the race of trappers has nearly disappeared from the mountain gorges, where they built their rude lodges, where they set their traps for the wily beaver, and where were their frequent combats with the savages, and with wild beasts not less formidable. In the school of men thus formed by hardship, exposure, peril, and temptation, our hero acquired all their virtues, and escaped their vices. He became noted through the extent of the trapping grounds, and on both sides of the Rocky Mountains, as a successful trapper, an unfailing shot, an unerring guide, and for bravery, sagacity, and steadiness in all circumstances. He was chosen to lead in almost all enterprises of unusual danger, and in all attacks on the Indians. At one time, with a party of twelve, he tracked a band of near sixty Crows, who had stolen some of the horses belonging to the trappers, cut loose the animals which were tied within ten feet of the strong fort of logs in which the Indians had taken shelter, attacked them, and made good his retreat with the recovered horses; an Indian of another tribe, who was with the trappers, bringing away a Crow scalp as a trophy. In one combat with the Blackfeet, Carson received a rifle ball in his left shoulder, breaking it. Save this, he has escaped the manifold dangers to which he has been exposed, without serious bodily injury. Of course, in so turbulent and unrestrained a life, there were not unfrequent personal rencounters among the trappers themselves, nor could the most peaceably-disposed always avoid them. These were most frequent and savage at the periods when the trappers went in to the 'rendezvous,' as were called the points where the companies kept their establishments for receiving the peltries and supplying the trappers. Here a few days of indulgence were commonly allowed himself by the trapper, and there was much drinking and gambling, and consequently fighting. Feuds, growing out of national feelings, would also naturally enough sometimes occur among the trappers—there being Canadians and Mexicans as well as the Americans; all having pride of race and country. On one occasion, a Frenchman, who ranked as a bully, had whipped a good many Canadians, and then began to insult the Americans, saying they were only worth being whipped with switches. At this, Carson fired up and said, '*He* was the most trifling one among the Americans, and to begin with him.' After some little more talk, each went off and armed himself—Carson with a pistol, the Frenchman with a rifle—and both mounted for the fight. Riding up until their horses' heads touched, they fired almost at the same instant, Carson a little the quickest, and, his ball passing through the Frenchman's hand, made him jerk up his gun, and sent the ball which was intended for Carson's heart grazing by his left eye and singeing his hair. This is the only serious personal quarrel of Carson's life, as he is, like most very brave men, of a peaceable and gentle temper.

"Col. Fremont owed his good fortune in procuring Carson's services, to an accidental meeting on a steamboat above St. Louis—neither having ever before heard of the other. It was at the commencement of Fremont's first expedition. Carson continued with it until, in its return, it had recrossed the mountains. His courage, fidelity, and excellent character, so far conciliated the good will of the commander, that, in his second expedition, he gladly availed himself again of Kit's services, on meeting with him, as he chanced to do, on the confines of New Mexico. Kit again left the party after its arrival this side of the mountains—not, however, until Fremont had obtained a promise from him to join the third expedition, in case one should be organized. Some incidents will be interesting, connected wtth this latter expedition, which was interrupted in its purely scientific character by the treachery of the Mexican chief (Castro) compelling Fremont to change his peaceful employment, and which, owing to the continuance of the war with Mexico, is not yet completed.

"In the interim between Fremont's second and third expeditions, Carson had settled himself near Taos, and had begun to farm, preparing to lead a quiet life, when he received a note from Fremont, written at Bent's Fort, reminding him of his promise, and telling him he would wait there for him. On this occasion Carson showed his strong friendship for his old commander, and the generous and unselfish nature of his feelings. In four days from receiving the note, Carson had joined the party, having sold house and farm for less than half the sum he had just expended upon it, and put his family under the protection of his friend, the late Gov. Bent, until he should return from a certainly long and dangerous journey. This protection, unfortunately, was taken from them in the late massacre at Taos, when Carson's brother-in-law was also one of the victims to the fury of the Mexicans against all connected with the Americans. Mrs. Carson saved her life by flight, leaving them to rob the house of every thing. Kendall, and all others who have written of their adventures in New Mexico, ascribe the highest character to the women of that country for modesty, generosity, quick sympathy, and all feminine virtues. To this amiable class belongs the wife of Carson, who has paid so dearly for her affection for him.

"The route of the third expedition led the party to the southern and western side of the Great Salt Lake—a region entirely unexplored, and filled, according to the superstitions and tales current among the Indians and the trappers of the mountains, with all imaginable horrors; a vast desert, void of vegetation and fresh water, abounding in quicksands and in brackish pools and rivers, with only subterranean outlets. This was the reputed character of the country, justifying at least the apprehension of lack of those indispensables to the voyageur of the wilderness—water and grass.

P

In truth, the southern border of the lake was found to be skirted with a salt plain of about sixty miles in width. Over this, as elsewhere, Carson, in his capacity of scout, was always with the advance party, to search for water and convenient places for camp— the usual signal of the prairies, a fire, serving, by its column of smoke, to find out where the advance were halting.

"The neighbourhood of the Rio Colorado and the Sierra Nevada of California, is infested with Indian tribes of Hippophagi, or Horse-Eaters, (as they may well be called,) who keep the northern parts of California in alarm, by sweeping down into the settlements, and carrying off horses and mules, which they use for food. With these savages the expedition had several skirmishes; but, owing to the perpetual vigilance which was exercised, neither men nor animals fell into the hands of the savages.

"When Fremont's party, in May, 1846, (not knowing of the existence of the war with Mexico,) retired from California, they proceeded north as far as the Tlamath lake, in Oregon, proposing to explore a new route into the Willhameth valley.

"A courier having overtaken Col. Fremont there, to say that Mr. Gillespie and five men were endeavouring to overtake him, he took ten men and returned sixty miles with the courier; making all haste, in order to reach them before night, and prevent any attack which the Indians might be tempted to make on a small party. These Tlamath Indians, by nature brave and warlike, have now a new source of power in the iron arrow-heads and axes furnished them by the British posts in that country. Their arrows can only be extracted from the flesh by the knife, as they are barbed, and of course are not to be drawn out. The events of that night and the days following, illustrate so fully the nightly dangers of an Indian country, and the treacherous nature of savages, that I will give them, and in Carson's own words:

"'Mr. Gillespie had brought the colonel letters from home—the first he had had since leaving the States the year before—and he was up, and kept a large fire burning until after midnight; the rest of us were tired out, and all went to sleep. This was the only night in all our travels, except the one night on the island in

the Salt Lake, that we failed to keep guard ; and as the men were
so tired, and we expected no attack now that we had sixteen in
party, the colonel didn't like to ask it of them, but sat up late himself. Owens and I were sleeping together, and we were waked at
the same time by the licks of the axe that killed our men. At
first, I didn't know it was that ; but I called to Basil, who was that
side, "What's the matter there ?—what's that fuss about ?" He
never answered, for he was dead then, poor fellow ; and he never
knew what killed him—his head had been cut in, in his sleep ; the
other groaned a little as he died. The Delawares (we had four
with us) were sleeping at that fire, and they sprang up as the Tlamaths charged them. One of them caught up a gun, which was
unloaded ; but, although he could do no execution, he kept them at
bay, fighting like a soldier, and didn't give up until he was shot
full of arrows—three entering his heart : he died bravely. As
soon as I had called out, I saw it was Indians in the camp, and I
and Owens together cried out 'Indians.' There were no orders
given ; things went on too fast, and the colonel had men with him
that didn't need to be told their duty. The colonel and I, Max-
well, Owens, Godey, and Stepp, jumped together, we six, and ran
to the assistance of our Delawares. I don't know who fired and
who didn't ; but I think it was Stepp's shot that killed the Tlamath
chief ; for it was at the crack of Stepp's gun that he fell. He had
an English half-axe slung to his wrist by a cord, and there were
forty arrows left in his quiver—the most beautiful and warlike
arrows I ever saw. He must have been the bravest man among
them, from the way he was armed, and judging by his cap. When
the Tlamaths saw him fall they ran ; but we lay, every man with
his rifle cocked, until daylight, expecting another attack.

   "'In the morning, we found, by the tracks, that from fifteen to
twenty of the Tlamaths had attacked us. They had killed three
of our men, and wounded one of the Delawares, who scalped the
chief, whom we left where he fell. Our dead men we carried on
mules ; but, after going about ten miles, we found it impossible to
get them any farther through the thick timber ; and, finding a
secret place, we buried them under logs and chunks, having no

way to dig a grave. It was only a few days before this fight that
some of these same Indians had come into our camp; and, although
we had only meat for two days, and felt sure that we would have
to eat mules for ten or fifteen days to come, the colonel divided
with them, and even had a mule unpacked to give them some
tobacco and knives.'

" The party then retraced its way into California; and, two days
after this rencontre, they met a large village of Tlamaths—more
than a hundred warriors. Carson was ahead with ten men, but
one of them having been discovered, he could not follow his
orders, which were to send back word and let Fremont come up
with the rest in case they found Indians. But as they had been
seen, it only remained to charge the village; which they did,
killing many, and putting to flight the rest. The women and
children, Carson says, 'we did not interfere with;' but they burnt
the village, together with their canoes and fishing-nets. In a
subsequent encounter, the same day, Carson's life was imminently
exposed. As they galloped up, he was rather in advance, when
he observed an Indian fixing his arrow to let fly at him. Carson
levelled his rifle, but it snapped; and in an instant the arrow
would have pierced him, had not Fremont, seeing the danger,
dashed his horse on the Indian, and knocked him down. 'I owe
my life to them two,' says Carson—'the colonel and Sacramento
saved me. Sacramento is a noble Californian horse which Capt.
Sutter gave to Col. Fremont in 1844, and which has twice made
the distance between Kentucky and his native valley, where he
earned his name by swimming the river after which he is called,
at the close of a long day's journey. Notwithstanding all his
hardships, (for he has travelled everywhere with his master,) he
is still the favourite horse of Col. Fremont.

" The hostile and insulting course of Castro drew Fremont into
retaliatory measures; and, aided by the American settlers, he pursued the Mexicans for some time; but, being unable to make them
stand and fight, (they always flying before him,) the flag of independence was raised at Sonoma on the 5th of July, 1846. Learning soon after of the existence of the war, the American flag was

promptly substituted, and the party proceeded to Monterey, where they found the fleet under Com. Sloat already in possession. Castro, with his forces, had retreated before Fremont; and, to prevent their escape into Sonora, Col. Fremont, with a hundred and sixty men, was offered the sloop of war 'Cyane' to carry them down to San Diego and facilitate the pursuit, as he hoped by that means to intercept Castro at Puebla de los Angeles. Then Carson, for the first time, saw the blue ocean, and the great vessels that, like white-winged birds, spread their sails above its waters. The vast prairies, whose immense green surface has been aptly likened to the sea, together with all objects ever seen upon it, were familiar to him; but it proved no preparation for actual salt water, and the pride and strength of the backwoodsmen were soon humbled by the customary tribute to Neptune. The forces were landed, and raised the flag at San Diego, and then they proceeded jointly to the capital, (Cuidad de los Angeles,) where, although from the detention at sea Castro had escaped, American authority was also established.

"From this point, on the 1st of September, 1846, Carson, with fifteen men, was despatched by Fremont with an account of the progress and state of affairs in that distant conquest. Carson was to have made the journey from Pueblo to Washington city and back, in 140 days. He pushed ahead accordingly, not stopping even for game, but subsisting on his mules, of which they made food as the animals broke down in the rapidity of the journey. He had crossed the wilderness, as he expected, in thirty days, when, meeting with Gen. Kearny's company within a few days of Santa Fé, he was turned back by that officer, to whose orders he believed himself subject, and with infinite reluctance resigned his despatches to another, and returned to guide Kearny's command into California.

"Gen. Kearny entered California without molestation, until the fight of San Pasqual; an official account of which has been published. In the charge made upon the Mexicans, Carson, as usual, was among the foremost, when, as he approached within bullet range of the enemy, who were drawn up in order of battle,

P 2

his horse stumbled and fell, pitching him over his head, and breaking his rifle in twain. Seizing his knife, he advanced on foot, until he found a killed dragoon, whose rifle he took, and was pressing on, when he met the mounted men returning from the charge, the Mexicans having galloped off. At the instance of Carson, the American party then took possession of a small rocky hill, near the scene of the battle, as the strongest position in reach. Not being in a situation to go forward, they encamped here; and the enemy collecting in force, they remained in a state of siege. There was little of either grass or water on the hill, and soon both animals and men began to suffer. The way was so thickly beset with the enemy, that the commander doubted the propriety of attempting to cut a passage through, when, after four days' siege, Carson and Passed Midshipman Beale, of the navy, (who had been sent to meet Kearny, with some thirty men, as a complimentary escort to San Diego,) volunteered to go to Capt. Stockton, at that place, and bring a reinforcement.

"This daring enterprise, these intrepid and resolute young men, accompanied by a Delaware Indian who was attached as a spy to Gen. Kearny's command, successfully accomplished, but not without extreme suffering and peril. The distance between the camp and San Diego was but thirty miles; but, as they had to make long detours, they travelled nearer fifty. They left the camp in the night of the 9th of December, crawling in a horizontal position through the enemy's lines. Their shoes made some noise; for which cause they took them off, and during the night unfortunately lost them. Lying by all day to avoid the enemy, they succeeded by the end of the second night in reaching their destination, and procuring the necessary reinforcement. Their feet and flesh torn and bleeding from the rocks and thorny shrubs, haggard from hunger, thirst, anxiety, and sleeplessness, they were, again nevertheless, in full performance of duty at the battles of the 8th and 9th of January.

"When Fremont, after meeting with and accepting the surrender of the Mexican forces, reached Los Angeles, Carson immediately returned to his command, and in the ensuing month was again selected to cross the desert, the wilderness, the mountains, and the prairies, to bring news of those far-off operations of its agents to the government in Washington. Leaving the frontier settlements of California on the 25th of February, Carson arrived in St. Louis about the middle of May—making the journey, notwithstanding the inclemency of the season, and an unavoidable detention of ten days at Santa Fé, in a shorter time than it was ever before accomplished. The unsettled state of the country—the war with Mexico, inciting the savage tribes to unusual license and daring—added much to the inevitable hazards and privations of the journey, rendering the most unceasing vigilance necessary night and day; while the speed with which the party travelled debarred them from the usual resource of travellers in uninhabited regions, and they were fain to resort to the unsavory subsistence of those Hippophagi of the Sierra Nevada; only converting the poor beasts to food, however, when they were travel-worn and exhausted.

"Fortunately, the journey was made in its extent without serious mishap, and Carson, with Lieut. Beale, his comrade in the night march to San Diego, and Lieut. Talbot, the young gentleman who led the gallant retreat of the little party of ten through the enemy's midst, a distance of three hundred miles from Santa Barbara to Monterey, are all now in Washington.

"Since Carson's arrival, solely through the appreciation by the President of his merit and services, he has received a commission of lieutenant in the rifle regiment of which Mr. Fremont is the lieutenant-colonel. The appointment was unsolicited and unexpected—the suggestion entirely of the President's own recognition of the deserts of this man of the prairies—a fact that is most honourable to the Executive, and makes the favour the more gratifying to the friends of Carson."

As soon as Col. Fremont was thus apprised of the arrival and action of Com. Shubrick and of Gen. Kearny, he started, (on 21st March, 1847,) from Los Angeles for Monterey, a distance of near 500 miles, without any attendants but a coloured man and two California gentlemen, Don Jesus Pico, who had been pardoned at

San Luis Obispo, and Don Andres Pico, both of whom had performed distinguished parts in hostilities against the Americans, but were then devoted to Col. Fremont in gratitude for clemency shown. From this fact is inferred the tranquillity of the country. Col. Fremont, simultaneously with his departure for Monterey, despatched W. H. Russell, Esq., to the United States, who, on his arrival, reported the general tranquillity of the country, and the faithful observance of the capitulation in his own language.

"These terms the Californians had faithfully observed up to the time of my coming away, and California presents a state of satisfied quietness, altogether different from New Mexico, (through which I passed on my return home,) or any other part of Mexico which we have conquered."

Col. Fremont having had an interview with Com. Shubrick and with Gen. Kearny, returned immediately to the City of the Angels, which he did not again leave until his departure for the United States.

Col. Fremont, when informed of the commission from the government as commander-in-chief, and of the orders with which Gen. Kearny arrived in California, declined, in writing, to obey his military orders, and continued to act as "governor and commander-in-chief of California;" alleging, as the grounds of this refusal, his own previous appointment as governor and commander by Com. Stockton, and the fact that the authority conferred on Gen. Kearny had become obsolete by the force of events not looked to by the government as to happen until after the arrival of Gen. Kearny in the territory. The chief of these events was the accomplishment of the conquest of California, which he alleged had been already achieved by Com. Stockton and himself, before the coming of Gen. Kearny, and the troops under his command.

(It is not the purpose of these sketches to commemorate any controversy between individuals whose gallantry did honour to their country, and to the branch of the service to which each belonged. It is enough here to say that the orders and achievements of every prominent actor have been given with entire impartiality, and, as far as the sources of information, common to the public, would admit of, in such narrative form as will, possibly, admit of the reader's determining questionable points for himself.)

On the 31st of May, 1847, Col. Fremont departed from Los Angeles, Upper California, (Col. Richard B. Mason, of First Dragoons, having been left by Gen. Kearny, as governor and commander-in-chief,) to return to the United States. His original engineering party of subordinates, hardy backwoodsmen, trappers, &c., who had encountered with him a series of adventures, uncontemplated on their enrolment for scientific purposes in 1845, returned under his charge. The party travelled with that of Gen. Kearny as far as Fort Leavenworth, where they arrived on the 22d of August, 1847. Here charges of disobedience of orders were preferred against Col. Fremont by Gen. Kearny, and a full and speedy trial asked in return. That trial is now progressing at Washington City.

From Fort Leavenworth, Col. Fremont paid a short visit to St. Louis, Mo., where his fellow citizens waited on him with their congratulations at his safe return, and the brilliancy of his achievements on his distant theatre of action. He was also tendered a public dinner by a large number of the most influential of all parties. This he declined, and in reply thus expressed himself:

"Placed in a critical and delicate position, where imminent danger urged immediate action, and where the principal difficulty lay in knowing full well what must be done, where, in a struggle barely for the right to live, every effort to secure our safety involved unusual and grave responsibilities, I could only hope from your forbearance a suspension of judgment until, with full possession of the facts, you would be able to determine understandingly."

And he hastened on to the seat of government.

CHAPTER IX.

Gen. Kearny—Upper California—Orders and Instructions—Departure from Santa Fé—Captain Johnston's Journal of the March—Meets Kit Carson—March renewed—Incidents of the Journey—Visit to Copper-mines—Apachas—Aztec Ruins—Casa de Montezuma—Pimos and Cocomaricopas Indians—Provisions fail—Capture of Castro's Horses, and of the Mail—Junction of the Gila and Colorado—Desert—Approach California—Signs of the Enemy—Letter to Com. Stockton—Capt. Gillespie—The Enemy—Battle of San Pasqual—Death of Captains Johnston and Moore, and Lieut. Hammond—Gen. Kearny, Lieut. Warner, Captains Gillespie and Gibson, wounded—Com. Stockton—Sailors and Marines—The Enemy—Battles of 8th and 9th January—Killed and Wounded—Occupation of City of the Angels—Col. Fremont joins Gen. Kearny—Joint Circular with Com. Shubrick—Lieut. Col. Cooke and Mormon Battalion—Proclamation of Lieut. Emory and Despatches—Capt. Tompkin's Artillery Company—Col. Stevenson's Regiment—Settlements and Towns, &c.—Decree of Gen. Kearny—Government established—Orders to take possession of Lower California—Gen. Kearny returns to United States—Route homewards—Dead Emigrants—Arrival—Reception.

GEN. KEARNY, in command of the Army of the West, had been directed by the Secretary of War, Wm. L. Marcy, to proceed across the Rocky Mountains to Upper California, (of which for various reasons it was "deemed important that military possession should be taken,") with what force he could spare, after taking and securing the possession of Santa Fé. The orders and instructions for the performance of Gen. Kearny's part in the attainment of this purpose of "the greatest importance," have been already sketched, as, also, "the prompt and energetic manner in which Gen. Kearny conducted to a successful termination the very difficult and distant enterprise,"* of the capture of Santa Fé and New Mexico.

Having made all his arrangements at Santa Fé, Gen. Kearny

---

* Report of the Secretary of War, Dec. 5, 1846, accompanying President's Message.

prepared as soon as possible, in accordance with the wishes of the executive, to set out on another difficult and distant enterprise.

The route to Upper California, recommended by his topographical engineers, and determined upon by Gen. Kearny, was to proceed from Santa Fé down the Rio Grande about 200 miles, thence to strike across to the Gila, and to move down that river near to its mouth, then to cross the Colorado—and thence, keeping near the Pacific, to Monterey.

On the 25th of September, 1846, Gen. Kearny set out on his long and exceedingly interesting journey. On the next day he had left Major Sumner's dragoon camp, thirteen miles from Santa Fé, and was *en route* with 300 United States dragoons for California. The dragoon horses were all sent back to the United States, and the command all mounted on mules, and the wagons drawn by the same hardy animals and by oxen, as it was not expected the country through which they were about to pass would afford the proper sustenance to the high-mettled chargers of the First Dragoons. Indeed, the grass had long been consumed for many miles around Santa Fé, and forage had been brought with great difficulty and expense from a distance, or the horses were picketed in distant places where they might find pasture.

The route of Gen. Kearny has been most ably and interestingly illustrated by the "*rough notes*" of his late lamented and accomplished aid-de-camp, Capt. A. R. Johnston, of the First Dragoons, who was unfortunately killed on the 6th December, 1846, at the battle of San Pasqual. They extend down to a few hours before his death, and imbody a great variety of curious and interesting facts. It is from these notes, that the latest and most authentic account of the protracted and fatiguing march of Gen. Kearny, through an important region of our continent, is to be found. From these "*notes*" it appears that Gen. Kearny continued his route through many villages of the New Mexicans, along the margin of the Rio Grande—down to Albuquerque, ("a town of some 6000 inhabitants"—elsewhere said,) where he crossed the Rio Grande, the ford being about two and a half feet deep. The inhabitable portion of New Mexico is represented as confined

to the immediate borders of the streams.   The bottoms on the
Rio Grande, down to this point, about one and a half mile wide,
and, elevated but a few feet above the level of the rapid and
regular streams of water, are rudely irrigated, but might, by
proper appliances, be made to support a population ten times
greater than the present number.   The rains of this country all
fall on the mountain-tops, which afford abundant evidence of volcanic action in their mineral substances.   From Albuquerque they
marched through a country generally destitute of wood, and
altogether of hard grained timber, and with excessive heat, until
October 8, when an express reached them on the right bank of
the Rio Grande, informing the General that the Navahoes had
attached the village of Palverdera, twelve miles down the river.
The alcalde had sent for help where they were still fighting.
Capt. Moore's company was forthwith sent in defence of the
Mexicans, and orders were despatched back to Col. Doniphan to
make a campaign in the Navaho country.   (The same which
he so ably executed.)   Capt. Moore next day reported that the
Navahoes, over 100, had driven off quite a quantity of stock, but
that, as both parties appeared to be afraid, no wounds were received.   On the 5th they reached Secoro, where they learned that
the best road to the river Gila was directly out from the Rio Grande
at that place.

On the 6th, a meeting took place, which is best described in
Capt. Johnston's own words:

"After marching about three miles, we met Kit Carson, direct
cn express from California with a mail of public letters for Washington.   He informs us that Col. Fremont is probably civil and
military governor of California ; and that about forty days since,
Com. Stockton, with the naval force, and Col. Fremont, acting in
concert, commenced to revolutionize that country, and place it
under the American flag ; that in about ten days their work was
done, and Carson, having received the rank of lieutenant, was
despatched across the country by the Gila, with a party to carry
the mail.   The general told him that he had just passed over the
country which we were to traverse, and he wanted him to go

back with him as a guide ; he replied, that he had pledged himself to go to Washington, and he could not think of not fulfilling
his promise. The general told him he would relieve him of all
responsibility, and place the mail in the hands of a safe person,
to carry it on. He finally consented, and turned his face to the
west again, just as he was on the eve of entering the settlements,
after his arduous trip, and when he had set his hopes on seeing
his family. It requires a brave man to give up his private feelings thus for the public good ; but Carson is one such. Honour
to him for it! Carson left California with 15 men—among them,
six Delaware Indians—faithful fellows. They had fifty animals ;
most of which they left on the road, or traded with the Apaches' ;
giving two for one. They were not aware of the presence of the
American troops in New Mexico. They counted upon feeling
their way along; and, in case the Mexicans were hostile, they
meant to start a new outfit and run across their country. When
they came to the Copper-mine Apaches, they first learned that an
American general had possession of the territory of New Mexico.
The Apaches were very anxious to be friendly with the Americans, and received them very cordially; much to their surprise.
The column moved on *ten miles*, and encamped under a beautiful
grove of cotton-woods ; and the General issued an order reducing
the command to 100 men, taking C and K companies with him,
and leaving B, G, and I companies under Major Sumner's command, in the new Mexican territory. The officers to march with
the expedition are Gen. Kearny, Captains Turner and Johnston ;
Major Swords, quartermaster ; Assistant-surgeon Griffin ; Lieut.
Warner and Emory, Topographical Engineers ; Capt. Moore, Lieutenants Hammond and Davidson, First Dragoons. Each company
has three wagons, with eight mules in each ; and the whole of the
other companies put under requisition to supply C and K companies with the best outfits. It went hard with some of the company
commanders to part with their fine teams—the accumulation of
many years in their companies ; but the public service being para-
mount, they submitted cheerfully. The Apaches came to us to-
day, and gave us four young men as guides."

Q

Next day, they took leave of their companions in arms, and on the day after had gone near 200 miles down the Rio Grande, from Santa Fé, but the stream was still unfit for navigation. They were then near the commencement of the Jornada del Muerto of 100 miles without water, (subsequently passed over by Col. Doniphan.)

The mountains at this point of their route appeared to become more lofty, and the "back-bone" of North America, to have been split open along here, and all the igneous rocks to have been thrust up in general parallelism, without making a continuous range along this stream, from which the waters of the Rio Grande run directly south, while those of the Arkansas, the Gila, and other streams flow east and west.

On the 9th, the mules began to give out in the teams, and the general determined to remain in camp, and send to Major Sumner, for mules to take back the wagons and other property not needed in packing. Carson reported the country as worse rather than better in front. Next morning they had frost and ice in camp. Two New Mexicans here brought mules for sale, representing they had them from the Apache Indians in trading. As this was contrary to the laws of the territory, Gen. Kearny confiscated all the mules they said they had gotten from the Apaches and sent them off. They said they knew it was contrary to law, and were willing to submit. The general gave them a paper, stating what he had done, and the reasons for it. They then asked for license to trade with the Apaches, which was granted them, and departed.

On the 13th, Lieut. Ingalls arrived with the pack-saddles, and the mail containing general orders Nos. 30 to 36, and letters which required answering. Here the door was closed to future communication with the United States, as they passed into the Apache country. On the 15th, they took a final departure from the Rio Grande, and its rugged gravel hills and harsh bottom-grass, tasting of salt, and ascended, at once, near 200 feet, to an elevated plain, deeply cut with the cañons of the streams. In this day's march, they saw a cañon (or deep cut) of fifty feet deep

and twenty wide, affording a passage for a stream, which, for a
short distance, was a fine leaping mountain stream, with overhanging trees, and fish playing in its waters, but then sank in the
sand and all became arid again.   Entered now upon a more pleasant country, as they approached the lesser peaks of the Sierra de
los Mimbres, covered with trees, shrubbery and grass. A view from
a peak near their camp is thus described :—"The view presented
was very grand ; the valley of the Rio Grande, widening to the
south as far as El Paso, and twenty to thirty miles wide, covered
with grass, lies below ; the peaks of mountains standing around
in the distance, like the frame of a picture.   It is evident at a
glance, that the lower part of New Mexico is by far the most
valuable."

The visit to the copper mines claims, from its interest, insertion
entire, as also does the next day's notes.

"*October* 19.—Visited the copper mines, and examined the old
excavations.   The veins of sulphuret of copper run through a
whitish silicious rock, like the blue veins running through white
marble ; they vary in their knees, but traverse the whole substance.   The rock breaks easily ; and the pick appears to be the
only tool used formerly.   Occasional veins of pure copper, very
yellow from the quantity of gold it contains, traverse the whole
mass.   I saw in the rollers, lying over the mine, masses of the
blue limestone, supposed to be cretaceous ; the water had filled
many of the abandoned chambers of the mine ; in others, the flies
had perched themselves in great numbers to pass the winter.
The fort which was built to defend the mines, was built in shape
of an equilateral triangle, with round towers at the corners ; it
was built of adobe, with walls four feet thick.   The fort was still
in tolerable preservation ; some remains of the furnaces were left,
and piles of cinders ; but no idea could be formed of the manner
of smelting the ore, except, that charcoal, in quantities, was used.
Several hundred dollars' worth of ore had been got ready for smelt-
ing when the place was abandoned.   McKnight, who was for
nine years a prisoner in Chihuahua, made a fortune here, and
abandoned the mines in consequence of the Apache Indians cut-

ting off his supplies. At one time, they took eighty pack-mules from him, (authority, Carson.) The mine is very extensive, and, doubtless, immensely valuable. Water is abundant, and pasture fine, and many lands which will furnish breadstuffs, by cultivation. Wood is very abundant, and particularly in the vicinity. Leaving the copper mines, the rocky masses soon show iron in the greatest abundance; then, going west, we came to the blue limestone, standing vertical, ranging south, and bent so as to lie level west. Through the seams of this limestone, some igneous rocks had been interjected, and occasional masses of iron ore, similar to that seen on the Blue and False Washita rivers. Then we came to a mountain mass of the same rock as of the copper mines. From this, westward, we came upon an amygdaloid of all sorts of igneous rocks. The hills were not very lofty, so that, gradually, we passed the great back-bone of America without perceiving it—the dividing ridge between the Atlantic and Pacific. The general set out to march fifteen miles to San Vicentia Spring; but finding no grass, he came on, expecting to find water—a Spanish guide said at three leagues, but it proved to be fifteen miles further, where we all arrived after night. Before we left the copper mines, some Apaches showed themselves; and as we came off, they rode upon a hill, made a smoke, and as we got opposite them on the road, commenced calling out to us, 'not to be afraid, but come on.' We replied, 'It is you that are afraid. Why don't you come on ?' They then approached, but motioned us all back but the guide, Carson, until he had a talk and satisfied them. Some of our mules gave out to-day. Three Apaches came to camp—distance, thirty miles.

"*October* 20.—The Apaches came to us this morning, as we did not start until late. Red Sleeve came with fifteen or twenty persons, some women; they ride small, but fine, horses. The high roads leading from this mountain to Sonora and California, show whence they came; they are partly clothed like the Spaniards, with wide drawers, moccasins, and leggins to the knees; they carry a knife, frequently in the right leggin, on the outside; their moccasins have turned-up square toes, their hair is long, and mostly they have no head-dress; some have hats, some fantastic helmets; they have some guns, but are mostly armed with lances and bows and arrows, their lances pointed with stone points. Carson remarked, yesterday, that he never knew how fine a weapon the bow and arrow was, until he had them fired at him in the night; at that time they are more sure than firearms, for they are fired by the feel rather than the arms. The vegetation westward from the copper mines grows thinner until we get to the Sierra del Buno, which is a mountain, covered black with forest growth; the pine is found here, live oak, three kinds, the gama and other fine grasses, some resembling timothy. A rain storm passed by the heads of the Gila last night; it is the first we have seen since we left Santa Fé; although high winds and heavy lightning betokened distant storms once or twice before, we have not yet been sprinkled upon. Trading mules is dull work, with the Apaches. Red Sleeve, Black Knife and Lasady, are the three principal chiefs of the Apaches on the west of the Del Norte. Somez is the head-man of those on the east of the Del Norte. There is another band about south-west of this; on the Panqatong mountain is another band. The Apaches near Taos are of the same stock with these—their whole people have not been together for a long time. The general gave Red Sleeve and two other chiefs papers to show he had talked with them, and that they had promised perpetual friendship with the Americans; they seemed all anxious to conciliate the Americans, and they did not forget the Shawnees; the copper mines are in their country, which lies north of the 32° of north latitude. Marched at 12 M., and descended a narrow, winding valley with a brisk running stream, two or three feet wide, meandering through it, with a few trees occasionally, and very tall grass. We found two small patches where the Apaches had made corn; the hills were high on each side, composed of rugged masses of volcanic rock, and very few trees. We followed this creek for five miles, and fell upon the famous Gila, a beautiful mountain stream, about thirty feet wide, and a foot deep on the shallows, with clear water and pebbly bed, fringed with trees and hemmed in by mountains; the bottom

Q 2

not more than a mile wide. The signs of beaver, the bear, the
deer, and the turkey, besides the tracks of herds of Indian horses,
were plain to be seen on the sand. We came down the river
about two miles and a half more, about south, and encamped at the
head of one of its cañons, preparatory to a long journey over
rocky hills to-morrow. Northward from where we struck the
river, is an open country, lying west of a very high mountain,
called the Gila Mountain, in which it is said the Salt forks also
head. Our camp was well supplied with fine fish from the river,
resembling, a little, the black bass; its flesh was not firm, but very
delicate. The California quail abounds in the bottoms. A new sort
of sycamore tree made its appearance here; it has a bark pre-
cisely like our own sycamore tree, or button-wood, and a leaf
resembling the maple; the leaves are now yellow with the frost,
as they are of the most deciduous plants. Found some of the
fruit of the black walnut of this country; it is about half the size
of our black walnut, and not rough on the outside as ours, but
shows the veins of the seams of the outer bark; the roses, the
hops, mosquits, and poison-oaks looked familiar, and some other
plants known in the United States, names unknown. Just as we
were leaving camp to-day, an old Apache chief came in and ha-
rangued the general, thus:—'You have taken Santa Fé; let us
go on and take Chihuahua and Sonora; we will go with you.
You fight for the soul, we fight for plunder, so we will agree perfectly: their people are bad Christians, let us give them a good
thrashing,' &c."

The route lay onwards through a wild country of occasional fertility and sterility—mountains, and valleys, and cañons—crossing and
recrossing the Gila—the San Francisco passed, as also the San Pedro,
&c.—meeting frequently parties of Apache Indians, but unable to
bring them to an interview at camp in any number, &c., until the
10th of November, and here the "notes" are given in detail:

"*November* 10.—Marched about eight o'clock; and after marching six miles, still passing plains which had once been occupied,
we saw to our left the "Casa de Montezuma." I rode to it, and
found the remains of the walls of four buildings; and the piles of

earth showing where many others had been. One of the buildings was still quite complete, as a ruin ; the others had all crum-
bled, but a few pieces of low broken wall. The large casa was
fifty feet by forty, and had been four stories high ; but the floors
and roof had long since been burnt out. The charred ends of the
cedar joist were still in the wall. I examined them, and found that
they had not been cut with a steel instrument. The joists were
round sticks, about four feet in diameter. There were four en-
trances—north, south, east, and west—the doors about four feet by
two ; the rooms as below, and had the same arrangement on each
story. There was no sign of a fire-place in the building. The
lower story was filled with rubbish, and above it was open to the
sky. The walls were four feet thick at the bottom, and had a
curved inclination inwards to the top. The house was built of a
sort of white earth and pebbles, probably containing lime, which
abounded on the ground adjacent. The walls had been smoothed
outside, and plastered inside ; and the surface still remained firm,
although it was evident they had been exposed to great heat from
the fire. Some of the rooms did not open to all the rest, but had
a hole, a foot in diameter, to look through ; in other places were
smaller holes. About two hundred yards from this building was
a mound, in a circle a hundred yards around the mound. The
centre was a hollow, twenty-five yards in diameter, with two
vamps or slopes going down to its bottom. It was probably a well,
now partly filled up. A similar one was seen near Mount Dallas.
A few yards further, in the same direction, northward, was a ter-
race, one hundred yards by seventy, about five feet high. Upon
this was a pyramid, about eight feet high, twenty-five yards square
at top. From this, sitting on my horse, I could overlook the vast
plain lying north-east and west, on the left bank of the Gila. The
ground in view was about fifteen miles—all of which, it would
seem, had been irrigated by the waters of the Gila. I picked up
a broken crystal of quartz in one of these piles. Leaving the
casa, I turned towards the Pimos, and travelling at random over
the plain, (now covered with mosquit,) the piles of earth and pottery showed for hours in every direction. I also found the remains

of a *sicia*, which followed the range of houses for miles. It had
been very large. When I got to camp, I found them on good
grass, and in communication with the Pimos, who came out with
a frank welcome. Their answer to Carson, when he went up and
asked for provisions, was, ' Bread is to eat, not to sell—take what you
want.' The general asked a Pimo who made the house I had seen.
' It is the Casa de Montezuma,' said he. ' It was built by the son
of the most beautiful woman who once dwelled in yon mountain.
She was fair, and all the handsome men came to court her, but in
vain. When they came, they paid tribute, and out of this small
store she fed all people in times of famine, and it did not diminish.
At last, as she lay asleep, a drop of rain fell upon her navel, and
she became pregnant, and brought forth a boy, who was the builder
of all these houses.' He seemed unwilling to talk about them ;
but said there were plenty more of them to the north, south, west,
&c. He said when he first knew this casa, it was in better preservation ; but that it had been burnt too long ago for any of them to
remember. I showed him the hieroglyphic, but he did not understand it. Some other Pimos and Cocomaricopas arrived, and messengers were sent to their village to buy water-melons and provisions, which soon came, although it was several miles. They
wanted white beads for what they had to sell, and knew the value
of money. Seeing us eating, the interpreter told the general he
had tasted the liquor of Sonora and New Mexico, and would like
to taste a sample of that of the United States. The dog had a
liquorish tooth, and when given a drink of French brandy, pro-
nounced it better than any he had ever seen or tasted. The Mari-
copa messenger came to ask the general what his business was,
and where he was going ? He said his people were at peace with
all the world, except some of their neighbours, the Apaches, and
they did not desire any more enemies. He was of course told to
say to his chief that our object was merely to pass peaceably
through their country ; that we had heard a great deal of the
Pimos, and knew them to be a good people ; we were all struck
with their unassumed ease and confidence in approaching our camp
—not like the Apaches, who bayed at us like their kindred wolves,

until the smell of tobacco and other (to them) agreeable things gave them assurance enough to approach us. The Pimos and Coco-maricopas live alongside of each other, but are a distinct people, speaking different languages ; the latter once lived near the mouth of the Gila. The Pimos have long lived at their present abode, and are known to all the trappers as a virtuous and industrious people. They and the Maricopas number over two thousand souls. At the river I saw a cinder, which might have been from the smelt-ing of some ore."

After a short rest here, they prepared to cross the Tesotal, a desert of forty miles, without water or grass. The animals were brought up to a well dug by the dragoons, and given as much water as they would drink, some of them swilling enormously, as if in anticipation of privation. This desert passed, their progress lay along the table-land until they gradually got into the bottom of the Gila again, at the point of Big Horn Mountain, on the 15th of November. Here their supply of beef gave out, and they were reduced to beans, corn, and the flesh of their horses.

Capt. Johnston's own words, as the interest of the narrative quickens, are resorted to.

(At the Pimos village, Gen. Kearny had heard a rumour of a force being raised in Sonora to interrupt him ; and by Lieut. Emory's capture of the mail, on the 22d, further particulars were obtained.)

"*November* 22.—Marched at the usual hour, and continued down the Gila. On the left bank, the first eight or nine miles, the road was rough ; passed through a cañon. The cañon was wide ; but we had to clamber along the edge of the hills. In many places the road was insecure, from its being a long declivity. After leaving this cañon, we found ourselves in a bottom, which lay to the west, and which proved to be the delta between the Gila and Colorado. We marched about twenty-one miles, and found ourselves near the junction of those rivers. We discovered the greatest abundance of recent signs of horses, and began to think, in truth, that Gen. Castro may have returned from Sonora with a large mounted force, to regain possession of California.

The signs proved to be very fresh, and indicated that, to whomsoever they belonged, they were not more than half a day off. The speculations, of course, were various, and all the knowledge of sign-studying put in practice. Carson went down the river, and discovered fresh signs of fires of half-a-dozen messes, with no military regularity, and a trail coming from the crossing half a mile wide, indicating a great number of loose animals. No trail could be discovered leading away from this place. The signs of very few men could be seen. A woman's track was found, a dead colt, colt tracks, and, finally, straggling men were seen. Fires were discovered in the bottom, up the Gila ; and Lieut. Emory went with twenty men to reconnoitre them, and found the camp of a party of Spaniards from California, with 400 or 500 animals, going to Sonora. He brought some of them to camp, and, as usual, they lied so much that we could get very little out of them. One of them told us, in confidence, that we would find 800 men in arms at the Pueblo, opposed to the Americans ; and that a party was at San Diego, friendly to the United States, of 200 ; and that three ships of war, he heard, were at San Diego, and advised us to be on our guard as we advanced. One of the others said the Mexicans were quiet at the Pueblo, and that the Americans had quiet possession of all the country. They were dismissed for the night, and the general determined not to lose so good a chance to get fresh animals. Camp on dry grass in the sand-hills.

"*November* 23.—The Mexicans came to camp on poor animals, and said they had no very good ones. They evidently are disposed to be shy and uncommunicative. One of them, who reported in confidence about the 800 men at Angeles, tells us that they had killed several Americans at the Puebla. They say the Jornada is fifty miles without water ; that they were lost upon it, and found water half way, by accident. One of them was caught by Lieut. Emory with a bundle of letters, some of which were to Gen. Castro—one giving an account of the rising of the Mexicans, and placing one Flores at their head at the Pueblo de los Angeles. Another letter to a different person, was to the effect that eighty Mexican cavalry had chased 400 Americans at the ravines between the Puebla and San Pedro, and had driven them back, and had captured a cannon called the Teazer. Their letters being opened, were re-sealed by Capt. Turner, and all returned to the man, who was discharged with them. These fellows tell various stories about the ownership of the horses. They acknowledge that a part of them belong to Gen. Castro. We are encamped one and a half miles south of the junction of the Gila and Colorado. These two rivers join together, and run through a stone hill, through which they have broken a passage, although there are bottom lands on either side of the hill, by which they may once have flowed. The place is remarkable; and, being the junction of two important rivers, (both of which are to a certain degree navigable —this point being also a point in the route from Sonora to California,) may one day fill a large space in the world's history. The Colorado disappears from here in a vast bottom. The last we can see of its cotton-woods is in the south-west, beyond which lies a low range of mountains—whether on the right or left bank, is not plain—probably on the right bank. Toiling about through the sand-hills, in thick boots, one is convinced that, to perform a journey on foot in this country, a moccasin with a thick but elastic sole is far preferable to the boot. The condition of our animals is sad enough to take the Jornada. Poor animals that have come with us from the United States will lay their bones on the desert. Some of the few horses we brought through, are not able to go on. An animal fat and well rested in New Mexico could have come well enough."

By the 28th, they had with great suffering passed the Jornada, or desert, of about ninety miles. Many of the animals they were obliged to leave to perish there.

The horses of which Capt. Johnston gives details, afterwards were found to have been sent by the Californians, under a small escort, thus far on their way for the benefit of Mexican reinforcements to be raised in Sonora. When taken, they had scarce recovered from crossing the Jornada, and returning over the same, made the capture almost useless.

On the 30th, the men killed a horse for food. On inspection, they were found all wellnigh naked—some of them barefoot and much weatherbeaten, but no signs of quailing in their swarthy sun-burnt faces.

The narrative of the four next days we give in the words of Capt. Johnston.

"*December* 1.—The first day of winter; we left camp at the usual hour, and found the air cold and chilly. The mountain peaks on the coast-range are covered with snow slightly. The whole of yesterday these peaks were covered with clouds, which drifted off in loose masses over the desert. This morning most of the clouds had disappeared, and a strong wind blew from the west. Our route for the day was devious, through narrow passes, without any great elevation—a bad road for our little howitzers, and impassable, without work for wagons. We marched eighteen miles, and encamped at the Vegas San Felipe, near the deserted Indian village; the rocks were mostly of mica-slate and granite. The water of the Vegas is apparently fresh, but the adjacent swamp is salt, and the grass bad for animals, especially at this season—the grass, the long, salty grass of the Del Norte, and the soda grass.

"*December* 2.—Marched at the usual hour. Our animals having spent a bad night, from the cold and bad grass, the few remaining horses, except one, gave out to-day, having been purged by the grass, and very much weakened. Our route was now over a rolling country. About six miles we met some Mexicans escaping out of the country, with women and children; we allowed them to pass free. They informed us of the existence of war still in this country, so that we count now upon meeting the enemy. It appears that there are no armed forces opposed to each other in the field; but that, generally, parties of California rancheros can be found in every quarter. We will probably have a long time with an unseen enemy, with no pitched battles. Arrived at Warner's ranch, very unexpectedly to them. This point is about sixty miles from San Diego, and perhaps eighty from the Pueblo. It is occupied by an American from Connecticut, who settled in this country and became naturalized, married, &c. He is now on the main route leading to Sonora, and of course is very much exposed to both parties. He is now said to be a prisoner in the hands of the Americans. Our approach to California improves to-day, and we came part of the day under the shade of fine live-oak trees, and, on the mountain-tops, clumps of lofty pines. As we came to Warner's, we got upon the western slope of mountains; and here nature had made pretty successful efforts to clothe her nakedness; the shrubs and trees almost hid the rocks of the mountains, and the hills had grass in abundance, but still nothing like the luxuriant growth of the prairies of Missouri, but doubtless a most enchanting sight when it is green, to one who has just crossed the desert. We found Warner's a place which would be considered a poor location in the United States, with a hot and a cold spring on his place—a good place for stock, but bad for grain, one would think. We are told wheat yields thirty-fold. The labour is performed by California Indians, who are stimulated to work by $3 per month and repeated floggings. We encamped a quarter of a mile west of the warm spring. Having heard of a herd of mules fifteen miles hence, belonging to Flores, the insurgent chief, Lieut. Davidson, with twenty-five men, was despatched, with Carson and Saunders, to see if we could get a remount; they started at dark. A Mr. Stokes, an Englishman, who lives fifteen miles hence, came to camp, and gave us information that Com. Stockton was at Diego, with the larger part of his naval force; that he had to remain neutral. A letter was sent to Com. Stockton; and it was determined to remain at this point until morning, and determine whether to march upon San Diego or the Pueblo, or to halt on the Sonora outlet, until it was known what was to be done with the American prisoners said to be in the hands of the rancheros. We hear that the Californians are very savage, killing any one of their people whom they suspect of treachery, and forcing those who are unwilling to join them. We were struck with the fact, that a furious wind blew in our faces as we approached the coast-range; but, after crossing it, we found all calm, and were told that there had been no wind.

R   13

"*December* 3. Lieut. Davidson and Carson returned about noon, with a large gang of tame and wild animals, most of which are said to belong to Flores, the Californian general. After them, came a party of French, English, and a Chilian, claiming their riding animals, as they were going out of the country, which the General gave them. Many of the animals from the herd were put into service, and arrangements made to secure the balance by driving them into some safe place in the mountain. Lay by for the rest of the day ; did not have time to examine the agua caliente, but it is said to be remarkable.

"*December* 4. Marched at 9, and took the route for San Diego to communicate with the naval forces, and to establish our depôt, not knowing yet in what state we would find the country. Marched 15 miles in a rain, cold and disagreeable, and encamped at Santa Isabella, a former ranch of the San Diego mission, now, by hook or crook, in the possession of an Englishman named Stokes. Here hospitality was held out to us. Stokes having gone to San Diego, we ate heartily of stewed and roast mutton and tortillas. We heard of a party of Californians of 80 men encamped a distance from this ; but the informant varied from 16 to 30 miles in his account, rendering it too uncertain to make a dash on them in a dark, stormy night, so we slept till morning."

Here end the "rough notes" of a gallant soldier. His profession called upon him to offer up his life at any moment the service of his country required it. Here he dropped the pen he had used with such ability, to draw his sword in combat—from whence he never returned to cheer his sorrowing companions-in-arms, in whose memory he ever lives, as he will in that of his country ; to use the language of Gen. Kearny—"a loss to his commander, to his regiment, and, more than all, to his country."

The rapid summary of the route given in Gen. Kearny's official despatches supplies the latitude of several places, and other omissions above, while conciseness and importance affords no excuse for its omission ; the narrative is therefore continued in the language of the "official" despatches.

HEAD-QUARTERS, ARMY OF THE WEST,
San Diego, Upper California, Dec. 12, 1846.

SIR: As I have previously reported to you, I left Santa Fé
(New Mexico) for this country on the 25th September, with 300
of the First Dragoons, under Major Sumner. We crossed to the
bank of the Del Norte at Albuquerque, (65 miles below Santa
Fé,) continuing down on that bank till the 6th October, when we
met Mr. Kit Carson, with a party of 16 men, on his way to
Washington city, with a mail and papers, an express from Com.
Stockton and Lieut. Col. Fremont, reporting that the Californias
were already in possession of the Americans under their command; that the American flag was flying from every important
position in the territory, and that the country was for ever free
from Mexican control; the war ended, and peace and harmony
established among the people. In consequence of this information, I directed that 200 dragoons, under Major Sumner, should
remain in New Mexico, and that the other 100, with two mountain
howitzers, under Capt. Moore, should accompany me as a guard
to Upper California. With this guard, we continued our march
to the south, on the right bank of the Del Norte, to the distance
of about 230 miles below Santa Fé, when, leaving that river on
the 15th October, in about the 33d deg. of latitude, we marched
westward for the Copper mines, which we reached on the 18th,
and on the 20th reached the river Gila, proceeded down the Gila,
crossing and recrossing it as often as obstructions in our front
rendered necessary; on the 11th November reached the Pimos
village, about 80 miles from the settlements in Sonora. These
Indians we found honest, and living comfortably, having made a
good crop this year; and we remained with them two days, to
rest our men, recruit our animals, and obtain provisions. On the
22d November, reached the mouth of the Gila, in latitude about
32 degrees—our whole march on this river having been nearly
500 miles, and, with but very little exception, between the 32d
and 33d parallels of latitude.

This river, (the Gila,) more particularly the northern side, is
bounded nearly the whole distance by a range of lofty mountains;

and if a tolerable wagon road to its mouth from the Del Norte is ever discovered, it must be on the south side. The country is destitute of timber, producing but few cotton-wood and musquit trees ; and though the soil on the bottom lands is generally good, yet we found but very little grass or vegetation, in consequence of the dryness of the climate and the little rain which falls here. The Pimos Indians, who make good crops of wheat, corn, vegetables, &c., irrigate the land by water from the Gila, as did the Aztecs, (the former inhabitants of the country,) the remains of whose sequias, or little canals, were seen by us, as well as the position of many of their dwellings, and a large quantity of broken pottery and earthenware used by them.

We crossed the Colorado about 10 miles below the mouth of the Gila, and marching near it about 30 miles further, turned off and crossed the desert—a distance of about 60 miles—without water or grass.

On the 2d December, reached Warner's rancho, (Agua Caliente,) the frontier settlement in California, on the route leading to Sonora. On the 4th we marched to Mr. Stokes's rancho, (San Isabella,) and on the 5th, were met by a small party of volunteers, under Capt. Gillespie, sent out from San Diego, by Com. Stockton, to give us what information they possessed of the enemy, 600 or 700 of whom are now said to be in arms and in the field throughout the territory, determined upon opposing the Americans and resisting their authority in the country. Encamped that night near another rancho (San Maria) of Mr. Stokes, about 40 miles from San Diego.

The journals and maps, kept and prepared by Capt. Johnston, (my aid-de-camp,) and those by Lieut. Emory, Topographical Engineers, which will accompany or follow this report, will render any thing further from me, on this subject, unnecessary.

Very respectfully, your obedient servant,

S. W. KEARNY,
Brigadier-general, U. S. A.

Brigadier-general R. JONES,
Adjutant-general, U. S. A.

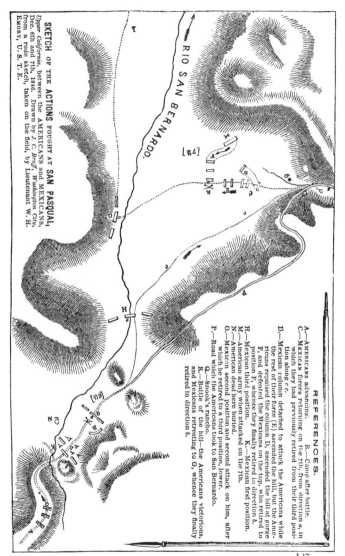

SKETCH OF THE ACTIONS FOUGHT AT SAN PASQUAL,

Upper California, between the AMERICANS and MEXICANS, Dec. 6th and 7th, 1846. Drawn by *J. C. Bruff, Washington City*, from a rude sketch, taken on the field, by Lieutenant W. H. EMORY, U. S. T. E.

RIO SAN BERNARDO.

REFERENCES.

A.—AMERICANS advancing. B.—Camp after battle.
C.—MEXICAN forces returning, on the 7th, from direction *a*, in which they had previously retired from their third position along *c c*.
D.—Mexican column detached to attack the Americans while the rest of their force (E) ascended the hill, but the Americans repulsed the column D, ascended the hill at gorge F, and defeated the Mexicans on the top, who retired to position F, whence they finally retired in direction *b*.
H.—Mexican third position. K.—Mexican first position.
M.—American army when attacked on the 7th.
N.—American dead here buried.
O.—Mexican second position and second attack on him, after which he retired to a third position, lower.
P.—Road which the Americans took to San Bernardo.
Q.—Snook's rancho.
R.—Battle of the hill—the Americans victorious, and Mexicans retreating to G, whence they finally retired in direction *b*.

HEAD-QUARTERS, ARMY OF THE WEST,
San Diego, Upper California, Dec. 13, 1846.

SIR: In my communication to you of yesterday's date, I brought the reports of the movements of my guard up to the morning of the 5th instant, in camp near a rancho of Mr. Stokes, (Santa Maria,) about 40 miles from San Diego.

Having learned from Capt. Gillespie, of the volunteers, that there was an armed party of Californians, with a number of extra horses at San Pasqual, three leagues distant, on a road leading to this place, I sent Lieut. Hammond, First Dragoons, with a few men to make a reconnoissance of them. He returned at two in the morning of the 6th instant, reporting that he had found the party in the place mentioned, and that he had been seen, though not pursued by them. I then determined that I would march for and attack them by break of day. Arrangements were accordingly made for the purpose. My aid-de-camp, Capt. Johnston, dragoons, was assigned to the command of the advanced guard of twelve dragoons, mounted on the best horses we had; then followed about fifty dragoons under Captain Moore, mounted, with but few exceptions, on the tired mules they had ridden from Santa Fé, (New Mexico, 1050 miles;) then about twenty volunteers of Captain Gibson's company under his command, and that of Capt. Gillespie; then followed our two mountain howitzers, with dragoons to manage them, and under the charge of Lieut. Davidson, of the 1st regiment. The remainder of the dragoons, volunteers, and citizens, employed by the officers of the staff, &c., were placed under the command of Major Swords, (quartermaster,) with orders to follow on our trail with the baggage, and to see to its safety.

As the day (December 6) dawned, we approached the enemy at San Pasqual, who was already in the saddle, when Capt. Johnston made a furious charge upon them with his advance guard, and was in a short time after supported by the dragoons; soon after which the enemy gave way, having kept up from the beginning a continued fire upon us. Upon the retreat of the enemy, Capt. Moore led off rapidly in pursuit, accompanied by the dragoons,

mounted on horses, and was followed, though slowly, by the others
on their tired mules ; the enemy, well mounted, and among the
best horsemen in the world, after retreating about half a mile, and
seeing an interval between Capt. Moore with his advance, and the
dragoons coming to his support, rallied their whole force, charged
with their lances, and, on account of their greatly superior numbers, but few of us in front remained untouched ; for five minutes
they held the ground from us, when our men coming up, we
again drove them, and they fled from the field, not to return to it,
which we occupied and encamped upon.

A most melancholy duty now remains for me : it is to report the
death of my aid-de-camp, Capt. Johnston, who was shot dead at
the commencement of the action ; of Capt. Moore, who was lanced
just previous to the final retreat of the enemy ; and of Lieut. Hammond, also lanced, and who survived but a few hours. We had
also killed two sergeants, two corporals, and ten privates of the
First Dragoons ; one private of the volunteers, and one man, an
engagé in the topographical department. Among the wounded
are myself, (in two places,) Lieut. Warner, Topographical Engineers, (in three places,) Capts. Gillespie and Gibson of the volunteers, (the former in three places,) one sergeant, one bugleman, and
nine privates of the dragoons ; many of these surviving from two
to ten lance wounds, most of them when unhorsed and incapable
of resistance.

Our howitzers were not brought into the action ; but coming to
the front at the close of it, before they were turned, so as to admit
of being fired upon the retreating enemy, the two mules before
one of them got alarmed, and freeing themselves from their drivers,
ran off, and among the enemy, and was thus lost to us.

The enemy proved to be a party of **160** Californians under An-
dreas Pico, brother of the late governor ; the number of their dead
and wounded must have been considerable, though I have no means
of ascertaining how many, as just previous to their final retreat,
they carried off all excepting six.

The great number of our killed and wounded proves that our
officers and men have fully sustained the high character and repu-

tation of our troops; and the victory thus gained over more than double our force, may assist in forming the wreath of our national glory.

I have to return my thanks to many for their gallantry and good conduct on the field, and particularly to Capt. Turner, First Dragoons, (assistant acting adjutant-general,) and to Lieut. Emory, Topographical Engineers, who were active in the performance of their duties, and in conveying orders from me to the command.

On the morning of the 7th, having made ambulances for our wounded, and interred the dead, we proceeded on our march, when the enemy showed himself, occupying the hills in our front, but which they left as we approached; till, reaching San Bernado, a party of them took possession of a hill near to it, and maintained their position until attacked by our advance, who quickly drove them from it, killing and wounding five of their number, with no loss on our part.

On account of our wounded men, and upon the report of the surgeon that rest was necessary for them, we remained at this place till the morning of the 11th, when Lieut. Gray, of the Navy, in command of a party of sailors and marines, sent out from San Diego by Com. Stockton, joined us. We proceeded at 10, a. m., the enemy no longer showing himself; and on the 12th, (yesterday,) we reached this place; and I have now to offer my thanks to Com. Stockton, and all of his gallant command, for the very many kind attentions we have received and continue to receive from them.

Very respectfully, your obedient servant,

S. W. KEARNY, *Brig. Gen. U. S. A.*

Brigadier-general R. JONES,

Adjutant-general U. S. A., Washington.

HEAD-QUARTERS ARMY OF THE WEST,
Ciudad de los Angeles, Upper California, Jan. 12, 1847.

SIR: I have the honour to report that, at the request of Com. R. F. Stockton, United States Navy, (who in September last assumed the title of governor of California,) I consented to take command of an expedition to this place, (the capital of the country,) and that, on the 29th December, I left San Diego with about 500 men, consisting of sixty dismounted dragoons under Capt. Turner, fifty California volunteers, and the remainder of marines and sailors, with a battery of artillery—Lieut. Emory (Topographical Engineers) acting as assistant adjutant-general. Com. Stockton accompanied us.

We proceeded on our route without seeing the enemy, till on the 8th instant, when they showed themselves in full force of 600 mounted men, with four pieces of artillery, under their governor, (Flores,) occupying the heights in front of us, which commanded the crossing of the river San Gabriel, and they ready to oppose our further progress. The necessary disposition of our troops was immediately made, by covering our front with a strong party of skirmishers, placing our wagons and baggage train in rear of them, and protecting the flanks and rear with the remainder of the command. We then proceeded, forded the river, carried the heights, and drove the enemy from them, after an action of about an hour and a half, during which they made a charge upon our left flank, which was repulsed; soon after which they retreated and left us in possession of the field, on which we encamped that night.

The next day (the 9th instant) we proceeded on our march at the usual hour, the enemy in our front and on our flanks: and when we reached the plains of the Mesa, their artillery again opened upon us, when their fire was returned by our guns as we advanced; and after hovering around and near us for about two hours, occasionally skirmishing with us during that time, they concentrated their force and made another charge on our left flank, which was quickly repulsed; shortly after which they retired, we continuing our march, and we (in the afternoon) encamped on the banks of the Mesa, three miles below this city, which we entered the following morning (the 10th instant) without further molestation.

Our loss in the actions of the 8th and 9th was small, being but one private killed, and two officers, Lieut. Rowan of the navy, and Capt. Gillespie, of the Volunteers, and eleven privates wounded. The enemy, mounted on fine horses, and being the

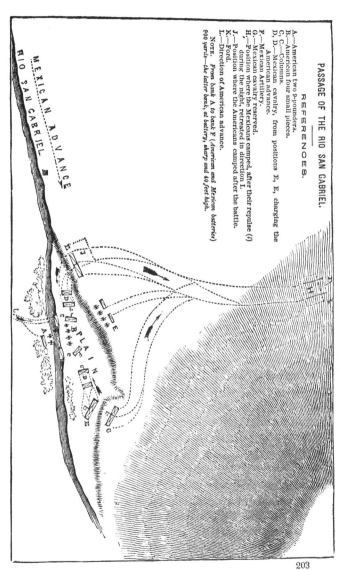

PASSAGE OF THE RIO SAN GABRIEL.

REFERENCES.

A.—American two 9-pounders.

B.—American four small pieces.

C, C.—Columns.

D, D.—Mexican advance.

F.—Mexican Artillery.

G.—Mexican cavalry reserved.

H.—Position where the Mexicans camped, after their repulse (?) during the night, retreated in direction I.

J.—Position where the Americans camped after the battle.

K.—Ford.

L.—Direction of American advance.

NOTE. *From bank A to bank F (American and Mexican batteries) 900 yards—the latter bank, at battery, sharp and 40 feet high.*

203

best riders in the world, carried off their killed and wounded, and we know not the number of them, though it must have been considerable.

Very respectfully, your obedient servant,

S. W. KEARNY,

Brigadier-general R. JONES,   *Brigadier-general.*

Adjutant-general, U. S. A., Washington.

Statement of killed and wounded in the action of the 8th January, 1847.

Killed.—Frederick Strauss, seaman, United States ship Portsmouth, artillery corps ; cannon-shot in neck.

Wounded.—1st. Jacob Hait, volunteer, artillery driver, wound in left breast; died on evening of 9th. 2d. Thos. Smith, ordinary seaman, United States ship Cyane, company D, musketeers, shot, by accident, through the right thigh ; died on night of the 8th. 3d. William Cope, seaman, United States ship Savannah, company B, musketeers, wound in the right thigh and right arm; severe. 4th. George Bantum, ordinary seaman, United States ship Cyane, pikeman, punctured wound of hand, accidental; slight. 5th. Patrick Cambell, seaman, United States ship Cyane, company D, musketeers, wound in thigh by spent ball; slight. 6th. William Scott, private, United States marine corps, ship Portsmouth, wound in the chest, spent ball; slight. 7th. James Hendry, seaman, United States ship Congress, company A, musketeers, spent ball, wound over stomach ; slight. 8th. Joseph Wilson, seaman, United States ship Congress, company A, musketeers, wound in right thigh, spent ball; slight. 9th. Ivory Coffin, seaman, United States ship Savannah, company B, musketeers, contusion of right knee, spent ball; slight.

Wounded on the 9th.—1st. Mark A. Child, private, company C, First Regiment United States Dragoons, gunshot wound in right heel, penetrating upwards into the ankle-joint; severe. 2d. James Cambell, ordinary seaman, United States ship Congress, company D, carbineers, wound in right foot, second toe amputated ; accidental discharge of his own carbine. 3d. George

s

Crawford, boatswain's mate, United States ship Cyane, company D, musketeers, wound in left thigh ; severe.   Lieut. Rowan, United States navy, and Capt. Gillespie, California battalion, volunteers, contused slightly by spent balls.

I am, sir, most respectfully, your obedient servant,

JOHN S. GRIFFIN,

Capt. Wm. H. Emory,   *Assistant Surgeon, U. S. N.*
Assistant Adjutant-general, U. S. forces.
Ciudad de los Angeles, *California, Jan.* 11, 1847.

Head-quarters, Army of the West,
Ciudad de los Angeles, Upper California, January 14, 1847.

Sir : This morning, Lieutenant-colonel Fremont, of the regiment of mounted riflemen, reached here with 400 volunteers from the Sacramento ; the enemy capitulated with him yesterday, near San Fernando, agreeing to lay down their arms, and we have now the prospect of having peace and quietness in this country, which I hope may not be interrupted again.

I have not yet received any information of the troops which were to come from New York, nor of those to follow me from New Mexico, but presume they will be here before long.   On their arrival, I shall, agreeably to the instructions of the President of the United States, have the management of affairs in this country, and will endeavour to carry out his views in relation to it.

Very respectfully, your obedient servant,

S. W. KEARNY,

Brigadier-general R. Jones,   *Brigadier-general.*
Adjutant-general, U. S. A., Washington.

It will be seen that Col. Fremont reported his command, as above, to Gen. Kearny.   It was a few days afterwards, that unhappy difficulties arose between the parties in high command as to their relative powers.   These ended in Gen. Kearny's proceeding to San Diego, and from thence, by water, to Monterey, where, as will be seen by the joint "Circular," given in another chapter, Gen. Kearny was assigned, on the 1st of March, 1847, under authority of the President, "the direction of the operations on

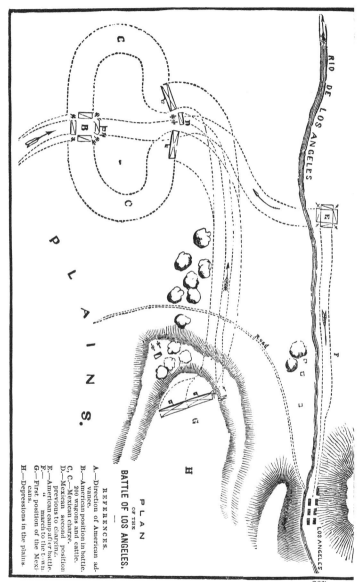

PLAN
OF THE
BATTLE OF LOS ANGELES.

REFERENCES.

A.—Direction of American advance.
B.—American position in battle.
C, C.—Mexican charge.
D.—Mexican second position 200 wagons and cattle.
E.—American camp after battle, previous to charging.
F.—" " march to the
G.—First position of the Mexicans.
H.—Depressions in the plains.

RIO DE LOS ANGELES

P L A I N S.

Road

LOS ANGELES

land," and invested " with administrative functions of government over the people and territory occupied by the forces of the United States."

At San Diego, Lieutenant-colonel Cooke joined Gen. Kearny with the Mormon Battalion, which he had brought in—with arms bright, fine health, excellent discipline, and without any serious loss from their long and weary march, and was posted at the mission of San Luis Rey to check any reinforcements to the Californians from the State of Sonora.

The following is Gen. Kearny's proclamation on assuming the civil government of California. Its re-translation from the Spanish may involve some inaccuracies, however substantially accurate the copy may otherwise be.

Proclamation to the People of California.

The President of the United States having devolved upon the undersigned the civil government of California, he enters upon the discharge of his duties with an ardent desire to promote as far as is possible the interests of the country and well being of the inhabitants.

The undersigned is instructed by the President to respect and protect the religious institutions of California, to take care that the religious rights of its inhabitants are secured in the most ample manner, since the Constitution of the United States allows to every individual the privilege of worshipping his Creator in whatever manner his conscience may dictate.

The undersigned is also instructed to protect the persons and property of the quiet and peaceable inhabitants of the country against each and every enemy, whether foreign or domestic ; and now assuring the Californians that his inclinations, no less than his duty, demand the fulfilment of these instructions, he invites them to use their best efforts to preserve order and tranquillity, to promote harmony and concord, and to maintain the authority and efficacy of the laws.

It is the desire and intention of the United States to procure for California as speedily as possible a free government like that of

s 2   14

their own territories, and they will very soon invite the inhabitants
to exercise the rights of free citizens in the choice of their own
representatives, who may enact such laws as they deem best
adapted to their interest and well-being. But until this takes
place, the laws actually in existence, which are not repugnant to
the Constitution of the United States, will continue in force until
they are revoked by competent authority; and persons in the exercise of public employments will for the present remain in them,
provided they swear to maintain the said constitution, and faithfully discharge their duties.

The undersigned by these presents absolves all the inhabitants
of California of any further allegiance to the Republic of Mexico, and
regards them as citizens of the United States. Those who remain
quiet and peaceable will be respected and protected in their rights;
but should any one take up arms against the government of this
territory, or join such as do so, or instigate others to do so—all
these he will regard as enemies, and they will be treated as such.

When Mexico involved the United States in war, the latter had
not time to invite the Californians to join their standard as friends,
but found themselves compelled to take possession of the country
to prevent its falling into the hands of some European power. In
doing this, there is no doubt that some excesses, some unauthorized
acts, were committed by persons in the service of the United States,
and that in consequence some of the inhabitants have sustained
losses in their property. These losses shall be duly investigated,
and those who are entitled to indemnification shall receive it.

For many years California has suffered great domestic convul-
sions; from civil wars, like poisoned fountains, have flowed
calamity and pestilence over this beautiful region. These fountains
are now dried up; the stars and stripes now float over California,
and as long as the sun shall shed its light, they will continue to
wave over her, and over the natives of the country, and over those
who shall seek a domicile in her bosom; and under the protection
of this flag, agriculture must advance, and the arts and sciences
will flourish like seed in rich and fertile soil.

Americans and Californians! from henceforth one people. Let

us then indulge one desire, one hope; let that be for the peace and tranquillity of our country. Let us unite like brothers, and mutually strive for the mutual improvement and advancement of this our beautiful country, which within a short period cannot fail to be not only beautiful, but also prosperous and happy.

Given at Monterey, capital of California, this 1st day of March, of the year of our Lord, 1847, and of the Independence of the United States the 71st.

S. W. KEARNY,

Brigadier-general U. S. A., and Governor of California.

On the 2d of March, Gen. Kearny ordered the government archives to Monterey,—the reorganization of the California battalion, &c.

Early in this month, Lieut. Emory, the adjutant-general of Gen. Kearny's forces, and Lieut. Gray of the navy, were sent home with important despatches for the government, and arrived in Washington in the latter part of April following.

Capt. Tompkins and his company, of the Third United States Artillery, arrived very early in February, and were stationed at Monterey.

Military supplies of the quarter-master's department had been personally obtained from the Sandwich Islands by the strenuous exertions of Major Swords.

On the 6th of March, Col. Stevenson arrived in the ship T. H. Perkins, at San Francisco, with 250 of the New York California Volunteers. The residue of the regiment followed soon after.

Col. Stevenson was ordered to occupy Monterey with four companies, and Lieutenant-colonel Burton, with three companies of the same regiment, was stationed at Santa Barbara.

In the mean time a large proportion of the emigrants who came to California the year before, and who had been immediately and almost to a man called up to bear arms in defence of the American flag, were with characteristic energy seeking settlements.

Towns and settlements were in progress. Fortifications were being permanently erected at the most prominent assailable points.

At the Bay of San Francisco, a town of the same name arose, and the site of the town is said to be the "most commanding commercial position on the entire western coast of the Pacific ocean."

Decree of Governor Kearny.

I, Brigadier-general S. W. Kearny, Governor of California, by virtue of authority in me vested by the President of the United States of America, do hereby grant, convey and release unto the town of San Francisco, the people, or corporate authorities thereof, all the right, title and interest of the government of the United States, and the Territory of California, in and to the beach and water lots on the east front of said town of San Francisco, included between the points known as the Rincon and Fort Montgomery, excepting such lots as may be selected for the use of the United States government by the senior officers of the army and navy now there ; provided, the said ground hereby ceded shall be divided into lots, and sold by public auction to the highest bidder, after three months' notice previously given—the proceeds of said sale to be for the benefit of the town of San Francisco.

Given at Monterey, capital of California, this 10th day of March, 1847, and the seventy-first year of the Independence of the United States.   S. W. KEARNY,
Brigadier-general and Governor of California.

Another town was located at Monterey Bay. In fact, government was established, a legislative council elected, civil officers appointed, &c.

The time of the Mormon battalion, stationed at Monterey and at San Diego, expired on the 16th of July, when the land forces would consist of Col. Stevenson's regiment, one company of dragoons, (at Los Angeles,) and one of light artillery, at Monterey. With this force and naval co-operation, there existed no reason to believe that the peaceful relations of the country would be again disturbed.

The last act of Gen. Kearny was to order Lieut. Col. Burton to proceed by sea to Lower California, and, disembarking at La Paz, to take possession of that country.

On the 31st of May, 1847, Gen. Kearny having devolved the government on Col. Richard B. Mason, of the First Dragoons, as governor and commander-in-chief, set out on his return to the United States.

Gen. Kearny's party consisted of Captains Turner and Cooke, of the First Dragoons, and Major Thomas Swords of the United States quartermaster department, all officers who had largely and honourably participated in the conquest of California and New Mexico, with Lieut. Radford, of the United States navy, who had distinguished him at Mazatlan and in California. Willard P. Hall of Missouri, who personated in New Mexico the citizen soldier, aiding in its conquest as a private, and called from the ranks to frame, with Doniphan and Kearny, its laws, now returned, to find himself elected by the free suffrage of his fellow citizens of Missouri, their representative in Congress, together with Dr. Sanderson of Missouri, and Lieut. Col. Fremont with his original engineering party.

The hazards and difficulties of their route contrast strangely with the luxurious comforts of railroads, steamboats, stages and turnpikes which traverse almost any equal distance of the extremes of this wide Union. Their journey becomes the more interesting that it affords some idea of the sufferings of the unprepared and unprovided Mormons and emigrants, in a winter's passage of the Rocky Mountains.

Did our design admit of detail, large and most interesting extracts would be here made of Gen. Kearny's, and others', route homewards, from the journal of a gallant and highly intelligent officer of his staff. The outlines must, however, suffice; excepting that the burial of the dead emigrants claims a place in full.

"There was colder weather in March, in California, than had been experienced there for twenty years. Before reaching Sutter's, the party were forced to swim four or five mountain torrents, swollen by the melting snow to the breadth of rivers—the baggage and provisions were crossed in skin boats made upon the spot. Their progress was slow, and most laborious and hazardous; and one of the officers, Major Cooke, lost by an upset, save saddle and blankets, his entire outfit, even to papers and specie."

The last rancho was left on the 18th of June. On the 21st they struck the Juba, which was overflowing, hence they passed higher up, and crossed the Sierra Nevada, on which the snow was fifteen feet deep, and through which the mules were constantly breaking and burying themselves. The mountain torrents were all swollen as the winter suddenly changed to spring, while the snow beneath their feet and overhanging from the mountain cliffs, threatened to engulf or overwhelm them alternately or simultaneously. Thus they passed the remains of (or rather clothes of) Strattan, an emigrant, who, becoming snow-blind, had been abandoned by his companions, and here starved to death. The party of Gen. Kearny experienced great pain from the reflection of the snow, having to protect their eyes with their handkerchiefs.

"On the 22d, they had gone five miles beyond the beautiful Turkey lake, surrounded by mountains capped with snow, when they came to 'Cannibal Camp,' so called from the deplorable state to which a party of emigrants were reduced in the year 1846. They had been overtaken by the snow and built cabins, intending to winter. But the snow fell to the depth of twenty-five or thirty feet, and out of eighty, forty-five perished there. Those that survived lived on those that perished of starvation. The party found a skull that had been sawn in two to reach its contents—with five perfect skeletons, and other remains. These were buried in the best manner the means of the party admitted of. In fact, it is stated, that from the time of their entering the mountains they had been constantly passing the remains of some poor emigrant.

"On the eastern slope, they were forced to pass trackless mountains of black rock, by the Trucky (or Salmon Trout) river. In the narrow pass, the road (made in autumn) very frequently crosses it; some of its small branches presented, besides a swimming deep torrent, hundreds of yards of dangerous bog and mire. On this river they were visited by the 'Digger Indians.'

"The party were nearly out of provisions of all sorts when they met the first emigrants at the falls of Snake river, (Lewis Fork,)

25 miles beyond Fort Hall. They passed by that trading-post on the 15th of July. On Bear river they obtained a recruit of horses and mules from the Snake Indians.

"The party came the new road, about 50 miles, without water: from Green river to Big Sandy. Besides some companies who went round by Bridger's Fort, they met about 940 wagons of emigrants—all, or nearly all, bound to Oregon. The last were met between the North Fork of Platte and Sweet Water, on the 28th July; they were believed to be, and considered themselves, too late to reach Oregon; and spoke of passing the winter at Fort Bridger. They left St. Joseph about the 6th of June.

"At Fort Laramie the party found many lodges of Sioux, who were quite friendly. They left that fort on the 3d inst. Next day they met 685 wagons of Mormons, who were advancing very slowly in parties of fifty; they had come all the way by the north bank of the Platte—they expecting to winter on the great Salt Lake; and this, they assert, is to be the final resting-place of their people. Incredible numbers of buffaloes were passed through for several days, near the junction of the two Plattes. No Indians were encountered after this time.

"The party was only 66 days from the settlements of California to Fort Leavenworth, and made not a day's stop—averaging for the last 57 days 31 miles: whole distance near 2,200 miles."

From Fort Leavenworth, Gen. Kearny paid a short visit to his family at St. Louis, Mo., where his friends and fellow-citizens greeted his return with congratulations and festivities, from which he hastened to Washington City, to attend an important court-martial, which, if it evince the fact of any discord between commanders as to relative rank, prerogative or deserving, can subtract nothing from the united or individual gallantry of the conquest of California and New Mexico.

CHAPTER X.

Col. Sterling Price—Lieut. Col. Willock—Missouri mounted Volunteers—Gen.
Kearny—Col. Doniphan—Col. Price remains at Santa Fé—Conspiracy—
Gov. Bent's Proclamation—Organization of Government—Sickness of Troops
—Enterprise and Amusements—Revolution—Murder of Gov. Bent and others
—Americans to be put to death—Letters intercepted—Enemy approaching
Santa Fé—Troops called together—Advance on the Enemy—Battles of Ca-
nada and Embudo—Battle of the Pueblo de Taos—Death of Capt. Burgwin
—Funerals and graves of Bent and Burgwin—People urged to rise—Massa-
cres—Fight at Moro—Capt. Henley killed—Capt. Morin destroys the Town—
The Father-in-law of Archuleta—Leaders delivered up—Tried and Executed
—State of Affairs in New Mexico—Revolutionary Spirit—Route between
Santa Fé and Fort Leavenworth dangerous—Lieut. Peck—Incidents of the
Desert—Indians very Hostile—Engagement with Apaches—Lieut. Brown
killed—Surprise and Capture of Los Pias—Loquesta, &c.—Prisoners—Exe-
cutions—Expiration of Terms of Service of Volunteers—Lieut. Love's Battle
with the Indians—Indian Aggression—Measures taken to Repress and Punish
—No organized resistance in New Mexico—Arrival of new Levies—Col.
Price created a Brigadier-general—Visits Missouri to return to Santa Fé.

UNDER an apprehension that the force which left Fort Leavenworth, in June, 1846, might not be sufficient fully to effect the
purposes of the expedition, which was, if found practicable, to
pass on to *California*, after conquering and securing *New Mexico*,
the President of the United States had accepted the services of an
additional regiment and battalion of Missouri mounted Volunteers,
who were sent on to Santa Fé, as reinforcements, and to augment
Gen. Kearny's disposable force for California; but they had not
joined him when he departed for that country, on the 25th of
September. The commanders of these reinforcements were Col.
Sterling Price, who had resigned his seat in Congress to serve
under the eagles of the republic, and Lieut. Col. Willock, of Missouri.

The prompt and energetic manner in which Gen. Kearny conducted the Santa Fé expedition has been sketched. When he
determined to leave for Upper California, with only about one

hundred men, orders were left with Col. Doniphan to make the march to Chihuahua, (which he so gloriously executed,) on the arrival of Col. Price, then daily expected.

Col. Price, thus left in command of the residue of the army of the west, had been instructed to occupy Santa Fé, Taos, and other points of New Mexico with his troops.

On the departure of Gen. Kearny for California, the inhabitants, not only at Santa Fé, but throughout the whole of New Mexico, were represented to be well satisfied with the change which had taken place, and the general had reported that "there could no longer be apprehended any organized resistance to our troops in that territory."*

Rumours of a revolution, however, began to be spoken of among the Mexicans in about two months after his departure, but the apparent willingness with which they submitted to the new government established over them, lulled all into the belief of a quiet submission.

An attempt to produce a revolution was concerted at the house of Thomas Ortiz, where, on the night of the 15th of December, met Don Thomas Ortiz, Don Diego Archuleta, Don Nicholas Pino, Don Santiago Armijo, Don Miguel Pino, Don Manuel Charaez, Don Domingo Boca, Don Pablo Dominguez, and Don Juan Lopez. These principal chiefs of the revolt conspired to surprise the guards, and to take bloody possession of Santa Fé., Ortiz was to be in chief command, and Archuleta second in authority. The first plan was for the conspirators to assemble with all their men, on Saturday evening, the 19th of December, in the parish church. Thence dividing themselves into several parties they were to sally forth, some to seize the pieces of artillery, others to go to the quarters of Col. Price, and others to go to the palace of Governor Bent, if he should be in Santa Fé, and if not, to send an order to Taos to seize him, thinking him the one who would give them most trouble. This was agreed upon by all. The church bell was to be the signal for the assault, from the forces concealed in

---

* Report of Secretary of War, Dec. 5, 1846.

T

the building, and for those which Don Diego Archuleta should have brought near the city. Midnight was the time agreed upon: all were to enter the plaza at the same moment, seize the pieces of artillery, point them into the streets, &c.

The time was afterwards postponed, and the attempt was to have been made on Christmas night, when a great number of New Mexicans were expected to congregate in Santa Fé, for the purpose of attending the ceremonies of the Catholic church, and that they might gain over the whole department. For this last purpose, Archuleta was to go to the valley of Taos, and the leaders to different sections of the country, but the whole plot was disclosed to the Americans by Mexican women, and the authorities were able to secure a good many of the leaders. Ortiz and Archuleta fled. No positive evidence could be obtained against the other leaders, and they were released upon promise of good behaviour. Confidence was again restored. The Mexicans, previous to the receipt of the news of Col. Doniphan's capture of Chihuahua, were very haughty—they would jostle the Americans in the street—refuse to speak with them, except to offer wagers that Col. Doniphan was a prisoner in Chihuahua. As soon, however, as intelligence of the battle was received, they became crest-fallen, and full of friendly professions. This appearance of amity was wholly deceptive. The fire of revenge was still burning beneath.

It was at this time that the following proclamation was issued :

Charles Bent, governor of the Territory of New Mexico, to the inhabitants :

Fellow-citizens : A concurrence of extraordinary events crowd upon me, and furnish me with materials to address you for the first time. I will not make use of eloquent or sublime language, for truth needs not the ornaments of flattery to cause an impression— its attractions are inherent, and will always obtain credence.

I arrived in this country for the first time in 1829; from my first acquaintance with it, your ingenuous and frank character aroused my sympathy, which has now taken deep root, and I joined my destiny to yours. New Mexico became my adopted country; all my interests are centered in its soil, and the more so at present, since joined to the United States, my native country, you compose a part of the Union, the cradle of liberty.

Gen. S. W. Kearny took military possession of this Territory on the 18th of August of last year, and he experienced the most lively pleasure in finding that without the force of arms, without mourning, or tears, you acknowledged the republican government, to which you now belong. You are now governed by new laws, and you now enjoy the free government promised to you by his proclamation. Use this liberty with moderation. This will enable you to gather the rich fruits which await you for the future.

Those who composed this blind opposition; who, notorious for their vices, and full of ambition, aspired to the first offices—and those who thought to bind the people slaves to their caprices, undeceived, and finding that they could not obtain the offices conferred on honest and meritorious men—Thomas Ortiz and the old revolutionist Diego Archuleta—rushed forward desperately to head a revolution against the present government. They collected in this capital, in the middle of last month, a few heedless and unprincipled persons, who, after attending their meetings, were persuaded to seize the standard of rebellion. This treason was discovered very opportunely, and smothered at its birth; they are now fugitives, but their doctrines are still disseminated among the people, and cause some anxiety, as the discontented who remain give publicity to their destructive plans.

The organic law and the statutes are the basis on which these anarchists repose; they say that contributions and land are the maxims of the present government; that it wishes to levy the former and deprive you of the possession of the latter—astounding falsehood! Examine the laws from the beginning to the end, and you will not find a single page that upholds the falsity. The statutes, it is true, impose duties on commerce, and on distilleries, but in no manner do they impose taxes on the people. There is, likewise, an office established for the registering of land-titles, but this is to secure to you the titles of your property, and not to despoil you of them, as the revolutionists would induce you to believe. They likewise avail themselves of other means to create alarm, deceiving you by the report that troops are coming from the interior to reconquer this country. What succour can you expect from the department of Chihuahua, your nearest neighbour, when there the spirit of party has crushed and reduced to a nullity its inhabitants?

Col. Doniphan, who was advancing on the Pueblo del Paso with his regiment, was attacked by a superior force at the Punto del Brazito—in a few minutes they were routed with the loss of thirty men. Such, my friends, are the futility and artifices with which these turbulent spirits would delude you! Listen not, I beseech you, to their false and poisonous doctrines—remain quiet in your domestic occupations, that under the protection of the laws, you may enjoy the unspeakable blessing offered, and uniting with your government you may point out any measures which may tend to the improvement of your country, and thus enjoy, individually, all the happiness which your best friend wishes you.

Santa Fé, January 5, 1847.   CHARLES BENT.

The organization of the government had progressed until the numerous appointments, civil officers, &c., of the territory had been filled up—clerks of courts, prefects, or county judges, sheriffs, &c., had been made. Among these, James White Leal, a volunteer of Capt. Hudson's company, was appointed attorney for Taos, or the northern judicial district, and Stephen Lee, formerly of St. Louis, but then a citizen, became the sheriff of the same.

In the meanwhile, there had been considerable sickness among the troops, which resulted in thinning their ranks, and in a conclusion that, of the Missourians, the troops from the city of St. Louis best preserved their health, those from St. Louis county next, and the country troops least successfully. Many died from nearly every company of the volunteers.

Nothing daunted, however, the spirit of enterprise among them set every thing in motion. Mills were established, fortifications erected, troops drilled, and a printing-press established. Nor were amusements wanting. A Thespian society was organized, principally from the men of St. Louis, and a room in the palacio was permitted by the governor to be fitted up as a theatre—scenes painted, an orchestra organized, and, in fact, all appointments provided. The gentlemen undertook *all* the characters, and were well sustained by crowded houses. These dramatic entertainments had most potent charms for the men of Col. Price's regiment. As a relic of the time, "the bill" for the night of the 25th of December is here given:

SANTA FE THEATRE!
ON CHRISTMAS NIGHT

Will be presented the tragedy of

BARBAROSSA!

Achmet	Mr. McSorley.
Othman	Livingston.
Yuseff	Eldridge.
Aladin	Hinton.
Barbarossa	Thomas.
Sadi	Work.
Hassan	Johnson.
Slave	Doty.
Zaphira	Miss Shands.
Irene	Chambers.

After which,

LA POLKA!
By an American gentleman and Spanish lady.

☞ Mr. CHAMBERS, (from Chicago,) the young Dempster, will sing "The Maniac," "Irish Emigrant's Lament," "The Old Arm Chair," and the "Blind Boy."

After which, the farce of

FORTUNE'S FROLIC!

Robin Roughhead	Mr. McSorley.
Snacks	Livingston.
Mr. Frank	Shands.
Rattle	Thomas.
Clown	Fox.
Miss Nancy	Miss Kennerly.
Dolly	Chambers.
Margery	Miller.

The whole to conclude with the

VIRGINIA MINSTRELS!
SONGS—"The Old Coloured Gentleman," "Get along home, you Spanish Gals," "Blue Tail Fly," and "You aint good looking and you can't come in."

☞ Doors open at 6; curtain rises at 6½.

T 2

At this period the Americans at Santa Fé had only about **500** effective men—the rest were on the sick list—or were, in detachments, at distant points of the country, whither the horses had been sent to graze, on account of the want of forage of any kind within any reasonable distance of Santa Fé, or were garrisoning outposts. The civil government went into active operation. On the first of December, Judge Hougton opened his first court at Santa Fé, and delinquents became amenable to the laws, and to punishment, on condemnation, after a fair trial.

Gov. Charles Bent had, previous to his installation, resided at Taos, whither, confiding in this apparent tranquillity, he went, on the 14th of January, to attend to some private business.

The Pueblos of Taos were accounted the most warlike and the bravest race in Mexico; certainly the circumstances of the murder of Gov. Bent, on the 19th, evince their extreme barbarity. Two Pueblo Indians had been confined in the calaboose at Taos, for crime. The Indians from their village, two miles distant, came to the prison and demanded their release from the sheriff, Stephen L. Lee, who, perceiving his life in danger, was about to comply, when the prefect, Cornelius Vigil, a Mexican, came in and forbid it. The Indians immediately killed him and Lee, and released the prisoners. They then proceeded towards the residence of Gov. Bent; but before their arrival he was informed of their approach. He instantly dressed himself, (for it was early,) and seized his pistols. A woman in the house advised him to fight, but he said it would be useless with such a crowd of savages. His object was to get into the streets to find assistance, or to escape. From one of the rooms of his house there was a window opening into that of another person, which was immediately on the street. Through this he was passing when he received two arrows from the Indians, who had covered the house-tops. He got to the door, and asked assistance from persons present: their answer was that they could do nothing—that he must die. By this time, the Indians found means to get into the house, when they shot him through the body and killed him. Tomas, who was taken after the battle at Pueblo de Taos, then took the governor's pistol, and shot him in the face.

They then scalped him, stretched his body on a board with brass nails, and paraded it through the streets with savage yells. The fate of Mr. Leal, the district-attorney, was still more horrible, for they murdered him with all the refinement of savage barbarity. They shot arrows into his body for some time, not sufficiently deep to destroy life, and, after that, they shot them into his face and eyes, and then scalped him alive. After torturing him thus for a long time, they finally despatched him, and threw his body into the street. They also murdered and scalped the son of Judge Baubien, who had just returned from school in the United States, and a friendly Mexican, named Harvimeah.

They then despatched messengers to inform the country people below that a blow had been struck, and invited their aid to prosecute the revolt. These messengers were arrested, and fell into the hands of the Americans—one by the alcalde of Moro, and the other by a Frenchman of Cañada. The latter, hearing that a man had gone down, saddled his horse, and with his rifle, started in pursuit. He headed off the messenger, and presenting his rifle, demanded the letter, which was delivered to him. Being unable to read, he carried it to the next alcalde, and again cocked his rifle, and ordered him to read it. Thus possessed of the facts, he galloped to Santa Fé, and laid the whole before Col. Price, who describes the subsequent events, in an official despatch:

HEAD-QUARTERS, ARMY IN NEW MEXICO,
Santa Fé, Feb. 15, 1847.

SIR: I have the honour to submit to you a short account of the recent *revolution* in this Territory, and a detailed report of the operations of the forces under my command, consequent upon the rebellion.

About the 15th of December last I received information of an attempt to excite the people of this territory against the American government. This rebellion was headed by Thomas Ortiz and Diego Archuleta. An officer, formerly in the Mexican service, was seized, and on his person was found a list of all the disbanded Mexican soldiers in the vicinity of Santa Fé. Many other persons, supposed to be implicated, were arrested, and a full investigation proved that many of the most influential persons in the northern part of this territory were engaged in the rebellion. All attempts to arrest Ortiz and Archuleta proved unsuccessful, and these rebels have, without doubt, escaped in the direction of Chihuahua.

After the arrest above mentioned and the flight of Ortiz and Archuleta, the rebellion appeared to be suppressed; but this appearance was deceptive.

On the 14th of January, Gov. Bent left this city for Taos. On the 19th of the same month, this valuable officer, together with five other persons, were seized at Don Fernando de Taos by the Pueblos and Mexicans, and murdered in the most inhuman manner the savages could devise. On the same day, seven Americans were murdered at the Arroya Honda, and two others on the Rio Colorado. The names of the unfortunate persons thus brutally butchered are as follows:

At Don Fernando de Taos.—Charles Bent, governor; Stephen Lee, sheriff; James W. Leal, circuit attorney; Cornelio Vigil, (a Mexican,) prefect; Narcisus Baubien, (son of the circuit judge;) Parbleau Harvimeah, (a Mexican.)

At the Arroya Honda.—Simeon Turley, Albert Turbush, William Hatfield, Louis Tolque, Peter Robert, Joseph Marshall, William Austin.

At the Rio Colorado.—Mark Head, William Harwood.

It appeared to be the object of the insurrectionists to put to death every American and every Mexican who had accepted office under the American government.

News of these events reached me on the 20th of January; and letters from the rebels, calling upon the inhabitants of the Rio Abajo for aid, were intercepted. It was now ascertained that the enemy was approaching this city, and that their force was continually being increased by the inhabitants of the towns along their line of march.

In order to prevent the enemy from receiving any further reinforcements in that manner, I determined to meet them as soon as possible. Supposing that the detachment of necessary troops would weaken the garrison of Santa Fé too much, I immediately ordered up from Albuquerque, Major Edmonson, Second Regiment Missouri mounted Volunteers, and Capt. Burgwin, with their respective commands, directing Capt. Burgwin to leave one company of dragoons at this post, and to join me with the other. Major Edmonson was directed to remain in Santa Fé.

Capt. Giddings, company A, Second Regiment Missouri mounted Volunteers, was also ordered to join me with his company, upon the arrival of Capt. Burgwin.

Leaving Lieutenant-colonel Willock in command of this post, on the 23d of January, I marched from this place at the head of companies D, Capt. McMillin, K, Capt. Williams, L, Capt. Slack, M, Capt. Halley, and N, Capt. Barber, of the Second Regiment Missouri mounted Volunteers, Capt. Angney's battalion of infantry, and a company of Santa Fé volunteers, commanded by Capt. St. Vrain. I also took with me four mountain howitzers, which I placed under the command of Lieut. A. B. Dyer, of the Ordnance. My whole force composed 353 rank and file, and, with the exception of Capt. St. Vrain's company, were all dismounted. On the march, Capt. Williams was taken sick, and the command of company K devolved upon Lieut. B. F. White. On the 24th of January, at half-past one P. M., our advance, Capt. St. Vrain's company, discovered the enemy in considerable force near the town of Cañada, their position, at that time, being in the valley bordering the Rio del Norte. Preparations were immediately made by me to attack them; and it became necessary for the troops to march more rapidly than the ammunition and provision wagons could travel, in order to prevent the escape of the enemy, or to frustrate them in any attempt they might make to occupy commanding positions. As I entered the valley, I discovered them beyond the creek on which the town is situated, and in full possession of the heights commanding the road to Cañada, and of three strong houses at the bases of the hills. My line of battle was immediately formed—the artillery, consisting of four twelve-

15

pounder mountain howitzers, being thrown forward on the left flank and beyond the creek, the dismounted men occupying a position where they would be, in some degree, protected by the high bluff bank of the stream, from the fire of the enemy, until the wagon train could be brought up. The artillery opened on the houses occupied by the enemy, and on the more distant height, on which alone the guns could be brought to bear. The enemy discovering the wagons to be more than a mile in the rear, sent a large party to cut them off; and it became necessary to detach Capt. St. Vrain's company for their protection. This service was rendered in the most satisfactory manner. So soon as the wagon train had been brought up, I ordered Capt. Angney to charge with his battalion of infantry, and dislodge the enemy from the house opposite the right flank, and from which a warm fire was being poured on us. This was done in the most gallant manner. A charge was then ordered to be made upon all the points occupied by the enemy in any force. Capt. Angney, with his command, supported by Lieut. White's company, charged up one hill, while Capt. St. Vrain's company turned the same, in order to cut off the enemy when in retreat. The artillery, supported by Captains McMillen, Barber, and Slack, with their respective companies, at the same time took possession of some houses, (enclosed by a strong corial densely wooded with fruit trees, from which a brisk fire was kept up by the enemy,) and of the heights beyond them. Capt. Halley's company was ordered to support Capt. Angney. In a few minutes my troops had dislodged the enemy at all points, and they were flying in every direction. The nature of the ground rendered pursuit hopeless ; and it being near night, I ordered the troops to take up quarters in the town. The number of the enemy was about 1500. Lieut. Irvine was wounded. In this charge, my loss was two killed and six wounded. Of the killed, one was a teamster, who volunteered in Capt. Angney's company. The loss of the enemy was thirty-six killed ; wounded not ascertained. The next morning, the enemy showed themselves in some force (I think not less than 400) on the distant heights. Leaving a strong guard in the town, I marched in pursuit of them; but they were so shy, and retreated so rapidly, that, finding it impossible to get near them, I returned to town.

While at Cañada, a number of the horses belonging to Capt. Slack's company were brought in by Lieut. Holcomb.

On the 27th, I advanced up the Rio del Norte as far as Luceros, where, early on the 28th, I was joined by Capt. Burgwin, commanding company G, First Dragoons, and company A, Second Regiment Missouri mounted Volunteers, commanded by Lieut. Boone. Capt. Burgwin's command was dismounted, and great credit is due to him and his officers and men for the rapidity with which a march so long and arduous was performed. At the same time Lieut. Wilson, First Dragoons, who had volunteered his services, came up with a six-pounder, which had been sent for from Cañada.

My whole force now comprised 479 rank and file. On the 29th I marched to La Joya, where I learned that a party of sixty or eighty of the enemy had posted themselves on the steep slopes of the mountains which rise on each side of the cañon or gorge, which leads to Embudo. Finding the road by Embudo impracticable for artillery or wagons, I detached Capt. Burgwin, in that direction, with his own company of dragoons and the companies commanded by Capt. St. Vrain, and Lieut White. This detachment comprised 180 rank and file.

By my permission, Adjutant R. Walker, Second regiment Missouri mounted Volunteers, accompanied Capt. Burgwin. Lieut. Wilson, First Dragoons, also volunteered his services as a private in Capt. St. Vrain's company.

Capt. Burgwin, pushing forward, discovered the enemy, to the number of between six and seven hundred, posted on the sides of the mountains, just where the gorge becomes so contracted as scarcely to admit of the passage of three men marching abreast.

The rapid slopes of the mountains rendered the enemy's position very strong, and its strength was increased by the dense masses of cedar and large fragments of rock which everywhere offered them shelter. The action was commenced by Capt. St. Vrain, who, dismounting his men, ascended the mountain on the left, doing much execution. Flanking parties were thrown out on either side, commanded respectively by Lieut. White. Second regiment Missouri mounted Volunteers, and by Lieut. McIlvaine and Taylor, First Dragoons. These parties ascended the hills rapidly, and the enemy soon began to retire in the direction of Embudo, bounding along the steep and rugged sides of the mountains with a speed that defied pursuit. The firing at the pass of Embudo had been heard at La Joya, and Capt. Slack, with twenty-five mounted men, had been immediately despatched thither. He now arrived and rendered excellent service by relieving Lieut. White, whose men were much fatigued. Lieuts. McIlvaine and Taylor were also recalled; and Lieut. Ingalls was directed to lead a flanking party on the right slope, while Capt. Slack performed the same duty on the left. The enemy having by this time retreated beyond our reach, Capt. Burgwin marched through the defile, and debouching into the open valley in which Embudo is situated, recalled the flanking parties, and entered that town without opposition, several persons meeting him with a white flag.

Our loss in this action was one man killed, and one severely wounded, both belonging to Capt. St. Vrain's company. The loss of the enemy was about twenty killed, and sixty wounded.

Thus ended the battle of the pass of Embudo.

On the 30th, Capt. Burgwin marched to Trampas, where he was directed to await the arrival of the main body, which, on account of the artillery and wagons, was forced to pursue a more southern route. On the 31st, I reached Trampas; and being joined by Capt. Burgwin, marched on to Chamisal with the whole command. On the 1st of February, we reached the summit of the Taos mountain, which was covered with snow to the depth of two feet; and on the 2d, quartered at a small village called Rio Chicito, in the entrance of the valley of Taos. The marches of the 1st and 2d were through deep snow. Many of the men were frostbitten, and all were very much jaded with the exertions necessary to travel over unbeaten roads, being marched in front of the artillery and wagons, in order to break a road through the snow. The constancy and patience with which the troops bore these hardships,

deserve all commendation, and cannot be excelled by the most
veteran soldiers.   On the 3d, I marched through Don Fernando de
Taos, and finding that the enemy had fortified themselves in the
Pueblo de Taos, proceeded to that place.   I found it a place of
great strength, being surrounded by adobe walls and strong pickets.
Within the enclosure and near the northern and southern walls,
arose two large buildings of irregular pyramidal form to the height
of seven or eight stories.   Each of these buildings was capable
of sheltering five or six hundred men.   Besides these, there were
many smaller buildings, and the large church of the town was
situated in the north-western angle, a small passage being left between it and the outer wall.   The exterior wall and all the enclosed buildings were pierced for rifles.   The town was admirably
calculated for defence, every point of the exterior walls and pickets
being flanked by some projecting building, as will be seen from
the enclosed drawing.

After having reconnoitered the town, I selected the western
flank of the church as the point of attack ; and about 2 o'clock,
P. M., Lieut. Dyer was ordered to open his battery at the distance
of about 250 yards.   A fire was kept up by the six-pounder and
the howitzers, for about two hours and a half, when, as the ammunition wagon had not yet come up, and the troops were suffering from cold and fatigue, I returned to Don Fernando.   Early on
the morning of the 4th, I again advanced upon Pueblo.   Posting
the dragoons under Capt. Burgwin, about 260 yards from the
western flank of the church, I ordered the mounted men under
Capts. St. Vrain and Slack, to a position on the opposite side of
the town, whence they could discover and intercept any fugitives
who might attempt to escape towards the mountains, or in the
direction of Don Fernando.   The residue of the troops took ground
about 300 yards from the northern wall.   Here, too, Lieut. Dyer
established himself with the six-pounder and two howitzers, while
Lieut. Hassendeubel, of Major Clark's battalion light artillery,
remained with Capt. Burgwin, in command of two howitzers.   By
this arrangement a cross-fire was obtained, sweeping the front and
eastern flank of the church.

U

All these arrangements having been made, the batteries opened upon the town at 9 o'clock, A. M.   At 11 o'clock, finding it impossible to breach the walls of the church with the six-pounder and howitzers, I determined to storm that building.   At a signal, Capt. Burgwin, (First regiment United States Dragoons,) at the head of his own company, and that of Capt. McMillin, (of the volunteers,) charged the western flank of the church, while Capt. Angney, Infantry battalion, and Capt. Barber, and Lieut. Boon, Second regiment Missouri mounted Volunteers, charged the northern wall.   As soon as the troops above mentioned had established themselves under the western wall of the church, axes were used in the attempt to breach it; and, a temporary ladder having been made, the roof was fired.   About this time, Capt. Burgwin, at the head of a small party, left the cover afforded by the flank of the church, and penetrating into the corral in front of that building, endeavoured to force the door.   In this exposed situation, Capt. Burgwin received a severe wound which deprived me of his valuable services, and of which he died on the 7th instant.   Lieuts. McIlvaine, First United States Dragoons, and Royall and Lackland, Second regiment mounted Volunteers, accompanied Capt. Burgwin into the corral; but the attempt on the church door proved fruitless, and they were compelled to retire behind the wall.   In the mean time, small holes had been cut into the western wall, and shells were thrown in by hand, doing good execution. The six-pounder was now brought around by Lieut. Wilson, who at the distance of two hundred yards, poured a heavy fire of grape into the town.   The enemy during all this time kept up a destructive fire upon our troops.   About half-past 3 o'clock, the six-pounder was run up within sixty yards of the church, and after ten rounds, one of the holes which had been cut with the axes was widened into a practicable breach.   The gun was now run up within ten yards of the wall—a shell was thrown in—three rounds of grape were poured into the breach.   The storming party —among whom were Lieut. Dyer, of the ordnance, and Lieuts. Wilson and Taylor, First Dragoons, entered and took possession of the church without opposition.   The interior was filled with dense smoke, but for which circumstance our storming party would have suffered great loss. A few of the enemy were seen in the gallery, where an open door admitted the air, but they retired without firing a gun. The troops left to support the battery on the north, were now ordered to charge on that side. The enemy abandoned the western part of the town. Many took refuge in the large houses on the east, while others endeavoured to escape toward the mountains. These latter were pursued by the mounted men under Capts. Slack and St. Vrain, who killed fifty-one of them, only two or three men escaping. It was now night, and our troops were quietly quartered in the houses which the enemy had abandoned. On the next morning, the enemy sued for peace, and thinking the severe loss they had sustained would prove a salutary lesson, I granted their supplication, on the condition that they should deliver up to me Tomas—one of their principal men, who had instigated and been actively engaged in the murder of Gov. Bent and others. The number of the enemy at the battle of Pueblo de Taos was between six and seven hundred. Of these, about one hundred and fifty were killed—wounded not known. Our own loss was seven killed, and forty-five wounded. Many of the wounded have since died.

The principal leaders in this insurrection were Tafoya, Pablo Chavis, Pablo Montoya, Cortez, and Tomas, a Pueblo Indian. Of these, Tafoya was killed at Cañada; Chavis was killed at Pueblo; Montoya was hanged at Don Fernando on the 7th instant, and Tomas was shot by a private while in the guard room at the latter town. Cortez is still at large. This person was at the head of the rebels in the valley of the Mora.

In the battles of Cañada, Embudo, and Pueblo de Taos, the officers and men behaved admirably. Where all conducted themselves gallantly, I consider it improper to distinguish individuals, as such discrimination might operate prejudicially against the just claims of others.

I have the honour to be, very respectfully, your obedient servant,

STERLING PRICE,

Col. commanding the army in New Mexico.

The ADJUTANT-GENERAL *of the Army, Washington, D. C.*

Early in the morning of the 5th, the women had come in crowds to the victors, on their knees, with white flags, crosses, images, &c., begging for mercy; and very soon the men followed them. Col. Price listened to their supplications. They brought forward much of the property that had been taken from the American citizens whom they had murdered. This was restored to their relatives.

This campaign of nineteen days was made without tents, and with marches through, and nights spent in snow from two to three feet deep, and here it may be mentioned that this winter was deemed the most severe that had occurred in New Mexico for many years.

Missouri had abundant cause of gratulation in the gallantry of her citizen soldiery, for this was a contest not alone against Mexicans, but against the most warlike tribe of Indians, and a fastness the strongest in New Mexico, and by them regarded as impregnable. The chivalry and daring of the attack and capture of the church at Pueblo could scarce atone in its confessedly glorious results for the loss of the gallant Burgwin and his comrades. The heroic conduct of the United States Dragoons was well attested by their loss in killed and wounded, as it was by their efficiency.

At Santa Fé, the 13th was a day of mourning. In the morning, the funeral of Burgwin, than whom the army did not furnish a better specimen of the combination of the gentleman with the officer, took place with all the honours due to his rank, and more to his merits. In the afternoon, the mangled remains of the lamented Governor Bent were buried by the Masonic fraternity, assisted by all the military of the place. At least 1300 Americans were present, and a vast concourse of Mexicans, at a funeral pageant such as was never witnessed before in that country.

Their graves are on a little knoll, just under the western angle of Fort Marcy.

As soon as Col. Price received the first intimation of the murder at Taos of Gov. Bent and others, and of insurrectionary movements at St. Miguel, he sent an order to Capt. Henley, who had been stationed in that neighbourhood, as well to take charge of the grazing parties as to protect Capt. Murphy, who had been sent to St. Louis and was daily expected back with United States funds for the troops, to collect all his forces, and to put down any attempt at a revolution, and to give convoy to Capt. Murphy's small train.

Anonymous letters had, immediately on the outbreak at Taos, been sent to all the surrounding settlements, urging the people to rise and massacre the Americans. One of these was received at Moro, a town on the east side of the mountains. On the 19th, eight Americans were at that place, and they were immediately killed. Among them were L. L. Waldo, and Benjamin Prewitt, both old traders. At the date of these massacres, Capt. Henley, with his grazing party of 90 men, was near Moro. The insurgents soon became formidable and fortified the town. Capt. Henley determined to attack in this position, and fought them for several hours, killing fifteen and wounding many, with eighteen prisoners, who were subsequently sent to Santa Fé. In the engagement, Henley was killed, when, finding that the insurgents could not be driven from their position, the first lieutenant withdrew for rein-forcements, which arrived at Vegas about the 28th of January, under Capt. Morin. The party then proceeded to Moro, but on its approach the inhabitants of the place fled. Moro had a popu-lation of about 2000, nearly all of whom took to the mountains. Capt. Morin then destroyed the place, with the exception of three houses, occupied by invalids, as also a large quantity of grain, then much wanted by the army in New Mexico, thus, unfortunately causing some of the horrors of war to be felt as well by the victors as by the enemy.

Besides the prisoners sent to Santa Fé from Moro town, Col. Price brought with him the father-in-law of Archuleta, who fought him at Cañada. He took both these persons on his way to Taos, carried them to that place, and finally turned them over to the civil authority of Santa Fé. The father-in-law was a venerable looking old man of about sixty-five, and suffered much while crossing the high mountains through deep snow, in mid-winter. There was no doubt of his having participated largely in the revolution. He was wealthy, and lived in good style. An interesting interview took place on the return, between Col. Price and the mother of Archuleta. She called on him and begged her son's release, and, with streaming eyes, told him he was her only comfort—that her other son had fled, and that she was alone in the world. Col. Price told her it was painful to him to be the cause of any sorrow to her, but that his duty to his country would not allow him to liberate her son. She replied that she would pledge all she was worth, if he would release him, that he would never engage in another revolution. Col. Price could not listen to her proposal. She then offered to bail him in any amount, to which it was replied that the civil authority alone could decide on that matter. Subsequently tried and condemned, they were humanely ordered to be pardoned by the President of the United States as soon as he came to a knowledge of the case.

After the fight at Taos, the Pueblo Indians, the late allies of the Mexicans, delivered up to Col. Price the ringleaders in the assassination and rebellion, and professed a wish to be friendly with the Americans, declaring they had been deceived by false representations of the Mexicans, and of plunder largely held out to them.

After these events, the Mexicans were, as far as possible, disarmed and deprived of their ammunition. The civil government resumed its functions under the secretary of state, acting as governor, and the trials of the rebels took place, and resulted in the condemnation of many who were engaged in the revolt. Their execution then took place. Early in April, Col. Price occupied Santa Fé, with about 450 troops. The remainder of his forces were stationed through the country, some guarding the horses and stock, and others garrisoning posts, as was the position of affairs previous to the insurrection.

The execution of the sentences of the courts on the criminals much excited the Mexicans, still at this time all was quiet, but it was believed to be that stubborn and sullen quiet which superior force alone compels.

In this state of affairs—in a country greatly exhausted of its resources—and, at any time, deficient in means to sustain a large mounted force, especially around Santa Fé, with reinforcements to be brought above one thousand miles, over the trackless and desert plains of the far west, and through hostile or thieving Indians, it was apparent that the troops at Santa Fé, and in New Mexico, would be required to exercise the greatest vigilance, in order to retain the conquered territory.

Nor was it long before the inimical spirit of the population gave occasion for activity, though not in any attempt at wide-spread insurrection, but in such isolated acts of hostility as, if successful to any extent, might have lead to a general revolt.

Reports came of parties of Mexicans having gone from the frontiers to rob on the plains, and of their allying themselves with the Chasjeune Indians, and some other savage tribes ; that Cortes, a Mexican outlaw, had enlisted the Cumanches, and threatened the eastern frontier, as well as all Americans on the Santa Fé trail to the United States, &c. Over this trail, it had for some time before required an efficient party to check the attacks or depredations of the savages who infested it, lured thither by the hope of plunder. With these Indians, Mexicans were found united. The Arrapohoes and Pawnees also, infested the route, so that a small government train with stores for the use of the troops at Santa Fé, had been cut off and the teamsters murdered, and that several other lives and much property had been lost.

At this time, whatever small party ventured to traverse the long and difficult route to or from Santa Fé and Fort Leavenworth, encountered with great certainty many adventures, as well as imminent risks of their lives. Lieuts. Abert and Peck, of the Topographical Engineers, had gone out with Gen. Kearny. They had remained at Santa Fé, when Gen. Kearny departed for California, and, subsequently, made under orders left for them,* an examination and survey of New Mexico, which, when published, must be

---

* Lieut. Emory, chief of the Engineer staff of Gen. Kearny, left these orders, and accompanied the general to California. No opportunity was neglected by this officer to take astronomical observations, as well as to make topographical reconnoissances. In these he was most ably seconded by Lieut. William H. Warner, both of the Topographical Engineer corps.

of exceeding interest, from their known ability. Lieut. Abert returned from New Mexico, in December, and January, 1847, over the plains. His journal of this trip has been published, and vividly details the hardships and dangers of the enterprise. Lieut. Peck, with Messrs. Woods and Sanford, left Santa Fé soon after the Taos insurrection, and when the insurgents were being brought to punishment. His party was small, and, after they had been out a few days, they were attacked by greatly superior numbers of Cumanches, who, though driven off for the time, succeeded in stealing ten of their mules and horses. This they effected by engaging and drawing off the men from their pack animals, or in a variety of ways common to Indian strategy—in fact, both as warriors and strategists, the Cumanches were generally found to be more warlike and skilful than the Mexicans. On the second day, the Indians in greater numbers renewed the fight, and succeeded in running off thirty-five of the horses and mules, but not without heavy loss to themselves. All of the small party displayed the utmost intrepidity in facing the enemy. A musket-ball struck the pistol of Lieut. Peck, and took the impression of the manufacturer's name, plain as if purposely made upon it, while his clothes were lanced through, and a man wounded by his side. Others were equally warmly engaged, and had a long and protracted struggle before they were able to drive the "Arabs of the Desert" (as they have been appropriately called) off from their prey. That night they were joined by Mr. McKnight, from Chihuahua, passed Midshipman E. Beale, of the United States navy, C. Toplin, Christopher Carson, Theodore Talbot, of the army, Robert E. Russell, and others from the Pacific coast. The names given are connected with principal events sketched in this work; and it was a singular incident that the far distant and widely separated branches of the "Army of the West"—Chihuahua—Santa Fé— and California—as well as the naval co-operation, should here be represented, and have to tell their adventures at a camp in the desert, and while yet in danger from the Cumanches, out of a contest with whom they had just emerged, and knew not at what moment they might have to renew, and here to listen to news of their companions in arms, and of distant achievements before unknown to each other.

At the bend of the Arkansas, the party thus reinforced had their camp attacked by another tribe of Indians, Pawnees, who fired many arrows into it, and attempted to excite a stampede among the horses, but as the Indians appeared with but one gun, they were more easily driven off. These gentlemen arrived, finally, at the settlements without further loss. They reported the Indians as very hostile, and as intending to attack every party which they might think themselves strong enough to contend with. In fact, these dangers and difficulties were encountered by all small parties who attempted the route between Santa Fé and the American settlements; some of them in a more eminent degree. It is now known that a force has been sent out, under Col. Gilpin, to punish the Indians, and protect the route.

In New Mexico, the Apache Indians had now become troublesome. Despite their treaty with Col. Doniphan, they had suffered themselves to be excited to hostilities against the Americans by some of the leading insurrectionists who had escaped, and penetrated their country.

Forces were detached against them. On the 29th of May, 1847, an engagement took place at the Red River cañon, about one hundred and fifty miles south-east of Santa Fé, between a detachment of about 175 men under Major Edmonson, and a band of Mexicans and Apaches numbering four hundred. These had combined to commit depredations on American property, and a few days previous succeeded in stealing 150 horses from traders and others. Major Edmonson was crossing a slough at the mouth of the cañon, which was very miry, and many of his horses being in weak condition, were unable to get through the morass. Here he suddenly came upon the enemy, and engaged the Mexicans and Indians for about two hours on foot, when he was compelled to retreat. Lieut. Elliott, in command of 27 men, principally Laclede Rangers, gallantly posted his men on a point of rocks and kept the enemy from advancing upon the retiring forces until they got out of their difficult position.   All the horses were either shot down or captured.

Lieutenant-colonel Willock was ordered, early in June, from Taos to Santa Fé, the terms of service of most of his men being at this time about to expire.   In fact, the terms of the whole volunteer force then in New Mexico were near expiration.

A small detached party under Lieut. Brown were surprised, and all killed by the Mexicans about this time.

Major Edmonson had again encountered the enemy with artillery, and had captured, with considerable loss on the part of the Mexicans, the town of Los Pias, and was in July following up his successes—here the narrative of one of his officers must serve for our sketches.

The insurrectionists under their leaders, Gen. Gonsales and the outlaw Cortes, surprised and dispersed, and the recapture of a great number of American horses by our troops.

SANTA FE, *August* 4, 1847.

MESSRS. EDITORS : At the destruction of the town of LOS PIAS, on the 6th of July last, by the troops under the command of Major Edmonson, we found upon the prisoners then taken, letters written by one Gonsales and others, leaders of the late projected insurrection, giving a plan of their intended operations, and asking the citizens to be in readiness for action at a moment's warning ; stating, also, that the Americans were already weakened by the departure to the States of a number of troops : that others were to start in a few days, and amongst them the company of artillerists, Capt. Fischer's ; and that spies would be kept constantly on the road to give information of their (the artillerists') departure, at which time they entertained no doubt of being able to strike a final and decisive blow.   The prisoners also stated that many of their men, with their arms, had gone to the town of Loquesta, to join their leader, Gen. Gonsales.

Loquesta is a town of considerable size, and admirably located for defence, being situated on the San Miguel river, surrounded by mountains of an almost inaccessible character.   The prisoners stated that Cortes and his party were at or near Anton Chico, a frontier town situate on the San Miguel river, some fifteen or twenty miles below Loquesta. Having disposed of the prisoners taken at the storming of Los Pias, by sending them to Santa Fé for trial, Major Edmonson, with the companies of Capts. Horine and Holloway, and two pieces of artillery, started on the 15th of July to the town of Anton Chico, a distance of about forty-five miles.

Upon our arrival at the latter place, at daylight the following morning, we found the town deserted, except by a few old men, women, and children, from whom we extracted the information that their men, with their arms, had likewise gone to the town of Loquesta. Pursuing our march, and when within about five miles of the latter town, a Mexican—supposed to be a spy—was captured by our scouting party, who informed us that from four to six hundred armed Mexicans, under their leaders Gonsales and Cortes, were then in the town of Loquesta. Upon our arrival on the heights commanding a view of the town, we discovered the enemy dispersing in every direction to the mountains. We, however, succeeded in capturing about fifty prisoners; the mule, saddle, bridle and sabre of Gen. Cortes; and a great number of American horses and Cumanche and Apache Indian horses, obtained from those Indians in exchange for horses stolen by the Mexicans from the American troops.

The enemy had evidently made great preparation for defence, as their houses were generally barricaded and fortified, and their goods and valuables either hid in the mountains or buried. Our prisoners informed us that the great panic amongst the Mexican troops was produced by our sudden and unexpected approach, together with the fact that we had with us artillery, which I think they never intend to face again if they can avoid it.

It is but justice to the troops—being part infantry, and having with them artillery drawn by oxen—to state that the march from Los Vegos, by Anton Chico, to Loquesta, a distance of between fifty-five and sixty miles, was performed in less than twenty-four hours, over a rough and mountainous country, and a great portion of the distance without even a road to guide them ; to which extraordinary march may be attributed their success on the occasion.

We are endeavouring, here in Santa Fé, to raise a new regiment. Three companies have already been mustered in, and two others reported ready for being mustered. They are composed principally of discharged volunteers and wagoners.

Six of the prisoners charged with the murder of Lieut. Brown and his party were executed on the 3d inst., in Santa Fé, by sentence of a drum-head court-martial. The balance, it is supposed, will be released for want of sufficient testimony.

Yours, respectfully,   J. H. BOURMAM,
Second Lieut. Co. F, Second Reg. Mo. Mounted Vol.

The troops alluded to as departed and departing, were the companies of Capts. Fischer and Dent, and portions of the original commands of Capts. Weightman and Hudson, which left Fort Leavenworth with Gen. Kearny, were left at Santa Fé by Col. Doniphan after Gen. Kearny's departure for California, and had been mustered into service on the 6th of June, 1846 ; consequently their term of service, for one year, had expired, and they were sent home, and arrived in good season, at St. Louis, in the latter part of August, 1847, where they were greeted with every distinction by their fellow-citizens.

Lieut. Love, of the First Dragoons, arrived with a train of wagons, and specie for the troops. The difficulties that beset his march are best described by an officer of his command of eighty United States Dragoons :

CAMP ON BATTLE-GROUND,
Arkansas River, 1st July, 1847.

DEAR SIR : Previous to your receiving this, you will no doubt have heard of our engagement with the Indians on the 26th ult., and of my being engaged on that occasion ; and from the very severe wound I received from a ball in the side, which is lodged backwards and cannot be extracted, left me in a very weak and uncertain state ; however, I feel now much easier, and being anxious that you should have in part at least the particulars, I avail myself of an opportunity of writing by traders who are going to the States. On the 23d, we arrived at the Pawnee Fork, and there met two government trains of provision wagons destined for Santa Fé, and learned from them that the day previous the Indians charged on them as their cattle were grazing, wounding three men —one severely—and driving off from traders and a return train of government wagons under Mr. Bell, some seventy yoke of oxen, leaving twenty wagons and a considerable quantity of provisions and other property without the means of transportation. The wagons and property were burned to prevent their falling into the hands of the Indians. Next day, (the 24th,) we travelled up to the Fork and encamped, and on the 25th to this place, on which day I was in charge of the guard, and the night passed over without any alarm, although every vigilance and precaution was used. Next morning, the 26th, immediately after reveillé, Hayden's train, which was encamped about five hundred yards due west from the guard-tent, drove their oxen from the corell to graze. All were scarcely out, when a large band of Cumanches and Mexicans emerged from a ravine called Coon creek, about two hundred yards west, and charged furiously on the teamsters and herdsmen, wounding three and driving off one hundred and thirty yoke of government oxen and thirty yoke belonging to a trader who was accompanying them. One conspicuous Indian rode within carbine range—I fired and killed the horse from under him, and, as far as could be ascertained, wounded himself; however, he was soon behind another Indian. In the mean time the camp was armed, and some eighteen or nineteen mounted dragoons were ordered out under my command, for the purpose of retaking the cattle. When my command reached within one hundred and fifty yards of the enemy, I halted, and formed in extended line, expecting to rally on a body of teamsters who were out as footmen; then charged on the Indians, and forced them to retreat. As they were just retreating, a large body of well-mounted Indians crossed the river between me and the camp on my left, and charged us in the rear with great fury, and preventing us from rallying, but to cut our way through them. About this time I was shot, and charged on

X   16

by several Indians. I made my sabre, however, drink blood, having killed one and wounded another. Every man in my little command fought bravely and manfully, and five of my poor fellows were killed defending themselves to the last, and selling their lives at a dear rate, and six wounded—three more besides myself severely wounded. The killed were Arlidge, Deckhart, Short, Gaskill, and Blake. The wounded, myself, Vancaster, Lovelace, and Ward, severely—and Burk and Wilson slightly. The severe loss we met with I attribute to the almost unmanageable state of the horses, all being new in the service, and to the Indians being permitted to charge on us from behind. The enemy took off the cattle, scalped three men, and took off the horses, equipments, arms and ammunition, and the clothes of the dead. The Indians, when in a body, numbered about 500. I make no comments, I merely give you the facts as they occurred before me. The Indians were all armed with lances measuring from twelve to fifteen feet in length, bows and arrows, and a great many with rifles and muskets. There were some white men among them. Several of our men saw them as well as myself. The air was actually as dark as if a flight of birds were hovering over us, from the balls, lances, and arrows that were flying through the air. Twelve or fifteen of the enemy are known to have fallen—perhaps more—but were immediately carried off. Four of their horses were left dead on the ground. Since then, we remain here, merely changing positions, for the purpose of pastime. To-morrow, I understand, we will proceed again on our route, arrangements being made to take all the trains along, with somewhat less team, however. The Indians have attacked every train that has gone out or come in this year, and are bound to attack every train that will follow. These infernal Cumanches, Pawnees, and Arrapahoes deserve a castigation that would ever after keep them quiet, and which they are sure some day to receive.

Lieut. Love was in a most distressing situation. Never has man suffered, I believe, more in one day than he suffered. Here were twelve wagons, with six mules to each—provisions, and all the specie, that he could not by any possible means abandon, as another large force were ready to attack the camp if he were to go out with a large force ; and yet he saw the awful situation in which we were placed, and could not give us the slightest aid or assistance. I am convinced that he acted prudently and wisely ; for it has been his special care to take all the precautions that an experienced officer could take to save his men and animals ever since he commenced his march.

Such was the character of the Indian aggression on the route to New Mexico. The violence was, however, confined to the Cumanches, and to a small portion of the Arrapahoes, and the band of Pawnees south of the Platte. This violence the United States government took effectual measures to quell, by placing a competent force under the command of Col. Gilpin, who had signally distinguished himself with Doniphan in Chihuahua.

In August, all organized resistance to the troops had ceased in New Mexico, the elections were held, and the persons principally concerned in the late insurrectionary struggles had been tried, and those convicted had been executed. Six of the murderers of Lieut. Brown were of this number.

New levies had arrived and were arriving to replace the volunteers whose constant and arduous services entitled them to their discharge as soon as their enlistments expired.

Col. Price, on the 20th of July, 1847, was made a brigadier-general, and commands at Santa Fé, whence he lately returned for a short visit to Missouri.

APPENDIX.

No. 1.

Letter of the Secretary of War to Gen. Kearny.

[CONFIDENTIAL.]   WAR DEPARTMENT,
Washington, June 3d, 1846.

SIR: I herewith send you a copy of my letter to the governor of Missouri for an additional force of 1000 mounted men.

The object of thus adding to the force under your command is not, as you will perceive, fully set forth in that letter, for the reason that it is deemed prudent that it should not, at this time, become a matter of public notoriety; but to you it is proper and necessary that it should be stated.

It has been decided by the President to be of the greatest importance in the pending war with Mexico to take the earliest possession of Upper California. An expedition with that view is hereby ordered, and you are designated to command it. To enable you to be in sufficient force to conduct it successfully, this additional force of 1000 mounted men has been provided, to follow you in the direction of Santa Fé, to be under your orders, or the officer you may leave in command at Santa Fé.

It cannot be determined how far this additional force will be behind that designed for the Santa Fé expedition, but it will not probably be more than a few weeks. When you arrive at Santa Fé with the force already called, and shall have taken possession of it, you may find yourself in a condition to garrison it with a small part of your command, (as the additional force will soon be at that place,) and with the remainder press forward to California. In that case you will make such arrangements, as to being followed by the reinforcements before mentioned, as in your judgment may be deemed safe and prudent. I need not say to you that, in case you conquer Santa Fé, (and with it will be included the department or state of New Mexico,) it will be important to provide for retaining safe possession of it. Should you deem it prudent to have still more troops for the accomplishment of the objects therein designated, you will lose no time in communicating your opinion on that point, and all others connected with the enterprise, to this department. Indeed, you are hereby authorized to make a direct requisition for it upon the governor of Missouri.

It is known that a large body of Mormon emigrants are *en route* to California, for the purpose of settling in that country. You are desired to use all proper means to have a good understanding with them, to the end that the United States may have their co-operation in taking possession of, and holding, that country. It has been suggested here that many of these Mormons would willingly enter into the service of the United States, and aid us in our expedition against California. You are hereby authorized to muster into service such as can be induced to volunteer; not, however, to a number exceeding one-third of your entire force. Should they enter the service they will be paid as other volunteers, and you can allow them to designate, so far as it can be properly done, the persons to act as officers thereof. It is understood that a considerable number of American citizens are now settled on the Sacramento river, near Suter's establishment, called "Nueva Helvetia," who are well-disposed towards the United States. Should you, on your arrival in the country, find this to be the true state of things there, you are authorized to organize and receive into the service of the United States such portion of these citizens as you may think useful to aid you to hold the possession of the country. You will, in that case, allow them, so far as you shall judge proper, to select their own officers. A large discretionary power is invested in you in regard to these matters, as well as to all others in relation to the expeditions confided to your command.

The choice of routes by which you will enter California, will be left to your better knowledge and ampler means of getting accurate information. We are assured that a southern route (called the Caravan route, by which the wild horses are brought from that country into New Mexico) is practicable; and it is suggested as not improbable that it can be passed over in the winter months, or, at least, late in autumn. It is hoped that this information may prove to be correct.

In regard to the routes, the practicability of procuring needful supplies for men and animals, and transporting baggage, is a point to be well considered. Should the President be disappointed in his cherished hope that you will be able to reach the interior of Upper California before winter, you are then desired to make the best arrangement you can for sustaining your forces during the winter, and for an early movement in the spring. Though it is very desirable that the expedition should reach California this season, (and the President does not doubt you will make every possible effort to accomplish this object,) yet, if in your judgment, it cannot be undertaken with a reasonable prospect of success, you will defer it, as above suggested, until spring. You are left unembarrassed by any specific directions in this matter.

It is expected that the naval forces of the United States, which are now, or will soon be, in the Pacific, will be in possession of all the towns on the seacoast, and will co-operate with you in the conquest of California. Arms, ordnance, munitions of war, and provisions, to be used in that country, will be sent by sea to our squadron in the Pacific, for the use of the land forces.

Should you conquer and take possession of New Mexico and Upper California, or considerable places in either, you will establish temporary civil governments therein—abolishing all arbitrary restrictions that may exist, so far as it may be done with safety. In performing this duty, it would be wise and prudent to continue in their employment all such of the existing officers as are known to be friendly to the United States, and will take the oath of allegiance to them. The duties at the custom-houses ought, at once, to be reduced to such a rate as may be barely sufficient to maintain the necessary officers without yielding any revenue to the government. You may assure the people of those provinces that it is the wish and design of the United States to provide for them a free government with the least possible delay, similar to that which exists in our territories. They will then be called on to exercise the rights of freemen in electing their own representatives to the territorial legislature. It is foreseen, that what relates to the civil government will be a difficult and unpleasant part of your duty, and much must necessarily be left to your own discretion.

In your whole conduct you will act in such a manner as best to conciliate the inhabitants, and render them friendly to the United States.

It is desirable that the usual trade between the citizens of the United States and the Mexican provinces should be continued as far as practicable, under the changed condition of things between the two countries. In consequence of extending your expedition into California, it may be proper that you should increase your supply for goods to be distributed as presents to the Indians. The United States superintendent of Indian affairs at St. Louis will aid you in procuring these goods. You will be furnished with a proclamation* in the Spanish language, to be issued by you, and circulated among the Mexican people, on your entering into or approaching their country. You will use your utmost endeavours to have the pledges and promises therein contained carried out to the utmost extent.

I am directed by the President to say that the rank of brevet brigadier-general will be conferred on you as soon as you commence your movement towards California, and sent round to you by sea, or over the country, or to the care of the commandant of our squadron in the Pacific. In that way, cannon, arms, ammunition, and supplies for the land forces, will be sent to you.

Very respectfully, your obedient servant,

W. L. MARCY,
Secretary of War.

Col. STEPHEN W. KEARNY,
Fort Leavenworth, Missouri.

Letter of the Secretary of War to Gen. Kearny.

WAR DEPARTMENT,
Washington, June 5, 1846.

SIR: I enclosed to you a few copies of a proclamation prepared for Gen. Taylor, to issue to the Mexicans. I discover that there are parts of it that will not answer our purpose for Santa Fé or Upper California. You will not, therefore, use these copies. It is intended to make the needful alterations in it, and thus altered, send on copies† to you before you will have occasion to distribute them. I must, however, urge you not to use those which have been forwarded.

Yours, respectfully,

Col. S. W. KEARNY.   W. L. MARCY.

---

* No proclamation for circulation was ever furnished to Gen. Kearny. A few copies of that prepared for and sent to Gen. Taylor were forwarded to Gen. Kearny, but he was requested not to use them. These copies were the only proclamations sent by the War Department to him, and I am not aware that he ever used any of them. See letter of the Secretary of War to Gen. Kearny, of the 6th of June, 1846, a copy of which is, with the papers, sent to the President, in answer to the resolution of the House of Representatives, of the 15th of December, 1846.   W. L. MARCY.

† No proclamation, modified as proposed, was sent.   W. L. MARCY.

No. 2.

Letter of the Secretary of War to General Kearny.

WAR DEPARTMENT,

Washington, September 12, 1846.

SIR: A volunteer regiment raised in the State of New York, engaged to serve during the war with Mexico, and to be discharged wherever they may be at its termination, if in a territory of the United States, has been mustered into service, and is about to embark at the port of New York for California. This force is to be a part of your command; but, as it may reach the place of its destination before you are in a condition to subject it to your orders, the colonel of the regiment, J. D. Stevenson, has been furnished with instructions for his conduct in the mean time. I herewith send you a copy thereof, as well as a copy of the instructions of the Navy Department to the commander of the naval squadron in the Pacific; a copy of a letter to General Taylor, with a circular from the Treasury Department; a copy of a letter from General Scott to Captain Tompkins; and a copy of general regulations relative to the respective rank of naval and army officers. These, so far as applicable, will be looked upon in the light of instructions to yourself. The department is exceedingly desirous to be furnished by you with full information of your progress and proceedings, together with your opinion and views as to your movements into California, having reference as to time, route, &c. Beyond the regiment under the command of Colonel S. Price, and the separate battalion called for at the same time by the President from the governor of Missouri, a requisition for one regiment of infantry was issued on the 18th of July last; but the information subsequently received here induced the belief that it would not be needed; and the difficulty of passing it over the route at so late a period in the season, with the requisite quantity of supplies, &c., was deemed so great, that the orders to muster it into service have been countermanded. It will not be sent. Your views as to the sufficiency of your force, and the practicability of sustaining a larger one, &c., are desired.

I am, with great respect, your obedient servant,

W. L. MARCY,

Secretary of War.

Gen. S. W. KEARNY, *Fort Leavenworth, Missouri.*

No. 3.

Letter of the Secretary of War to Colonel Stevenson.

WAR DEPARTMENT,

September 11, 1846.

SIR: The transports having on board the regiment under your command are destined to the Pacific, and will repair to our naval squadron now on the coast of California. Instructions, with a copy of which you are herewith furnished, have been given to the naval commander on the station in regard to his operations, and you are directed to co-operate with him in carrying out his plans, so far as the land forces may be needed for that purpose. Without undertaking to give specific instructions as to the movements of our forces in that quarter—for much must be left to the judgment of the commanding officers—it is proper to state that the military occupation of California is the main object in view. There are three points deemed to be worthy of particular attention. These are San Francisco, Monterey, and San Diego. It is important to have possession of the bay of San Francisco and the country in that vicinity. The necessity of having something like a permanent and secure position on the coast of California, and probably at this place, will not be overlooked. Assuming that such a position will be found and selected in the bay of San Francisco, it is expected that a fortification, such as the means at your command may enable you to construct, will be erected, and that the heavy guns heretofore sent out, and those taken by the transports, to the extent needed, will be used for its armament. This work should be designed for a two-fold object—the protection of the vessels in the bay, and the security of the land forces. The selection of the site will be an important matter. It should be preceded by a careful examination of the place with reference to both objects, and the location made under the advice and direction of the commanding naval officer. It may, however, be that your first debarkation will not be at this point. The circumstances which may be found to exist on your arrival in that region must control in this matter.

It is probable that Monterey will have been taken by our naval force before the land troops reach that coast, and they may be needed to hold possession of it. This place is also to be secured by fortifications or temporary works from an attack either by sea or land. Judging from the information we have here of what will be the state of things on your arrival on the coast of California, it is concluded that these will be found to be the important points, and the possession of them essential to the objects in view in prosecuting the war in that quarter; but the particular mention of them is by no means intended as instructions to confine our military operations to them. As to the third place suggested, San Diego, less is known of it than the other two. Should the naval commander determine to take and hold possession of it, and need the land force, or a part of it for that purpose, you will of course yield to his views in that respect. Whatever is done upon the coast of California, or of any other part of Mexico, will require, it is presumed, the co-operation of the land and naval forces, and it is not doubted that this co-operation will be cordially rendered.

The point, or points of debarkation of the regiment under your command, should be settled as speedily as practicable after your arrival upon the Mexican coast, and the transports discharged. The land forces will, thereafter, be attended with the vessels of the squadron. The ordnance, ammunition, arms, and all descriptions of public property which are not required on shore, or cannot be safely deposited there, will be transferred to the public ships. Upon them the land forces must rely for bringing supplies, where water transportation is necessary. If the exigency of the service requires these forces to remove from one place to another on the coast, the public vessels will furnish the means of doing so.

The regiment under your command, as well as the company of Captain Tompkins, which has preceded it, is a part of General Kearny's command; but it may be that he will not be in a situation to reach you, by his orders, immediately on your debarkation. Until that is the case, yours will be an independent command, except when engaged in joint operations with the naval force.

It is not expected that you will be able to advance far into the country; nor is it advisable for you to undertake any hazardous enterprises. Until you shall fall under the command of General Kearny, your force will be mostly, if not wholly, employed in seizing and holding important possessions on the sea-coast.

The government here have received information, which is deemed to be reliable, though not official, that our squadron in the Pacific had taken possession of Monterey, as early as the 6th of July last.

There is reason to believe that California is not favorably disposed to the central government of Mexico, and will not be disposed to make a vigorous resistance to our operations in that quarter. Should you find such to be the state of things there, it will be of the greatest importance that the good will of the people towards the United States should be cultivated. This is to be done by liberal and kind treatment. They should be made to feel that we come as deliverers. Their rights of person, property, and religion, must be respected and sustained. The greatest care must be taken to restrain the troops from all acts of license or outrage; the supplies drawn from the country must be paid for at fair prices; and, as far as practicable, friendly relations should be established. In the event of hostile resistance, your operations must be governed by circumstances; and you must use the means at your command to accomplish the objects in view—the military occupation of the country. It is not, however, expected that much can be done, if preparations shall have been made to resist, until the forces under General Kearny shall have entered the country.

You are directed to embrace every opportunity to communicate with this department, and to furnish it with not only a full account of your movements and operations previous to your coming under the direct command of General Kearny, but with such other information as may be useful for the department to possess in regard to conducting the war in that quarter.

Your attention is particularly directed to that portion of the instructions to the commanding officer of the squadron in the Pacific, herewith, which has reference to the joint operation of the land and naval force, and you will conform your conduct thereto.

You are also furnished with an extract from instructions to General Kearny, giving directions for the course of conduct to be pursued while in the military occupation of any portion of the enemy's country—together with a copy of a letter to General Taylor, enclosing one from the Secretary of the Treasury in regard to commercial intercourse with such parts of the enemy's ports, &c., as may be in possession of our forces. These are to be regarded as instructions to you, should you find yourself placed in the circumstances therein contemplated. You will take the earliest opportunity to make the commanding officer of the squadron in the Pacific fully acquainted with your instructions and the accompanying papers. Where a place is taken by the joint action of the naval and land force, the naval officer in command, if superior in rank to yourself, will be entitled to make arrangements for the civil government of it while it is held by the co-operation of both branches of the military force. All your powers, in this respect, will of course be devolved on General Kearny, whenever he shall arrive in California and assume the command of the volunteer regiment. As soon as practicable, you will furnish him with a copy of this communication, and the other papers herewith transmitted.

Very respectfully, your obedient servant,

W. L. MARCY,
Secretary of War.

Col. J. D. STEVENSON,
Commanding Regiment of Volunteers, Governor's Island, harbour of New York.

No. 4.

Extract of Letter of Major General Scott to Lieut. Tompkins.

[CONFIDENTIAL.]   HEAD-QUARTERS OF THE ARMY,
                                               Washington, June 20, 1846.

SIR: As the commander of a company of the 3d artillery, you have been ordered to embark with the same on board of the United States ship the Lexington, now lying in the harbour of New York, and bound to the north-west coast of America.

I am now to inform you that, with your company, you are destined to act in conjunction with the United States naval forces in the Pacific, against the republic of Mexico, with which we are at war. The commander of that squadron may desire to capture and to hold certain important points, as Monterey, and towns or posts in San Francisco bay. The company under your command may be needed for both purposes, and you will, on consultation, give your co-operation.

It is not intended to place you under the orders, strictly speaking, of any naval officer, no matter how high in rank. That would be illegal, or at least without the authority of any law; but you will be held responsible, when associated in service, whether on land or water, with any naval officer, without regard to relative rank, to co-operate in perfect harmony and with zeal and efficiency. Great confidence is reposed in you, in those respects, as also in your intelligence, judgment, temper, and prowess. See in this connection paragraphs 24, 25, and 26, in the old *General Regulations for the Army,* (edition of 1825,) a copy of which book I handed to you in my office.

Your condition, and that of your company, on board the Lexington, commanded by Lieutenant ———— of the navy, or other United States vessel to which you may be transferred, will be that of *passengers,* not *marines ;* but in the event of the ship finding herself in action, you, and the company under your command, will not fail to show yourselves at least as efficient as any equal number of marines whatsoever. In such case, again, the utmost harmony, upon consultation, would be indispensable ; and in no case will you fail, so far as it may depend upon your best exertions, to conciliate such harmony.

On the landing of the ordnance and ordnance stores belonging to the army, placed on board of the Lexington, you will take charge of the same, unless you should be joined for that purpose by an ordnance officer, in which case you will give him aid and assistance in that duty.

On effecting a successful landing in the enemy's country, it may be necessary, after consultation with the naval commander, as above, and with his assistance, to erect and defend one or more forts, in order to hold the conquered place or places. In such service you will be on your proper element.

It is proper that I should add, you may find on the north-west coast an army officer, with higher rank than your own, when, of course, you will report to him by letter, and if ashore, come under his command.

It is known that you have made requisitions for all the proper supplies which may be needed by your company, for a considerable time after landing. Further supplies, which may not be sent after you from this side of the continent, you will, when ashore, in the absence of a naval force, and in the absence of a higher officer of the army, have to purchase on the other side ; but always in strict conformity with regulations. On board, it is understood that your company will be subsisted from the stores of the ship or navy.

Should you not come under the orders of an army officer, or should you not be landed by the naval commander, as above, you will remain on board of the squadron, and be sent home on some ship of the same.

I need scarcely add that, afloat or ashore, you will always maintain the honour, &c.

No. 5.

Letter from General Kearny to General Wool.

HEAD-QUARTERS ARMY OF THE WEST,
Santa Fé, New Mexico, August 22, 1846.

GENERAL: I have to inform you, that on the 18th instant, without firing a gun or spilling a drop of blood, I took possession of this city, the capital of the department of New Mexico; and that I have this day issued a proclamation claiming the whole department, with its original boundaries, for the United States, and under the title of "the Territory of New Mexico."

Every thing here is quiet and peaceable. The people now understand the advantages they are to derive from a change of government, and are much gratified with it.

I have more troops (Missouri volunteers) following in my rear. On their arrival, there will be more than necessary for this Territory. I will send the surplus to you. Should you not want them, you can order them to Major General Taylor, or to their homes, as you may think the good of the public service requires.

I am destined for Upper California, and hope to start from here in the course of a few weeks. Success attend you.

Very respectfully, your obedient servant,
S. W. KEARNY,
Brig. Gen. U. S, A.

Brig. Gen. JNO. E. WOOL,
U. S. Army, Chihuahua.

No. 6.

[SECRET AND CONFIDENTIAL.]

UNITED STATES NAVY DEPARTMENT,
Washington, June 24, 1845.

SIR: Your attention is still particularly directed to the present aspect of the relations between this country and Mexico. It is the earnest desire of the President to pursue the policy of peace ; and he is anxious that you, and every part of your squadron, should be assiduously careful to avoid any act which could be construed as an act of aggression.

Should Mexico, however, be resolutely bent on hostilities, you will be mindful to protect the persons and interests of citizens of the United States near your station ; and, should you ascertain beyond a doubt that the Mexican government has declared war against us, you will at once employ the force under your command to the best advantage. The Mexican ports on the Pacific are said to be open and defenceless. If you ascertain with certainty that Mexico has declared war against the United States, you will at once possess yourself of the port of

San Francisco, and blockade or occupy such other ports as your force may permit.

Yet, even if you should find yourself called upon by the certainty of an express declaration of war against the United States to occupy San Francisco and other Mexican ports, you will be careful to preserve, if possible, the most friendly relations with the inhabitants; and, where you can do so, you will encourage them to adopt a course of neutrality.

Should you fall in with the squadron under Commodore Parker, you will signify to him the wish of the department that, if the state of his vessels will admit of it, he should remain off the coast of Mexico until our relations with that power are more definitely adjusted; and you will take directions from him, as your senior officer, communicating to him these instructions.

The great distance of your squadron, and the difficulty of communicating with you, are the causes for issuing this order. The President hopes most earnestly that the peace of the two countries may not be disturbed. The object of these instructions is to possess you of the views of the government in the event of a declaration of war on the part of Mexico against the United States—an event which you are enjoined to do every thing consistent with the national honour, on your part, to avoid.

Should Commodore Parker prefer to return to the United States, he has permission from the department to do so. In that event, you will command the united squadron.

Very respectfully, your obedient servant,
GEORGE BANCROFT.

Commodore JOHN D. SLOAT,
Commanding United States naval forces in the Pacific.

No. 7.

UNITED STATES NAVY DEPARTMENT,
Washington, May 13, 1846.

COMMODORE: The state of things alluded to in my letter of June 24, 1845, has occurred. You will therefore now be governed by the instructions therein contained, and carry into effect the orders then communicated with energy and promptitude, and adopt such other measures for the protection of the persons and interests, the rights and the commerce of the citizens of the United States, as your sound judgment may deem to be required.

When you establish a blockade, you will allow neutrals twenty days to leave the blockaded ports; and you will render your blockade absolute, except against armed vessels of neutral nations.

Commending you and your ships' companies to Divine Providence,

I am, respectfully, your obedient servant,
GEORGE BANCROFT.

Commodore JOHN D. SLOAT,
Commanding U. S. Squadron, Pacific.

Y

No. 8.

UNITED STATES NAVY DEPARTMENT,
Washington, May 15, 1846.

COMMODORE: By my letter of the 13th instant, forwarded to you through different sources, in triplicate, of which a copy is enclosed, you were informed of the existing state of war between this government and the republic of Mexico, and referred to your instructions, bearing date, June 24th, 1845, in reference to such a contingency, and directed to " carry into effect the orders then communicated, with energy and promptitude, and adopt such other measures for the protection of the persons and interests, the rights and the commerce of the citizens of the United States, as your sound judgment may deem to be required."

I transmit you herewith, by the hands of Midshipman McRae, whom you will employ on your station, a file of papers, containing the President's message, and the proceedings of Congress relative to the existing state of war with Mexico. The President, by authority of Congress, has made proclamation of war between the United States and Mexico. You will find a copy of the proclamation in the papers enclosed.

You will henceforth exercise all the rights that belong to you as commander-in-chief of a belligerent squadron.

You will consider the most important public object to be to take and to hold possession of San Francisco, and this you will do without fail.

You will also take possession of Mazatlan and of Monterey, one or both, as your force will permit.

If information received here is correct, you can establish friendly relations between your squadron and the inhabitants of each of these three places.

Enymas is also a good harbour, and is believed to be defenceless. You will judge about attempting it.

When you cannot take and hold possession of a town, you may establish a blockade, if you have the means to do it effectually, and the public interest shall require it.

With the expression of these views, much is left to your discretion, as to the selection of the points of attack, the ports you will seize, the ports which you will blockade, and as to the order of your successive movements.

A connection between California, and even Sonora, and the present government of Mexico, is supposed scarcely to exist. You will, as opportunity offers, conciliate the confidence of the people in California, and also in Sonora, towards the government of the United States; and you will endeavour to render their relations with the United States as intimate and as friendly as possible.

It is important that you should hold possession, at least, of San Francisco, even while you encourage the people to neutrality, self-government, and friendship.

You can readily conduct yourself in such a manner as will render your occupation of San Francisco and other ports a benefit to the inhabitants.

Com. Biddle has left, or will soon leave, China. If occasion offers, you will send letters for him to our agent at the Sandwich Islands, conveying to him the wish of the department that he should appear, at once, off California or Sonora.

You will inform the department, by the earliest opportunity, of those ports which you blockade. You will notify neutrals of any declaration of blockade you may make, and give to it all proper publicity. Your blockade must be strict, permitting only armed vessels of neutral powers to enter; but to neutrals already in the ports, you will allow twenty days to leave them.

The frigate "Potomac" and sloop "Saratoga" have been ordered to proceed as soon as possible into the Pacific; and Capt. Aulick in the Potomac, and Commander Shubrick in the Saratoga, directed to report to you at Mazatlan, or wherever else they may find your forces. You would do well, if occasion offers, to send orders to Callao and Valparaiso, instructing them where to meet you.

Other reinforcements will be sent you as the exigencies of the service may require.

You will communicate with the department as often as you can; and you will, if practicable, send a messenger with despatches across the country to the Del Norte, and so to Washington.

Very respectfully, your obedient servant,
GEORGE BANCROFT.

Commodore JOHN D. SLOAT.
Commanding U. S. naval forces in the Pacific.

No. 9.

UNITED STATES NAVY DEPARTMENT,
Washington, June 8, 1846.

COMMODORE: You have already been instructed, and are now instructed, to employ the force under your command, first, to take possession of San Francisco; next, to take possession of Monterey; next, to take possession of such other Mexican ports as you may be able to hold; next, to blockade as many of the Mexican ports in the Pacific as your force will permit; and to watch over American interests and citizens, and commerce, on the west coast of Mexico.

It is rumoured that the province of California is well disposed to accede to friendly relations with the United States. You will encourage the people of that region to enter into relations of amity with our country.

In taking possession of their harbours, you will, if possible, endeavour to establish the supremacy of the American flag without any strife with the people of California.

The squadron on the east coast of Mexico, it is believed, is in the most friendly relations with Yucatan. In like manner, if California separates herself from our enemy, the central Mexican government, and establishes a government of its own under the auspices of the American flag, you will take such measures as will best promote the attachment of the people of California to the United States; will advance their prosperity; and will make that vast region a desirable place of residence for emigrants from our soil.

Considering the great distance at which you are placed from the department, and the circumstances that will constantly arise, much must be left to your discretion. You will bear in mind generally that this country desires to find in California a friend, and not an enemy; to be connected with it by near ties; to hold possession of it, at least during the war; and to hold that possession, if possible, with the consent of its inhabitants.

The sloop of war "Dale," Commander McKean, sailed from New York, on the 3d instant, to join your squadron. The "Lexington," Lieut. Bailey, will sail as soon as she can take on board her stores. The "Potomac" and "Saratoga," have also been ordered to the Pacific.

I am, sir, very respectfully, your obedient servant,

GEORGE BANCROFT.

Commodore JOHN D. SLOAT,
Commanding U. S. naval forces in the Pacific ocean.

No. 10.

Extract from the General Regulations of the Army—edition of 1825.

ARTICLE 6.—*Relative rank and precedence of land and sea officers.*

24. The military officers of the land and sea services of the United States shall rank together as follows: 1st. A lieutenant of the navy with captains of the army. 2d. A master commandant with majors. 3d. A captain of the navy, from the date of his commission, with lieutenant-colonels. 4th. Five years thereafter with colonels. 5th. Ten years thereafter, with brigadier-generals; and 6th. Fifteen years after the date of his commission, with major-generals. But, should there be created in the navy the rank of rear-admiral, then such rank only shall be considered equal to that of major-general.

25. Nothing in the preceding paragraph shall authorize a land officer to command any United States vessel or navy yard; nor any sea officer to command any part of the army on land; neither shall an officer of the one service have a right to *demand* any compliment, on the score of rank, from an officer of the other service.

26. Land troops *serving* on board a United States vessel as marines, shall be subject to the orders of the sea officer in command thereof. Other land troops, embarked on board such vessels for transportation merely, will be considered, in respect to the naval commanders, as passengers; subject, nevertheless, to the internal regulations of the vessel.

No. 11.

NAVY DEPARTMENT, *August* 17, 1846.

COMMODORE: The United States being in a state of war by the action of Mexico, it is desired by the prosecution of hostilities to hasten the return of peace, and to secure it on advantageous conditions. For this purpose orders have been given to the squadron in the Pacific to take and keep possession of Upper California, especially of the ports of San Francisco, of Monterey, and of San Diego; and also, if opportunity offer and the people favour, to take possession, by an inland expedition, of San Pueblo de los Angeles, near San Diego.

On reaching the Pacific, your first duty will be to ascertain if these orders have been carried into effect. If not, you will take immediate possession of Upper·California, especially of the three ports of San Francisco, Monterey, and

San Diego, so that if the treaty of peace shall be made on the basis of the *uti possidetis*, it may leave California to the United States.

The relations to be maintained with the people of Upper California are to be as friendly as possible. The flag of the United States must be raised, but under it the people are to be allowed as much liberty of self-government as is consistent with the general occupation of the country by the United States. You, as commander-in-chief of the squadron, may exercise the right to interdict the entrance of any vessel or articles that would be unfavourable to our success in the war into any of the enemy's ports which you may occupy. With this exception, all United States vessels and merchandise must be allowed, by the local authorities of the ports of which you take possession, to come and go free of duty; but on foreign vessels and goods reasonable duties may be imposed, collected, and disposed of by the local authorities, under your general superintendence.

A military force has been directed by the Secretary of War to proceed to the western coast of California for the purpose of co-operation with the navy, in taking possession of and holding the ports and positions which have been specified, and for otherwise operating against Mexico.

A detachment of these troops, consisting of a company of artillery under command of Captain Tompkins, has sailed in the United States ship Lexington. A regiment of volunteers, under Colonel Stevenson, will soon sail from New York, and a body of troops under Brigadier-general Kearny may reach the coast over Santa Fé. Copies of so much of the instructions to Captain Tompkins and General Kearny as relates to objects requiring co-operation are herewith enclosed.

By article 6 of the *General Regulations for the Army*, (edition of 1825,) which is held by the War Department to be still in force, and of which I enclose you a copy, your commission places you, in point of *precedence*, on occasions of ceremony or upon meetings for consultation, in the class of major-general; but no officer of the army or navy, whatever may be his rank, can assume any direct command, independent of consent, over an officer of the other service, excepting only when land forces are especially embarked in vessels of war to do the duty of marines.

The President expects and requires, however, the most cordial and effectual co-operation between the officers of the two services, in taking possession of and holding the ports and positions of the enemy, which are designated in the instructions to either or both branches of the service, and will hold any commander of either branch to a strict responsibility for any failure to preserve harmony and secure the objects proposed.

The land forces which have been, or will be sent to the Pacific, may be dependent upon the vessels of your squadron for transportation from one point to another, and for shelter and protection in case of being compelled to abandon positions on the coast. It may be necessary also to furnish transportation for their supplies, or to furnish the supplies themselves, by the vessels under your direction.

In all such cases you will furnish all the assistance in your power which will not interfere with objects that, in your opinion, are of greater importance.

You will, taking care, however, to advise with any land officer of high rank (say of the rank of brigadier-general) who may be at hand, make the necessary regulations for the ports that may be occupied.

Having provided for the full possession of Upper California, the next point of

Y 2   17

importance is the Gulf of California. From the best judgment I can form, you should take possession of the port of Guaymas. The progress of our arms will probably be such, that in conjunction with land forces you will be able to hold possession of Guaymas, and so to reduce all the country north of it on the gulf.

As to the ports south of it, especially Mazatlan and Acapulco, it is not possible to give you special instructions. Generally, you will take possession of, or blockade, according to your best judgment, all Mexican ports, as far as your means allow; but south of Guaymas, if the provinces rise up against the central government, and manifest friendship towards the United States, you may, according to your discretion, enter into a temporary agreement of neutrality. But this must be done only on condition that our ships have free access to their ports, and equal commercial rights with those of other nations; that you are allowed to take in water and fuel; to purchase supplies; to go to and from shore without obstruction, as in time of peace; and that the provinces which are thus neutral shall absolutely abstain from contributing towards the continuance of the war by the central government of Mexico against the United States.

Generally, you will exercise the rights of a belligerent, and bear in mind that the greater advantages you obtain, the more speedy and the more advantageous will be the peace.

Should Commodore Biddle be in the Pacific, off the shores of Mexico, at the time you arrive there, you will report yourself to him; and as long as he remains off the coast of Mexico, you will act under his direction in concert with him, communicating to him these instructions.

The Savannah, the Warren, and the Levant ought soon to return. If you hear of peace between the United States and Mexico, you will at once send them home.

If war continues, you will send them home singly, or in company, at the earliest day they can be spared. The Savannah will go to New York, and the Warren and Levant to Norfolk.

Very respectfully, yours,
GEORGE BANCROFT.

Com. W. B. Shubrick,
    Appointed to command the U. S. naval forces in the Pacific ocean.

No. 12.

[CONFIDENTIAL.]   United States Navy Department,
                                      Washington, November 5, 1846.

Commodore: Commodore Sloat has arrived in this city, and delivered your letter of the 28th July ult., with the copy of your address to the people of California, which accompanied it. The department is gratified that you joined the squadron before the state of the commodore's health rendered it necessary for him to relinquish his important command.

The difficulties and embarrassments of the command, without a knowledge of the proceedings of Congress on the subject of the war with Mexico, and in the absence of the instructions of the department, which followed these proceedings, are justly appreciated; and it is highly gratifying that so much has been done in anticipation of the orders which have been transmitted.

You will, without doubt, have received the despatches of the 15th of May last, addressed to Commodore Sloat; and I now send you, for your guidance, a copy of instructions to Commodore Shubrick of the 17th of August. He sailed early in September, in the razee Independence, with orders to join the squadron with the least possible delay. On his assuming the command, you may hoist a red pennant. If you prefer, you may hoist your pennant on the Savannah, and return home with her and the Warren.

The existing war with Mexico has been commenced by her. Every disposition was felt and manifested by the United States government to procure redress for the injuries of which we complained, and to settle all complaints on her part, in the spirit of peace and of justice which has ever characterized our intercourse with foreign nations. That disposition still exists; and whenever the authorities of Mexico shall manifest a willingness to adjust unsettled points of controversy between the two republics, and to restore an honourable peace, they will be met in a corresponding spirit.

This consummation is not to be expected, nor is our national honour to be maintained, without a vigorous prosecution of the war on our part. Without being animated by any ambitious spirit of conquest, our naval and military forces must hold the ports and territory of the enemy, of which possession has been obtained by their arms. You will, therefore, under no circumstances, voluntarily lower the flag of the United States, or relinquish the actual possession of Upper California. Of other points of the Mexican territory, which the forces under your command may occupy, you will maintain the possession or withdraw, as in your judgment may be most advantageous in the prosecution of the war.

In regard to your intercourse with the inhabitants of the country, your views are judicious and you will conform to the instructions heretofore given. You will exercise the rights of a belligerent; and if you find that the liberal policy of our government, in purchasing and paying for required supplies, is misunderstood, and its exercise is injurious to the public interest, you are at liberty to take them from the enemy without compensation, or pay such prices as may be deemed just and reasonable. The best policy in this respect depends on a knowledge of circumstances in which you are placed, and is left to your discretion.

The Secretary of War has ordered Col. R. B. Mason, 1st United States dragoons, to proceed to California, via Panama, who will command the troops and conduct the military operations in the Mexican territory bordering on the Pacific, in the absence of Brigadier-general Kearny. The commander of the naval forces will consult and co-operate with him in his command to the same extent as if he held a higher rank in the army. In all questions of relative rank, he is to be regarded as having only the rank of colonel.

The President has deemed it best for the public interests to invest the military officer commanding with the direction of the operations on land and with the administrative functions of government over the people and territory occupied by us. You will relinquish to Colonel Mason, or to General Kearny, if the latter shall arrive before you have done so, the entire control over these matters, and turn over to him all papers necessary to the performance of his duties. If officers of the navy are employed in the performance of civil or military duties, you will withdraw or continue them, at your discretion, taking care to put them to their appropriate duty in the squadron, if the army officer commanding does not wish their services on land.

The establishment of port regulations is a subject over which it is deemed by the President most appropriate that the naval commander shall exercise jurisdiction. You will establish these, and communicate them to the military commander, who will carry them into effect so far as his co-operation may be necessary, suggesting for your consideration modifications or alterations.

The regulation of the import trade is also confided to you. The conditions under which vessels of our own citizens and of neutrals may be admitted into ports of the enemy in your possession will be prescribed by you, subject to the instructions heretofore given. To aid you, copies of instructions to the collectors in the United States, from the Treasury Department, on the same subject, are enclosed. On cargoes of neutrals imported into such ports you may impose moderate duties, not greater in amount than those collected in the ports of the United States. The collection of these duties will be made by civil officers, to be appointed, and subject to the same rules as other persons charged with civil duties in the country. These appointments will be made by the military officers, on consultation with you.

The President directs me to impress most earnestly on the naval officers, as it is impressed on those of the army, the importance of harmony in the performance of their delicate duties while co-operating. They are arms of one body, and will, I doubt not, vie with each other in showing which can render the most efficient aid to the other in the execution of common orders, and in sustaining the national honour, which is confided to both.

You will make your communications to the department as frequent as possible.

The great distance at which your command is placed, and the impossibility of maintaining a frequent or regular communication with you, necessarily induce the department to leave much of the details of your operations to your discretion. The confident belief is entertained, that, with the general outline given in the instructions, you will pursue a course which will make the enemy sensible of our power to inflict on them the evils of war, while it will secure to the United States, if a definitive treaty of peace shall give us California, a population impressed with our justice, grateful for our clemency, and prepared to love our institutions and to honour our flag.

On your being relieved in the command of the squadron, you will hand your instructions to the officer relieving you.

I am, very respectfully, your obedient servant,

J. Y. MASON.

Commodore R. F. STOCKTON,
Commanding United States naval forces on the west coast of Mexico.

ADDENDA.

WAR DEPARTMENT, *Washington, January* 11, 1847.

SIR : Your communication from Santa Fé, of the 22d of September, accompanied by a copy of the laws prepared for the government of New Mexico, and established in that Territory, was received at this Department on the 23d of November last.

Soon after the meeting of Congress the President was called on by a resolution of the House of Representatives for the *orders* and instructions issued to the officers of the army and navy by him for the civil government of the territories which had been or might be acquired by our arms. I herewith send you a copy of the President's message, with the documents, sent to Congress in answer to that resolution. By this you will learn the President's views as to the power and authority to be exercised in the territories conquered and occupied by our forces.

These views are presented more in detail in instructions prepared under his directions by the Secretary of the Navy, bearing date this day, an extract of which is herewith transmitted for your information, and particularly for the guidance of your conduct. This document is so full and clear on all points, in regard to which you may desire the directions of the Government, that I do not deem it necessary to enlarge upon it.

It is proper to remark that the provisions of the laws which have been established for the government of the Territory of New Mexico go, in some few respects, beyond the line designated by the President, and propose to confer upon the people of that Territory political rights under the Constitution of the United States. Such rights can only be acquired by the action of Congress. So far as the code of laws established in New Mexico by your authority attempts to confer such rights, it is not approved by the President, and he directs me to instruct you not to carry such parts into effect.

Under the law of nations the Power conquering a territory or country has a right to establish a civil Government within the same, as a means of securing the conquest, and with a view to protecting the persons and property of the people; and it is not intended to limit you in the full exercise of this authority. Indeed, it is desired you should exercise it in such a manner as to inspire confidence in the people that our power is to be firmly sustained in that country. The territory in our military occupation, acquired from the enemy by our arms, cannot be regarded, the war still continuing, as permanently annexed to the United States, though our authority to exercise civil government over it is not by that circumstance the least restricted.

It is important that the extent and character of our possession in the territories conquered from the enemy should not be open to question or cavil. This remark, though having reference to all our acquisitions, is in an especial manner applicable to the Californias. As to Upper California, it is presumed no doubt can arise, but it may not be so clear as to Lower California. It is expected that our flag will be hoisted in that part of the country, and actual possession taken and continuously held of some place or places in it, and our civil jurisdiction there asserted and upheld.

A copy of this communication will be sent to the commanding officer at Santa Fé, with instructions to conform his conduct to the views herein presented.

Very respectfully, your obedient servant,

W. L. MARCY, *Secretary of War.*

Brig. Gen. S. W. KEARNY,
   Commanding U. S. Army in California, Mexico.

[CONFIDENTIAL.] NAVY DEPARTMENT,
January 11, 1847.

SIR : Your communications, dated at Monterey on the 18th and 19th of September, were received at the Department on the 26th December ultimo, by the hands of Mr. Norris, whose activity and intelligence in executing his orders entitle him to my thanks.

You will probably have received before this can reach you my despatches, which were intrusted to Lieut. Watson, of the United States Navy, under date of the 5th of November, in which, as Commander-in-chief of the United States naval forces in the Pacific, you were informed that the President " has deemed it best for the public interests to invest the military officer commanding with the direction of the operations on land, and with the administrative functions of government over the people and territory occupied by us."

Accompanying this, I send you copies of the President's annual message transmitted to Congress on the 8th of December ultimo, with the accompanying documents, including the reports of the War and Navy Departments. I also send you a printed copy of the document No. 19 of the House of Representatives.

You will perceive from these papers the view taken by the Executive of the measures which have been adopted by the military and naval commanders in those States of Mexico of which we have acquired possession by military conquest.

I see no reason to qualify the opinion which I expressed in my report, that " your measures in regard to the conquered territory are believed to be warranted by the laws of war." And, in answer to your suggestion that " a general approval by the Government of the United States of your conduct, if they do approve, to be published in the Californian, would have a good effect," I have been directed by the President to communicate a more full statement of his views of the principles which govern the conduct of our officers in the circumstances in which you have been placed, and on which the instructions heretofore given were based.

By the constitution of the United States the power to declare war is vested in Congress. The war with Mexico exists by her own act and the declaration of the Congress of the United States. It is the duty of the Executive to carry on the war with all the rights and subject to all the duties imposed by the laws of nations—a code binding on both belligerents.

The possession of portions of the enemy's territory, acquired by justifiable acts of war, gives to us the right of government during the continuance of our possession, and imposes on us a duty to the inhabitants who are thus placed under our dominion. The right of possession, however, is temporary, unless made absolute by subsequent events. If, being in possession, a treaty of peace is made and duly ratified, on the principle of *uti possidetis*, that is, that each of the belligerent parties shall enjoy the territory of which it shall be in possession at the date of the treaty, or if the surrender of the territory is not stipulated in the treaty so ratified, then the imperfect title, acquired by conquest, is made absolute, and the inhabitants, with the territory, are entitled to all the benefits of the federal constitution of the United States, to the same extent as the citizens of any other part of the Union.

The course of our Government in regard to California, or other portions of the territory of Mexico now or hereafter to be in our possession by conquest, depends on those on whom the constitution imposes the duty of making and carrying treaties into effect. Pending the war, our possession gives only such rights as the laws of nations recognise, and the government is military, performing such civil duties as are necessary to the full enjoyment of the advantages resulting from the conquest, and to the due protection of the rights of persons and of property of the inhabitants.

No political right can be conferred on the inhabitants thus situated, emanating from the Constitution of the United States. That instrument establishes a form of government for those who are within our limits and owe voluntary allegiance to it. Unless incorporated, with the assent of Congress, by ratified treaty, or by legislative act, as in the case of Texas, our rights over enemies' territory in our possession are only such as the laws of war confer, and theirs no more than are derived from the same authority. They are therefore entitled to no representation in the Congress of the United States.

Without anticipating what may be the terms of a treaty which it is hoped will be entered into between the two Republics, there will be no revocation of the orders, given in my despatch on the 5th of November last, that "under no circumstances will you voluntarily lower the flag of the United States, or relinquish the actual possession of California," with all the rights which it confers.

In the discharge of the duty of government in the conquered territory during our military possession, it has not been deemed improper or unwise that the inhabitants should be permitted to participate in the selection of agents to make or execute the laws to be enforced. Such a privilege cannot fail to produce ameliorations of the despotic character of martial law, and constitute checks, voluntarily and appropriately submitted to by officers of the United States, all whose institutions are based on the will of the governed.

I have regarded your measures, in authorizing the election of agents charged with making laws, or in executing them, as founded on this principle, and so far as they carry out the right of temporary government, under existing rights of possession, they are approved. But no officers created, or laws or regulations made to protect the rights or perform the duties resulting from our conquests, can lawfully continue beyond the duration of the state of things which now exists, without authority of future treaty or act of Congress.

At present it is needless, and might be injurious to the public interest, to agitate the question in California as to how long those persons who have been elected for a prescribed period of time will have official authority. If our right of possession shall become absolute, such an inquiry is needless, and if, by treaty or otherwise, we lose the possession, those who follow us will govern the country. The President, however, anticipates no such result. On the contrary, he foresees no contingency in which the United States will ever surrender or relinquish the possession of the Californias.

The number of official appointments with civil or military duties, other than those devolved on our army and navy by our own laws, should be made as small as possible, and the expenses of the local government should be kept within the limits of the revenues received in the Territory, if it can be done without detriment to the public interest.

Very respectfully, your obedient servant,   J. Y. MASON.

Commodore R. F. STOCKTON,
   Commanding U. S. Naval forces west coast of Mexico.

EXTRACT OF A LETTER, DATED

PUEBLA DES LOS ANGELES, CALIFORNIA, *June* 22, 1847.

DEAR SIR: The ship Loo Choo, one of the transports that brought out a portion of the New York regiment, being about to return home, I avail myself of the opportunity to write a few lines.

Since the departure of Gen. Kearny, who left some weeks ago for the United States, little of importance has transpired here. The country now, as then, is perfectly tranquil, and there is nothing to indicate a change of this desirable state of things, unless it be for the better. Some of the Californians who left their homes for Sonora, are returning here. They give deplorable representations of the condition of that country. I am advised by those who have come in, that many families, respectable residents of Sonora, are making arrangements to remove to California, and from a conviction that they will be sure of a permanent and good government under the American flag, and under the full belief that Mexico cannot extend to them aid and protection, and that farther persistence in rebellion will be unavailing.

Another reason for their acquiescence in a state of things which they cannot prevent, deserves to be mentioned in justice to the volunteers. The conduct of our troops since they set foot here has been such as to inspire the Californians with respect and confidence towards them and the nation of which they are, as it were, the representatives. This confidence and good feeling are manifested in a thousand ways which I have not the space to particularize. It is enough to say, that they seize upon every opportunity to avail themselves of the mechanical skill and ingenuity of the troops, when they are at liberty to engage in their wonted avocations at home; and at such times the troops have as much employment from the native inhabitants as they desire or can attend to.

We have now at this post nearly completed a strong fortress. It has been erected by the troops on a hill that commands the town and the surrounding country. This, of course, will effectually suppress any attempt at insurrection, as every effort must inevitably involve all engaged in it in a common calamity.

The Mormon force here and at San Diego consists of about 360 men. Their term of service expires on the 17th of July. They have been invited to re-enter the service for another year, but at present there is not much prospect of their doing so. This is extremely to be regretted, for they are an orderly, quiet, and peaceable set of men, submitting without resistance or a murmur to the severest discipline, and altogether a most useful and efficient body of men.

The regiment of New York volunteers is now very much scattered, being distributed among different posts, from Sutter's settlement on the Sacramento to La Paz in Lower California—a distance of 1500 miles. The regiment will never probably be together again while in service. They will dearly earn all they receive from the government. The hand of American industry and enterprise is plainly to be seen wherever our troops are stationed. Bricks are burned, ovens built, chimneys erected, saw-mills put into operation, and comfortable houses constructed wherever timber can be had.

Watches and clocks, too, are sent to these stations from a distance of fifty miles, to be repaired; cloths brought to be made into clothing; leather to be made into boots and shoes; and at one of the posts a tannery has been established; and at Monterey two of the New York volunteers, who are employed by the commissary, have opened a stall at which beef, lamb, veal, and mutton, can be purchased dressed in Fulton market style. They are doing remarkably well, and even the inhabitants who have been in the habit of slaughtering a bullock in the streets for their own use, are abandoning the habit and patronizing the New York butchers.

These are specimens of what is going forward here in the way of civilization and improvement under the sway of the United States government and its arms. All can do well here who choose to help themselves and become useful. But I have no more time to write.

THE END.